THE
VEGETARIAN
KITCHEN

Consultant Editor

Linda Fraser

LORENZ BOOKS

INTRODUCTION

Vegetarian food has finally become a major part of our cuisine. We no longer need to justify the inclusion of vegetarian dishes on restaurant menus, and a cookery book such as this is to be universally celebrated and not seen as catering to the few. With the plentiful supply of fresh vegetables, fruit, herbs, nuts, grains, pulses and pasta that is available to us, the possibilities of creating really exciting and varied recipes have never been greater.

It is not only vegetarians who can enjoy vegetarian food. The fresh, light and innovative recipes that have come to the forefront of new-style vegetarian cooking provide a tempting departure from many of the heavier, non-vegetarian dishes. This book gathers together some of the best recipes in the world, all of them packed with fabulous tastes and textures.

We are constantly being urged to choose a diet rich in the complex carbohydrates found in cereals, grains, fruits and vegetables, all of which are abundant in vegetarian cooking. If you include dairy products in your diet, restrict your intake of fat by choosing skimmed or semi-skimmed milk and low-fat yogurts and cheeses. By limiting the use of oils to unsaturated types, such as olive, sunflower, corn and peanut, you can reduce the level of fat in your diet considerably.

So whether you are a committed vegetarian, enjoy the occasional vegetarian meal, or just want something simple and satisfying, this book has a delicious recipe to suit every taste and occasion.

Fresh Vegetables

Thanks to the range of fresh produce, the choice for vegetarians has expanded enormously.

Aubergine
This vegetable is delicious grilled, fried or stuffed.

Beans
Cook broad beans, green beans and runner beans until just tender-crisp.

Broccoli
Quick to prepare, broccoli can be eaten raw or cooked.

Cabbage
There are many varieties of this nutritious vegetable – don't overcook.

Carrots
Sweet-flavoured carrots are delicious raw or cooked.

Cauliflower
Can be eaten raw or cooked.

Celeriac
This knobbly root vegetable tastes very similar to celery.

Celery
Delicious raw in salads.

Fennel
Aniseed-flavoured fennel can be eaten raw or cooked.

Leeks
A versatile vegetable with a subtle oniony flavour.

Lettuce
Buy fresh whole heads or in bags of mixed leaves.

Mushrooms
Use fresh or dried, cultivated and wild mushrooms.

Onions
Can be sautéed, roasted or even eaten raw in salads.

Parsnips
A sweet root vegetable with a distinct earthy flavour.

Peppers
Green peppers have a fresh raw flavour; red, orange and yellow peppers are sweeter.

Potatoes
Rich in Vitamin C, potatoes can be cooked in many ways.

Spinach
This dark leaf can be eaten raw in salads or cooked.

Swedes and turnips
Sweet and nutty flavoured – add to soups and casseroles.

Tomatoes
The basis of many dishes.

Dairy Products and Tofu

An important source of protein for vegetarians, these products are widely available.

Butter and margarine
Butter is a cow's milk product – choose unsalted butter for shallow frying. Margarine is made from vegetable oils.

Buttermilk
Skimmed milk with an added bacterial culture, which gives it a natural tangy flavour.

Cheeses
Choose strong-flavoured cheeses that melt well, such as Cheddar, Red Leicester or Gruyère, for sauces and toppings, or for adding to home-made pastry. Parmesan is a full-flavoured hard cheese, which is delicious finely grated and added to pasta, or pared into fine slivers to scatter over salads. If a recipe calls for blue cheese, use Roquefort or Stilton if a strong flavour is required, and dolcelatte or cambozola for a milder result. Use crumbly white feta in salads – its piquant, salty taste is delicious with crisp leaves. Fresh goat's cheese has an intense flavour. Mozzarella can be eaten raw, but melts well too and is perfect for topping pizzas and adding to baked pasta dishes.

Cream
Available in many forms, such as single, double, extra thick, clotted, whipping and soured cream, and crème fraîche.

Eggs
Rich in protein, eggs are used in sweet and savoury dishes.

Fromage frais
A creamy white fresh cheese sold in pots.

Milk
Cow's milk comes in different forms: skimmed, semi-skimmed and full-fat. Goat's milk and sheep's milk are also available.

Quark
This soft white cheese has a tangy flavour.

Tofu
This is an unfermented bean curd made from soya beans that absorbs flavours readily. Various forms are available, from silken tofu, which is useful for adding to sauces and is often used for desserts, to a firm type that can be cut into cubes and sautéed.

Yogurt
Available plain or flavoured, yogurt may be made with cow's, sheep's or goat's milk.

The Store Cupboard

Your store cupboard should be the backbone of your kitchen. Stock it sensibly and you'll always have the wherewithal to make a tasty meal.

Canned pulses

Chick-peas, cannellini beans, green lentils, haricot beans and red kidney beans survive the canning process well. Tip into a sieve, rinse under cold running water and drain well before use.

Canned vegetables

Although fresh vegetables are best for most cooking, some canned products are very useful. Artichoke hearts have a mild sweet flavour and are great for adding to stir-fries, salads, risottos or pizzas. Pimientos are canned whole red peppers, seeded and peeled. Use them for stews and soups. Canned tomatoes are an essential ingredient to have in the store cupboard. Additional useful items to include are ratatouille, water chestnuts and sweetcorn.

Mustard

Wholegrain or Dijon mustards are used in both cooking and salad dressings.

Oils

Ground nut or sunflower oils are bland and will not mask flavours. They are ideal for deep frying. Fiery chilli oil will liven up vegetable stir-fries, while aromatic sesame oil will give them a rich nutty flavour. A good olive oil will suit most purposes (except deep-frying – it is simply too expensive). Choose extra virgin olive oil, which has the best flavour, for making salad dressings and adding to pasta dishes.

Olives

Green and black olives are available in brine or olive oil, as well as a variety of tasty marinades. Olive paste is useful for pasta sauces.

Passata

This thick sauce is made from sieved tomatoes. It is mainly used in Italian cookery.

Pesto

This classic Italian sauce combines fresh basil, pine nuts, Parmesan cheese, garlic and olive oil, and is useful for flavouring pasta or grilled or roasted vegetables.

Soy sauce/shoyu

Soy sauce is a thin, salty, black liquid made from fermented soya beans. Shoyu, naturally brewed soy sauce, is fermented for much longer and so has fewer additives than soy sauce.

Stocks

There are three kinds of vegetable stocks. Granules are ideal for light soups and risottos, stock cubes have a stronger flavour and are good for hearty soups, while vegetable extracts have a robust taste that is delicious in casseroles.

Sun-dried tomatoes

These deliciously sweet tomatoes, baked in the sun and dried, are sold in bags or in jars, steeped in olive oil.

Tahini paste

Made from ground sesame seeds, this paste is used in Middle Eastern cookery and, with chick-peas, is the basis for hummus.

Tomato purée

This concentrated tomato paste is useful for adding flavour to sauces and is sold in cans, jars or tubes. A version made from sun-dried tomatoes is also available.

Vinegars

White or red wine vinegars and sherry vinegar are ideal for salad dressings. Balsamic vinegar, with its distinctive sweet flavour, can be used to liven up roasted vegetables.

Spices and Dry Goods

Ground and whole spices, grains, cereals, dried fruit, flours, nuts, seeds, pasta and noodles are invaluable for vegetarian cooking.

Spices

Cardamom
This fragrant spice is used in sweet and savoury dishes.

Chinese five-spice powder
This anise-flavoured spice is made from a mixture of anise pepper, star anise, cassia, fennel seed and cloves.

Cinnamon
A sweet spice available whole, as sticks of bark or ground.

Cloves
This strongly scented spice is often used ground, mixed with other spices for sweet and savoury dishes.

Coriander
This spice imparts a mildly hot, aromatic flavour.

Cumin
Sweet and pungent, with a distinctive taste, often used in Indian dishes.

Garam masala
An aromatic mixture of spices used widely in Indian dishes.

Turmeric
This ground spice has a strong, musty flavour and adds a deep-yellow colour to food. Sometimes used as a substitute for saffron.

Saffron
The most expensive spice, saffron has a pungent scent and a bitter-sweet taste. The threads are steeped in a little liquid before use.

Dry Goods

Barley
With its distinctive flavour and chewy texture, barley is often added to hearty soups and can be used as an alternative to rice in risottos.

Buckwheat
Nutty in texture and taste, this grain can be used as an alternative to rice in risottos and stir-fries, but is actually the seed from a type of grass.

Bulgur wheat
This whole wheat grain is steam-dried and cracked before sale, so only needs a brief soaking before use.

Couscous
Also made from wheat, this cracked grain is a staple in North Africa. It is usually steamed and served hot.

Dried fruit
Rich in dietary fibre, vitamins and minerals, dried fruits are delicious in a wide range of dishes including muesli.

Flours
Instead of white refined flour, try experimenting with other flours, such as whole-meal, buckwheat, soya or rye flours. Cornflour is often used as a thickening agent for sauces.

Millet
High in protein, millet is used extensively in South-East Asia and is cooked in the same way as rice.

Nuts and seeds
Almonds, brazil nuts, cashew nuts, pecans and walnuts, and such seeds as sunflower, sesame and pumpkin, are all valuable sources of protein and calcium. Add to salads or rice dishes.

Pasta and noodles
While fresh pasta and noodles are usually preferred, both for flavour and for speed of cooking, the dried products are valuable store cupboard ingredients.

Rice
Types include long grain, basmati, short grain for puddings, and risotto rice, such as arborio. Black wild rice (actually the seeds of an aquatic grass) is also good.

Equipment

Stocking up on every item in your local cookware shop will not make you a better cook, but some basic items are definitely worth investing in.

A few good saucepans in various sizes and with tight-fitting lids are a must. Heavy-based and non-stick pans are best. A large non-stick frying pan is invaluable because the food cooks faster when spread over a wider surface area. For the same reason, a good wok is essential. I suggest using a large saucepan or frying pan when the recipe calls for occasional stirring, and a wok for continuous movement, such as stir-frying.

Good-quality knives can halve your preparation time, but more importantly, a really sharp knife is safer than a blunt one. You can do yourself a lot of damage if your hand slips when you are pressing down hard with a blunt knife. For basic, day-to-day use, choose a good chopping knife, a small vegetable knife and a long serrated bread knife. If possible store knives safely in well-secured slotted racks. Drawer storage is not good for knives as the blades can easily become damaged when they are knocked around. If you do have to keep knives in a drawer, make sure they are stored with their handles

towards the front for safe lifting, and keep the blades protected in some way. Good sharp knives are essential and indispensable pieces of kitchen equipment, so it is worth taking care of them.

A few of the recipes in this book call for the use of a food processor, which does save time and effort but is not strictly necessary. Other essential pieces of kitchen equipment, which almost seem too obvious to mention, include chopping boards, a colander, a sieve, a grater, a whisk and some means of extracting citrus juice, be this a squeezer or a juicer.

For the cook who likes to work speedily and efficiently, where you store your equipment is an important factor to consider. Use your cooker as the pivot around which most of the action takes place. Hang pots, pans, whisks, spoons and strainers overhead within easy reach, keep a chopping board on an adjacent work surface and place ceramic pots with a variety of wooden spoons, spatulas, ladles, scissors, peelers and other kitchen utensils within easy reach.

wooden spatula

ladle

scissors

knives and peelers

vegetable knife

bread knife

whisks

draining spoon

serving spoon

grater

colander

chopping board

pans

wok

frying pan

Menus for Entertaining

When you have guests to feed, expand your vegetarian main course into an impressive meal. The menu suggestions below feature main course recipes from the book, accompanied by simple ideas for starters, accompaniments and desserts that can be rustled up in minutes.

Menu 1

Warm focaccia bread with salt crystals and olives

Asparagus Rolls with Herb Butter Sauce

Lentil Stir-fry served with a green salad

Summer berries with Kirsch and vanilla sugar

Menu 2

Grilled cherry tomato and basil salad

Mushrooms with Leeks and Stilton

Potato, Broccoli and Red Pepper Stir-fry

Baked banana and orange segments

Menu 3

Poached asparagus with crème fraîche and lemon

Ciabatta Rolls with Courgettes and Saffron

Red Fried Rice

Warm ginger cake with golden syrup

Menu 4

French bread slices with tapenade and mozzarella

Lemon and Parmesan Cappellini with Herb Bread

Fresh Spinach and Avocado Salad

Banana and amaretti with passion fruit cream

Menu 5

Fresh tomato and coriander with poppadoms

Bengali-style Vegetables

Cumin-spiced Marrow and Spinach

Spiced potato and cauliflower Fresh fruit to follow

Menu 6

Crudités with mayonnaise dip

Potato, Spinach and Pine Nut Gratin

Vegetable Kebabs with Mustard and Honey

Grilled mascarpone plums

TECHNIQUES

Once mastered, the techniques described here will help you to prepare vegetables speedily and with less waste, to produce better results with ease.

Peeling and Seeding Tomatoes

A simple and efficient way of preparing tomatoes.

1 Use a sharp knife to cut a small cross on the bottom of the tomato.

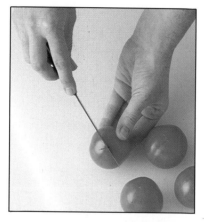

2 Turn the tomato over and cut out the core.

3 Immerse the tomato in boiling water for 10–15 seconds, then transfer to a bowl of cold water using a slotted spoon.

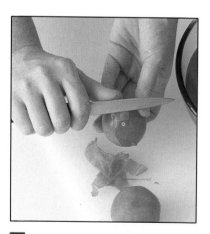

4 Lift out the tomato and peel (the skin should be easy to remove).

5 Cut the tomato in half crosswise and squeeze out the seeds.

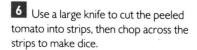

6 Use a large knife to cut the peeled tomato into strips, then chop across the strips to make dice.

Chopping Onions

Uniform-sized dice make cooking easy. This method can't be beaten.

1 Peel the onion. Cut it in half with a large knife and set it cut-side down on a board. Make lengthwise vertical cuts along the onion, cutting almost but not quite through to the root.

2 Make 2 horizontal cuts from the stalk and towards the root, but not through it.

3 Cut the onion crosswise to form small, even dice.

Slicing Onions

Use thin slices for sautéeing or to flavour oils for stir-frying, or use sweet onion slices in salads.

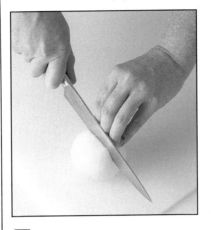

1 Peel the onion. Cut it in half with a large knife and set it cut-side down on a chopping board.

2 Cut out a triangular piece of the core from each half.

3 Cut across each half in vertical slices.

Shredding Cabbage

This method is useful for coleslaws, pickled cabbage or any cooked dish.

I Use a large knife to cut the cabbage into quarters.

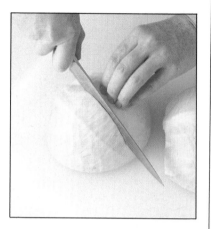

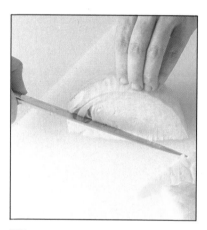

2 Cut out the core from each quarter.

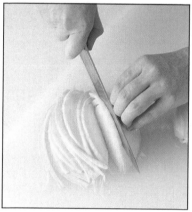

3 Slice across each quarter to form fine, even shreds.

Cutting Carrot Julienne

Thin julienne strips of any vegetable make decorative accompaniments, or can be used in stir-fries.

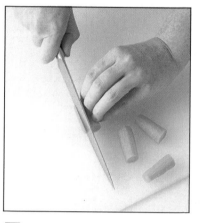

I Peel the carrot and use a large knife to cut it into 5 cm/2 in lengths. Cut a thin sliver from one side of each piece so that it sits flat on the board.

2 Cut into thin lengthwise slices.

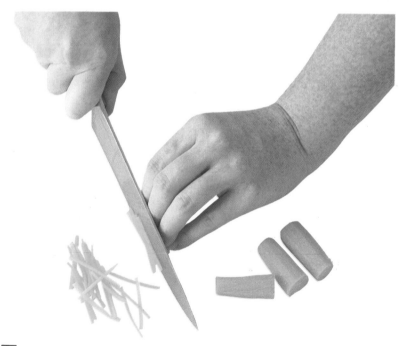

3 Stack the slices and cut through them to make fine strips.

Preparing Lemon Grass

Use the whole stem and remove it before cooking or chop the root.

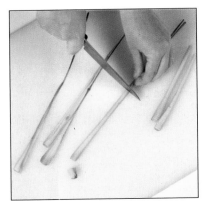

1 Cut off and discard the dry, leafy tops. Peel away any tough outer layers. Trim off the tops and end of the stem until you are left with about 10 cm/4 in.

2 Lay the lemon grass on a board. Set the flat side of a chef's knife on top and strike it firmly with your fist. Cut across the lemon grass to make thin slices.

Preparing Kaffir Lime Leaves

The distinctive lime-lemon aroma and flavour of Kaffir lime leaves are a vital part of Thai cooking.

COOK'S TIP
Buy fresh lime leaves in oriental stores and freeze them for future use. Dried lime leaves are also now available.

1 You can tear, shred or cut kaffir lime leaves. Using a small, sharp knife, carefully remove the centre vein. Cut the leaves crossways into very fine strips.

Preparing Fresh Ginger

Fresh root ginger can be used in slices, strips or finely chopped.

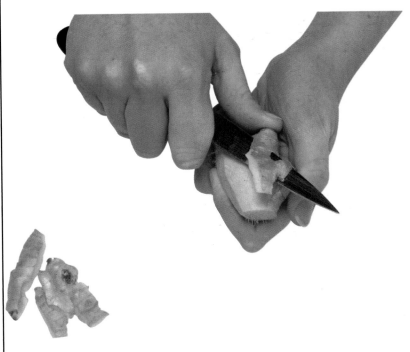

1 Using a small, sharp knife, peel the skin from the root ginger.

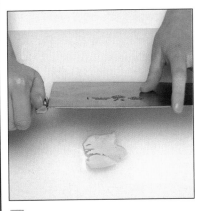

2 Place the ginger on a board, set the flat side of a cleaver or chef's knife on top and strike it firmly with your fist – this will soften the fibrous texture.

3 Chop the ginger as coarsely or finely as you wish, moving the blade backwards and forwards.

Preparing Beansprouts

Usually available from supermarkets, beansprouts add a crisp texture to stir-fries.

1 Pick over the beansprouts, discarding any pieces that are discoloured, broken or wilted.

2 Rinse the beansprouts under cold running water and drain well.

Preparing Spring Onions

Use spring onions in stir-fries to flavour oil, as a vegetable in their own right, or as a garnish.

1 Trim off the root and any discoloured tops with a sharp knife. For an intense flavour in a stir-fry, cut the entire spring onion into thin matchsticks.

2 Alternatively, slice the white and pale green part of the spring onion diagonally and stir-fry with crushed garlic, to flavour the cooking oil.

Chopping Coriander

Chop coriander just before you use it, the flavour will then be much better.

1 Strip the leaves from the stalks and pile them on a chopping board.

2 Using a cleaver or chef's knife, cut the coriander into small pieces, moving the blade back and forth until it is as coarsely or finely chopped as you wish.

Preparing Chillies

The flavour of chilli is wonderful in cooking, but fresh chillies must be handled with care.

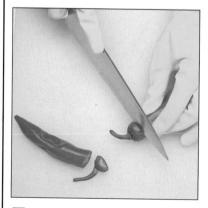

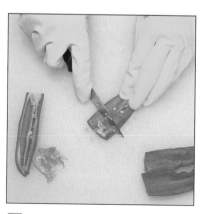

1 Wearing rubber gloves, remove the stalks from the chillies.

2 Cut in half lengthways. Scrape out the seeds and fleshy, white pith from each half, using a sharp knife. Chop or thinly slice according to the recipe.

Segmenting Oranges

Orange segments without any skin are useful for adding to salsas or serving alongside sweet dips.

1 Slice the bottom off the orange so that it will stand firmly on a chopping board. Using a sharp knife, remove the peel by slicing from the top to the bottom of the orange.

2 Hold the orange in one hand over a bowl. Slice towards the middle of the fruit, to one side of the segment, and then gently twist the knife to ease the segment away from the membrane and out of the orange. Repeat to remove all of the segments. Squeeze any juice from the remaining membrane into the bowl.

Preparing Avocados

Removing the flesh from avocados is easy to do.

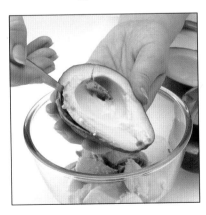

1 Cut around the avocado, twist to separate the halves, remove the stone, then scoop out the flesh into a bowl.

2 Mash the flesh well with a fork or a potato masher, or tip out on to a board and chop finely using a large knife.

Making Mayonnaise

Home-made mayonnaise tastes wonderful and is very quick and simple to prepare.

1 Place the egg yolks and lemon juice in a food processor or blender and process them briefly until lightly blended.

2 Pour the oil into a jug, then with the machine running pour in the oil in a slow, steady stream.

3 Once half the oil has been added, add the remaining oil more quickly. Continue processing until the mayonnaise is thick and creamy, add a little lemon juice and season with salt and pepper to taste.

French Dressing

French vinaigrette is the most widely used salad dressing and is appreciated for its simplicity and style. For the best flavour, use the finest extra-virgin olive oil and go easy on the vinegar.

Makes about 125 ml/4 fl oz/¹/₂ cup

INGREDIENTS
90 ml/6 tbsp extra-virgin olive oil
15ml/1 tbsp white wine vinegar
5ml/1 tsp French mustard
pinch of caster sugar

2 Add the mustard and sugar.

1 Place the olive oil and vinegar in a screw-top jar.

3 Replace the lid and shake well.

COOK'S TIP
Liquid dressings that contain extra-virgin olive oil should be stored at room temperature. Refrigeration can cause them to solidify.

French Herb Dressing

The delicate scents of fresh herbs combine especially well in a French dressing. Toss with a simple green salad and serve with good cheese and wine.

Makes about 125 ml/4 fl oz/¹/₂ cup

INGREDIENTS
60 ml/4 tbsp extra-virgin olive oil
30ml/2 tbsp ground nut or
    sunflower oil
15ml/1 tbsp lemon juice
60 ml/4 tbsp finely chopped fresh
    herbs, such as parsley, chives,
    tarragon and marjoram
pinch of caster sugar

2 Add the lemon juice, herbs and sugar.

1 Place the olive and groundnut oil in a screw-top jar.

3 Replace the lid and shake well.

Relishes

These relishes are very quick and easy to prepare and will liven up vegetable burgers and pies.

QUICK BARBECUE RELISH

Making use of storecupboard ingredients, this quick relish is ideal for an impromptu barbecue. It has a tangy flavour.

45ml/3 tbsp sweet pickle
15 ml/1 tbsp soy sauce
30 ml/2 tbsp tomato ketchup
10 ml/2 tsp prepared mustard
15 ml/1 tbsp cider vinegar
30 ml/2 tbsp brown sauce

1 Mix together the pickle, soy sauce, tomato ketchup and prepared mustard.

2 Add the vinegar and brown sauce and mix well. Cover and chill and use when required.

TOMATO RELISH

This cooked relish has a rich, concentrated tomato flavour. Serve it hot or cold with barbecued foods, or use to pep up a cheese sandwich.

15 ml/1 tbsp olive oil
1 onion, finely chopped
1 garlic clove, crushed
25 g/1 oz/2 tbsp flour
30 ml/2 tbsp tomato ketchup
300 ml/^{1}/2 pint/1^1/4 cups passata
5 ml/1 tsp sugar
15 ml/1 tbsp fresh parsley, chopped

1 Heat the oil in a pan. Add the onion and garlic clove and fry for 5 minutes. Add the flour and cook for 1 minute.

2 Stir in the tomato ketchup, passata, sugar and fresh parsley. Bring to the boil and cook for 10 minutes. Cover and chill and use when required.

COOK'S TIP

Barbecue and Tomato relishes should be used as quickly as possible, but will keep for a few days in the fridge.

VARIATION

For a hot and spicy version of this relish, add 10 ml/2 tsp chilli sauce and 1 green chilli, finely chopped at step two.

CUCUMBER RELISH

A cool, refreshing relish, it may also be used as a dip with crudités as a starter.

^{1}/2 cucumber
2 celery sticks, chopped
1 green pepper, seeded and chopped
1 garlic clove, crushed
300 ml/^{1}/2 pint/1^1/4 cups natural yoghurt
15 ml/1 tbsp chopped fresh coriander
freshly ground black pepper

1 Dice the cucumber and place in a large bowl. Add the celery, green pepper and crushed garlic.

2 Stir in the yoghurt and fresh coriander. Season with the pepper. Cover and chill. Use the same day.

Melon and Basil Soup

A deliciously refreshing, chilled fruit soup, just right for a hot summer's day.

Serves 4–6

INGREDIENTS
2 Charentais or rock melons
75 g/3 oz/⅓ cup caster sugar
175 ml/6 fl oz/¾ cup water
finely grated rind and juice of 1 lime
45 ml/3 tbsp shredded fresh basil
fresh basil leaves, to garnish

basil

caster sugar

lime

Charentais melon

1 Cut the melons in half across the middle. Scrape out the seeds and discard. Using a melon baller, scoop out 20–24 balls and set aside for the garnish. Scoop out the remaining flesh and place in a blender or food processor.

2 Place the sugar, water and lime zest in a small pan over a low heat. Stir until dissolved, bring to the boil and simmer for 2–3 minutes. Remove from the heat and leave to cool slightly. Pour half the mixture into the blender or food processor with the melon flesh. Blend until smooth, adding the remaining syrup and lime juice to taste.

3 Pour the mixture into a bowl, stir in the basil and chill. Serve garnished with basil leaves and melon balls.

COOK'S TIP
Add the syrup in two stages, as the amount of sugar needed will depend on the sweetness of the melon.

Chilled Fresh Tomato Soup

This effortless uncooked soup can be made in minutes.

Serves 4–6

INGREDIENTS
1.5 kg/3–3½ lb ripe tomatoes, peeled
  and roughly chopped
4 garlic cloves, crushed
30 ml/2 tbsp extra-virgin olive oil
  (optional)
30 ml/2 tbsp balsamic vinegar
freshly ground black pepper
4 slices wholemeal bread
low-fat fromage blanc, to garnish

wholemeal bread

garlic

fromage blanc

peppercorns

tomato

COOK'S TIP
For the best flavour, it is important to use only fully ripened, flavourful tomatoes in this soup.

1 Place the tomatoes in a blender with the garlic and olive oil if using. Blend until smooth.

2 Pass the mixture through a sieve to remove the seeds. Stir in the balsamic vinegar and season to taste with pepper. Leave in the fridge to chill.

3 Toast the bread lightly on both sides. Whilst still hot, cut off the crusts and slice in half horizontally. Place the toast on a board with the uncooked sides facing down and, using a circular motion, rub to remove any doughy pieces of bread.

4 Cut each slice into 4 triangles. Place on a grill pan and toast the uncooked sides until lightly golden. Garnish each bowl of soup with a spoonful of fromage blanc and serve with the melba toast.

Leek, Parsnip and Ginger Soup

A flavoursome winter warmer, with the added spiciness of fresh ginger.

Serves 4–6

INGREDIENTS
30 ml/2 tbsp olive oil
225 g/8 oz leeks, sliced
25 g/1 oz fresh ginger root, finely chopped
675 g/1½ lb parsnips, roughly chopped
300 ml/½ pint/1¼ cups dry white wine
1.1 litres/2 pints/5 cups vegetable stock or water
salt and freshly ground black pepper
low-fat fromage blanc, to garnish
paprika, to garnish

1 Heat the oil in a large pan and add the leeks and ginger. Cook gently for 2–3 minutes, until the leeks start to soften.

ginger

parsnips

vegetable stock

2 Add the parsnips and cook for a further 7–8 minutes.

leek

3 Pour in the wine and stock or water and bring to the boil. Reduce the heat and simmer for 20–30 minutes or until the parsnips are tender.

4 Purée in a blender until smooth. Season to taste. Reheat and garnish with a swirl of fromage blanc and a light dusting of paprika.

Broccoli and Almond Soup

The creaminess of the toasted almonds combines perfectly with the slight bitterness of the taste of broccoli.

Serves 4–6

INGREDIENTS
50 g/2 oz/⅔ cup ground almonds
675 g/1½ lb broccoli
850 ml/1½ pints/3¾ cups vegetable
    stock or water
300 ml/½ pint/1¼ cups skimmed
    milk
salt and freshly ground black pepper

ground almonds

skimmed milk

broccoli

1 Preheat the oven to 180°C/350°F/ Gas 4. Spread the ground almonds evenly on a baking sheet and toast in the oven for about 10 minutes, or until golden. Reserve ¼ of the almonds and set aside for the garnish.

2 Cut the broccoli into small florets and steam for 6–7 minutes or until tender.

3 Place the remaining toasted almonds, broccoli, stock or water and milk in a blender and blend until smooth. Season to taste.

4 Reheat the soup and serve sprinkled with the reserved toasted almonds.

Red Onion and Beetroot Soup

This beautiful vivid ruby-red soup will look stunning at any dinner party.

Serves 4–6

INGREDIENTS
15 ml/1 tbsp olive oil
350 g/12 oz red onions, sliced
2 garlic cloves, crushed
275 g/10 oz cooked beetroot, cut into sticks
1.1 litres/2 pints/5 cups vegetable stock or water
50 g/2 oz/1 cup cooked soup pasta
30 ml/2 tbsp raspberry vinegar
salt and freshly ground black pepper
low-fat yogurt or fromage blanc, to garnish
snipped chives, to garnish

garlic

red onion

beetroot

pasta

chives

1 Heat the olive oil and add the onions and garlic.

2 Cook gently for about 20 minutes or until soft and tender.

3 Add the beetroot, stock or water, cooked pasta shapes and vinegar and heat through. Season to taste.

4 Ladle into bowls. Top each one with a spoonful of yogurt or fromage blanc and sprinkle with chives.

COOK'S TIP
Try substituting cooked barley for the pasta to give extra nuttiness.

Courgette Soup with Small Pasta Shells

A pretty, fresh-tasting soup which could be made using cucumber instead of courgettes (zucchini).

Serves 4–6

INGREDIENTS
60 ml/4 tbsp olive or sunflower oil
2 medium onions, finely chopped
1.5 litres/2½ pints/6¼ cups
    vegetable stock
900 g/2 lb courgettes
115 g/4 oz/1 cup small soup pasta
fresh lemon juice
30 ml/2 tbsp chopped fresh chervil
salt and ground black pepper
soured cream, to serve

courgettes

onion

soup pasta

chervil

1 Heat the oil in a large saucepan and add the onions. Cover and cook gently for about 20 minutes until very soft but not coloured, stirring occasionally.

2 Add the stock and bring to the boil.

3 Meanwhile grate the courgettes and stir into the boiling stock with the pasta. Turn down the heat and simmer for 15 minutes until the pasta is tender. Season to taste with lemon juice, salt and pepper.

4 Stir in the chervil and add a swirl of soured cream before serving.

COOK'S TIP
If no fresh stock is available, instead of using a stock cube, use canned chicken or beef consommé instead.

Fresh Tomato and Bean Soup

A rich chunky tomato soup, with beans and coriander. Serve with olive ciabatta.

Serves 4

INGREDIENTS
900 g/2 lb ripe plum tomatoes
30 ml/2 tbsp olive oil
275 g/10 oz onions, roughly chopped
2 garlic cloves, crushed
900 ml/1½ pints/3¾ cups
   vegetable stock
30 ml/2 tbsp sun-dried tomato paste
10 ml/2 tsp paprika
15 ml/1 tbsp cornflour
425 g/15 oz can cannellini beans,
   rinsed and drained
30 ml/2 tbsp chopped fresh coriander
salt and pepper
olive ciabatta, to serve

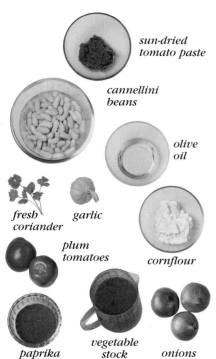

sun-dried tomato paste

cannellini beans

olive oil

fresh coriander

garlic

plum tomatoes

cornflour

paprika

vegetable stock

onions

1 First, peel the tomatoes. Using a sharp knife, make a small cross in each one and place in a bowl. Pour over boiling water to cover and leave to stand for 30–60 seconds.

2 Drain the tomatoes and peel off the skins. Quarter them and then cut each piece in half again.

3 Heat the oil in a large saucepan and cook the onions and garlic for 3 minutes, or until just beginning to soften.

4 Add the tomatoes to the onions, with the stock, sun-dried tomato paste and paprika. Season with a little salt and pepper. Bring to the boil and simmer for 10 minutes.

5 Mix the cornflour to a paste with 30 ml/2 tbsp water. Stir the beans into the soup with the cornflour paste. Cook for a further 5 minutes.

6 Adjust the seasoning and stir in the chopped coriander just before you serve with olive ciabatta.

Succotash Soup Plate

Succotash is a traditional North American Indian dish of sweetcorn and butter beans. This version is enriched with milk (you could use cream for ever-richer flavour) and it makes an appetizing and filling main course soup.

Serves 4

INGREDIENTS
50 g/2 oz/4 tbsp butter
1 large onion, chopped
2 large carrots, peeled and cut into
    short batons
900 ml/1½ pints/3¾ cups milk
1 vegetable stock cube
2 medium-sized waxy potatoes,
    peeled and diced
1 thyme sprig
225 g/8 oz/2 cups frozen sweetcorn
225 g/8 oz/3 cups frozen butter beans
    or broad beans
30 ml/2 tbsp chopped fresh parsley,
    to garnish

carrots   *sweetcorn*

thyme   *beans*

potatoes   *parsley*

1 Heat the butter in a large saucepan. Add the onion and carrots and cook over a gentle heat for 3–4 minutes, to soften without colouring.

2 Add the milk, stock cube, potatoes, thyme, sweetcorn and butter beans or broad beans. Simmer for 10 minutes until the potatoes are cooked through.

COOK'S TIP
Frozen sweetcorn and butter beans are best for flavour and convenience in this soup, although the canned variety may also be used.

3 Season to taste, ladle into soup plates and garnish with chopped fresh parsley.

Cauliflower, Flageolet and Fennel Seed Soup

The sweet, anise-liquorice flavour of the fennel seeds gives a delicious edge to this hearty soup.

Serves 4–6

INGREDIENTS
15 ml/1 tbsp olive oil
1 garlic clove, crushed
1 onion, chopped
10 ml/2 tsp fennel seeds
1 cauliflower, cut into small florets
2 × 400 g/14 oz cans flageolet beans,
    drained and rinsed
1.1 litres/2 pints/5 cups vegetable
    stock or water
salt and freshly ground black pepper
chopped fresh parsley, to garnish
toasted slices of French bread, to
    serve

flageolet beans

French bread

onion

garlic

cauliflower

fennel seeds

parsley

1 Heat the olive oil. Add the garlic, onion and fennel seeds and cook gently for 5 minutes or until softened.

2 Add the cauliflower, half of the beans and the stock or water.

3 Bring to the boil. Reduce the heat and simmer for 10 minutes or until the cauliflower is tender.

4 Pour the soup into a blender and blend until smooth. Stir in the remaining beans and season to taste. Reheat and pour into bowls. Sprinkle with chopped parsley and serve with toasted slices of French bread.

Creamy Parmesan and Cauliflower Soup with Pasta Bows

A silky smooth, mildly cheesy soup which isn't overpowered by the cauliflower. It is an elegant dinner party soup served with the crisp melba toast.

Serves 6

INGREDIENTS
1 large cauliflower
1.1 litres/2 pints/5 cups vegetable stock
175 g/6 oz/1½ cups pasta bows (farfalle)
150 ml/¼ pint/⅔ cup single cream
freshly grated nutmeg
pinch of cayenne pepper
60 ml/4 tbsp freshly grated Parmesan cheese
salt and pepper

FOR THE MELBA TOAST
3–4 slices day-old white bread
freshly grated Parmesan cheese for sprinkling
1.5 ml/¼ tsp paprika

cauliflower

pasta bows

Parmesan cheese

nutmeg

1 Cut the leaves and central stalk away from the cauliflower and discard. Divide the cauliflower into florets.

2 Bring the stock to the boil and add the cauliflower. Simmer for about 10 minutes or until very soft. Remove the cauliflower with a perforated spoon and place in a food processor.

3 Add the pasta to the stock and simmer for 10 minutes until tender. Drain, reserve the pasta, and pour the liquid over the cauliflower in the food processor. Add the cream or milk, nutmeg, and cayenne to the cauliflower. Blend until smooth, then press through a strainer. Stir in the cooked pasta. Reheat the soup and stir in the Parmesan. Taste and adjust the seasoning.

4 Meanwhile make the melba toast. Pre-heat the oven to 180°C/350°F/gas mark 4. Toast the bread lightly on both sides. Quickly cut off the crusts and split each slice in half horizontally. Scrape off any doughy bits and sprinkle with Parmesan and paprika. Place on a baking sheet and bake in the oven for 10–15 minutes or until uniformly golden. Serve with the soup.

Garlic, Chick-pea and Spinach Soup

This delicious, thick and creamy soup is richly flavoured and perfect for vegetarians.

Serves 4

INGREDIENTS

30 ml/2 tbsp olive oil
4 garlic cloves, crushed
1 onion, roughly chopped
10 ml/2 tsp ground cumin
10 ml/2 tsp ground coriander
1.2 litres/2 pints/5 cups
　　vegetable stock
350 g/12 oz potatoes, peeled and
　　finely chopped
425 g/15 oz can chick-peas, drained
15 ml/1 tbsp cornflour
150 ml/¼ pint/⅔ cup double cream
30 ml/2 tbsp light tahini (sesame
　　seed paste)
200 g/7 oz spinach, shredded
cayenne pepper
salt and pepper

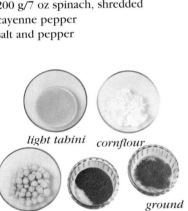

light tahini　　*cornflour*

chick-peas　*cayenne pepper*　*ground coriander*

double cream　*garlic*　*spinach*　*potatoes*

onion　*vegetable stock*　*ground cumin*　*olive oil*

1 Heat the oil in a large saucepan and cook the garlic and onion for 5 minutes, or until they are softened and golden brown.

2 Stir in the cumin and coriander and cook for a further minute.

3 Pour in the stock and add the potatoes. Bring to the boil and simmer for 10 minutes. Add the drained chick-peas and simmer for a further 5 minutes, or until the potatoes and chick-peas are just tender.

4 Blend together the cornflour, cream, tahini and plenty of seasoning. Stir into the soup with the spinach. Bring to the boil, stirring, and simmer for a further 2 minutes. Adjust the seasoning with salt, pepper and cayenne pepper to taste. Serve immediately, sprinkled with a little cayenne pepper.

Tomato and Fresh Basil Soup

A soup for late summer, when fresh tomatoes are at their most flavoursome.

Serves 4–6

INGREDIENTS
15 ml/1 tbsp olive oil
25 g/1 oz/2 tbsp butter
1 onion, finely chopped
900 g/2 lb ripe plum tomatoes, roughly chopped
1 garlic clove, roughly chopped
about 750 ml/1¼ pints/3 cups vegetable stock
120ml//4 fl oz/½ cup dry white wine
30 ml/2 tbsp sun-dried tomato paste
30 ml/2 tbsp shredded fresh basil, plus a few whole leaves, to garnish
150 ml/¼ pint/⅔ cup double cream
salt and ground black pepper

olive oil *garlic*
stock
butter
onion
double cream
white wine
basil
plum tomatoes *sun-dried tomato paste*

VARIATION
The soup can also be served chilled. Pour it into a container after sieving and chill for at least 4 hours. Serve in chilled bowls.

1 Heat the oil and butter in a large saucepan over a medium heat until foaming. Add the onion and cook gently for about 5 minutes, stirring frequently, until it is softened but not brown.

2 Stir in the chopped tomatoes and garlic, then add the stock, white wine and sun-dried tomato paste, with salt and pepper to taste. Bring to the boil, then lower the heat, half-cover the pan and simmer gently for 20 minutes, stirring occasionally to stop the tomatoes sticking to the base of the pan.

3 Process the soup with the shredded basil in a blender or food processor, then press through a sieve into a clean pan.

4 Add the double cream and heat through, stirring. Do not allow the soup to approach boiling point. Check the consistency and add more stock if necessary, then adjust the seasoning. Pour into heated bowls and garnish with whole basil leaves. Serve at once.

Vegetable Minestrone with Anellini

Serves 6–8

INGREDIENTS

large pinch of saffron strands
1 onion, chopped
1 leek, sliced
1 celery stick, sliced
2 carrots, diced
2–3 garlic cloves, crushed
600 ml/1 pint/2½ cups vegetable
    stock
2 x 400 g/14 oz cans chopped
    tomatoes
50 g/2 oz/½ cup frozen peas
50 g/2 oz/½ cup anellini soup pasta
5 ml/1 tsp caster sugar
15 ml/1 tbsp chopped fresh parsley
15 ml/1 tbsp chopped fresh basil
salt and ground black pepper

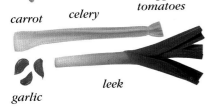

anellini   *frozen peas*   *onion*

saffron strands   *basil*   *stock*

parsley

chopped tomatoes

carrot   *celery*

garlic   *leek*

1 Soak the pinch of saffron strands in 15 ml/1 tbsp boiling water. Leave to stand for 10 minutes.

2 Meanwhile, put the prepared onion, leek, celery, carrots and garlic into a pan. Add the stock, bring to the boil, cover and simmer for 10 minutes.

3 Add the canned tomatoes, the saffron with its liquid, and the peas. Bring back to the boil and add the anellini. Simmer for 10 minutes until tender.

4 Season with salt, pepper and sugar to taste. Stir in the chopped herbs just before serving.

Stuffed Garlic Mushrooms with a Parsley Crust

These garlic mushrooms are perfect for dinner parties, or you could serve them in larger portions as a light supper dish with a green salad. Try them stuffed with a healthy dose of freshly chopped parsley.

Serves 4

INGREDIENTS
350 g/12 oz large mushrooms, stems removed
3 garlic cloves, crushed
175 g/6 oz/¾ cup butter, softened
50 g/2 oz/1 cup fresh white breadcrumbs
50 g/2 oz/1 cup fresh parsley, chopped
1 egg, beaten
salt and cayenne pepper
8 cherry tomatoes, to garnish

parsley

butter *egg*

garlic

mushrooms

breadcrumbs

1 Preheat the oven to 190°C/375°F/ Gas 5. Arrange the mushrooms cup side uppermost on a baking tray. Mix together the crushed garlic and butter in a small bowl and divide 115 g/4 oz/½ cup of the butter between the mushrooms.

2 Heat the remaining butter in a frying pan and lightly fry the breadcrumbs until golden brown. Place the chopped parsley in a bowl, add the breadcrumbs, season to taste and mix well.

3 Stir in the egg and use the mixture to fill the mushroom caps. Bake for 10–15 minutes until the topping has browned and the mushrooms have softened. Garnish with quartered tomatoes.

COOK'S TIP
If you are planning ahead, stuffed mushrooms can be prepared up to 12 hours in advance and kept in the fridge before baking.

Brie Parcels with Almonds

A sophisticated starter or light main course, served with crusty bread.

Serves 4

4 large vine leaves, preserved in
  brine
200 g/7 oz piece Brie cheese
30 ml/2 tbsp chopped fresh
  chives
30 ml/2 tbsp ground almonds
5 ml/1 tsp crushed black
  peppercorns
15 ml/1 tbsp olive oil
flaked almonds

vine leaves

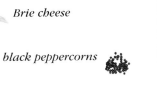

Brie cheese

black peppercorns

chives

flaked almonds

olive oil

ground almonds

1 Rinse the vine leaves thoroughly in cold water and dry them well. Spread the leaves out on a board.

2 Cut the Brie into four chunks and place each chunk on a vine leaf.

3 Mix together the chives, ground almonds, peppercorns and oil; then place a spoonful on top of each piece of cheese. Sprinkle with flaked almonds.

4 Fold the vine leaves over, to enclose the cheese completely. Brush with oil and cook on a hot barbecue for 3–4 minutes, until the cheese is hot and melting. Serve immediately.

Roasted Garlic Toasts

A delicious starter or accompaniment to vegetable dishes.

Serves 4

2 whole garlic heads
extra-virgin olive oil
fresh rosemary sprigs
ciabatta loaf or thick baguette
chopped fresh rosemary
salt and freshly ground black
    pepper

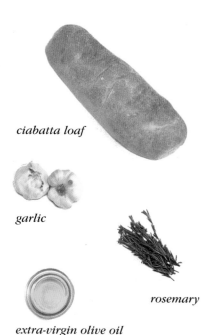

ciabatta loaf

garlic

rosemary

extra-virgin olive oil

1 Slice the tops from the heads of garlic, with a sharp knife.

2 Brush with oil, and then wrap in foil, with a few sprigs of rosemary. Cook on a medium–hot barbecue for 25–30 minutes, turning occasionally, until soft.

3 Slice the bread and brush generously with oil. Toast on the barbecue until golden, turning once.

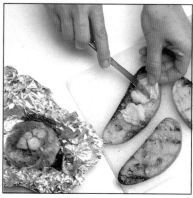

4 Squeeze the garlic cloves from their skins on to the toasts, then sprinkle the toasts with chopped fresh rosemary, a little extra olive oil and salt and pepper to taste.

COOK'S TIP

Roast a few aubergine, pepper or onion slices, to spread over the toasts, for variety.

Aubergine, Tomato and Feta Rolls

Grilled aubergines wrapped around tangy feta cheese, flavoured with basil and sun-dried tomatoes make a wonderful combination of sunshine flavours.

Serves 4

2 large aubergines
olive oil
10–12 sun-dried tomatoes in oil, drained
handful of large, fresh basil leaves
150 g/5 oz feta cheese
salt and freshly ground black pepper

olive oil

aubergines

feta cheese

basil

sun-dried tomatoes in oil

COOK'S TIP

Vegetarians or vegans could use tofu in place of the feta cheese. For extra flavour, sprinkle the tofu with a little soy sauce before wrapping.

1 Slice the aubergines lengthways into 5 mm/¼ in thick slices. Sprinkle with salt and layer in a colander. Leave to drain for about 30 minutes.

2 Rinse the aubergines in cold water and dry well. Brush with oil on both sides and grill on a hot barbecue for 2–3 minutes, turning once, until golden brown and softened.

3 Arrange the sun-dried tomatoes over one end of each aubergine slice and top with the basil leaves. Cut the feta into short sticks and place on top. Season with salt and pepper.

4 Roll the aubergine slices around to enclose the filling. Cook on the barbecue for a further 2–3 minutes, until hot. Serve with ciabatta bread.

Aubergine, Roast Garlic and Red Pepper Pâté

This is a simple pâté of smoky baked aubergine, sweet pink peppercorns and red peppers, with more than a hint of garlic!

Serves 4

INGREDIENTS
3 medium aubergines
2 red peppers
5 whole garlic cloves
7.5 ml/1½ tsp pink peppercorns in brine, drained and crushed
30 ml/2 tbsp chopped fresh coriander

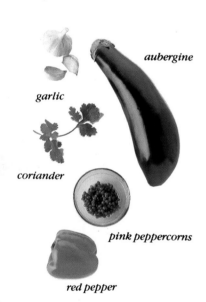

aubergine

garlic

coriander

pink peppercorns

red pepper

1 Preheat the oven to 200°C/400°F/Gas 6. Arrange the whole aubergines, peppers and garlic cloves on a baking sheet and place in the oven. After 10 minutes remove the garlic cloves and turn over the aubergines and peppers.

2 Peel the garlic cloves and place in the bowl of a blender.

3 After a further 20 minutes remove the blistered and charred peppers from the oven and place in a plastic bag. Leave to cool.

4 After a further 10 minutes remove the aubergines from the oven. Split in half and scoop the flesh into a sieve placed over a bowl. Press the flesh with a spoon to remove the bitter juices.

5 Add the mixture to the garlic in the blender and blend until smooth. Place in a large mixing bowl.

6 Peel and chop the red peppers and stir into the aubergine mixture. Mix in the peppercorns and fresh coriander and serve at once.

Grilled Mixed Peppers with Feta and Green Salsa

Soft smoky grilled peppers make a lovely combination with the slightly tart salsa.

Serves 4

INGREDIENTS

4 medium peppers in different
   colours
45 ml/3 tbsp chopped fresh flat-leaf
   parsley
45 ml/3 tbsp chopped fresh dill
45 ml/3 tbsp chopped fresh mint
½ small red onion, finely chopped
15 ml/1 tbsp capers, coarsely chopped
50 g/2 oz/¼ cup Greek olives, pitted
   and sliced
1 fresh green chilli, seeded and finely
   chopped
60 g/4 tbsp pistachios, chopped
75 ml/5 tbsp extra-virgin olive oil
45 ml/3 tbsp fresh lime juice
115 g/4 oz/½ cup medium-fat feta
   cheese, crumbled
25 g/1 oz gherkins, finely chopped

olives

feta cheese

green chilli

mint

pistachios

peppers

gherkins

red onion

1 Preheat the grill. Place the whole peppers on a tray and grill until charred and blistered.

2 Place the peppers in a plastic bag and leave to cool.

COOK'S TIP

Feta cheese is quite salty so if preferred, soak in cold water and drain well before using.

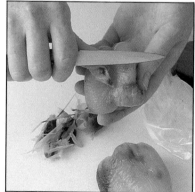

3 Peel, seed and cut the peppers into even strips.

4 Mix all the remaining ingredients together, and stir in the pepper strips.

Artichokes with Garlic and Herb Butter

It is fun eating artichokes and even more fun to share one between two people. You can always have a second one to follow so that you get your fair share!

Serves 4

INGREDIENTS
2 large or 4 medium
    globe artichokes
salt

FOR THE GARLIC AND HERB BUTTER
75 g/3 oz/6 tbsp butter
1 garlic clove, crushed
15 ml/1 tbsp chopped fresh
    mixed herbs

butter

garlic

mixed herbs

globe artichokes

1 Wash the artichokes well in cold water. Using a sharp knife, cut off the stalks level with the bases. Cut off the top 1 cm/½ in of leaves. Snip off the pointed ends of the remaining leaves with scissors and discard.

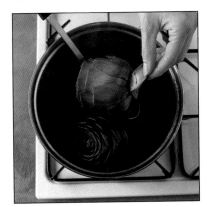

2 Put the prepared artichokes in a large saucepan of lightly salted water. Bring to the boil, cover and cook for about 40–45 minutes or until one of the lower leaves comes away easily from the choke when gently pulled.

4 Place the artichokes on individual serving plates and serve with the garlic and herb butter.

3 Drain upside down for a couple of minutes while making the sauce. Melt the butter over a low heat, add the garlic and cook for 30 seconds. Remove from the heat, stir in the herbs and then pour into one or two small serving bowls.

COOK'S TIP
To eat an artichoke, pull off each leaf and dip into the garlic and herb butter. Scrape off the soft, fleshy base with your teeth. When the centre is reached, pull out the hairy choke and discard it, as it is inedible. The base can be cut up and eaten with the remaining garlic butter.

Stuffed Vine Leaves

Based on the Greek dolmades, but with a vegetarian brown rice stuffing, this makes an excellent starter, snack or buffet dish.

Makes about 40

INGREDIENTS

15 ml/1 tbsp sunflower oil
5 ml/1 tsp sesame oil
1 onion, finely chopped
225 g/8 oz/1¼ cups brown rice
600 ml/1 pint/2½ cups vegetable stock
1 small yellow pepper, seeded and finely chopped
115 g/4 oz/½ cup ready-to-eat dried apricots, finely chopped
2 lemons
50 g/2 oz/⅔ cup pine nuts
45 ml/3 tbsp chopped fresh parsley
30 ml/2 tbsp chopped fresh mint
2.5 ml/½ tsp mixed spice
225 g/8 oz packet vine leaves preserved in brine, drained
30 ml/2 tbsp olive oil
freshly ground black pepper
lemon wedges, to garnish

TO SERVE

300 ml/½ pint/1¼ cups low-fat natural yogurt
30 ml/2 tbsp chopped mixed fresh herbs
cayenne pepper

yogurt   *cayenne pepper*

mint   *mixed herbs*

pine nuts

parsley   *olive oil*

onion

sunflower oil   *sesame oil*   *yellow pepper*   *vine leaves*

mixed spice

brown rice   *vegetable stock*   *dried apricots*   *lemons*

1 Heat the sunflower and sesame oils together in a large saucepan. Add the onion and cook gently for 5 minutes to soften. Add the rice, stirring to coat the grains in oil. Pour in the stock, bring to the boil, then lower the heat, cover the pan and simmer for 30 minutes, or until the rice is tender but *al dente*.

2 Stir in the chopped pepper and apricots, with a little more stock if necessary. Replace the lid and cook for a further 5 minutes. Grate the rind from one of the lemons then squeeze both.

3 Drain off any stock which has not been absorbed by the rice. Stir in the pine nuts, herbs, mixed spice, grated lemon rind and half the juice. Season with pepper and set aside.

5 Pack the parcels closely together in a shallow serving dish. Mix the remaining lemon juice with the olive oil. Pour the mixture over the vine leaves, cover and chill before serving. Garnish with lemon wedges. Spoon the yogurt into a bowl, stir in the chopped herbs and sprinkle with a little cayenne. Serve with the stuffed vine leaves.

4 Bring a saucepan of water to the boil and blanch the vine leaves for 5 minutes. Drain the leaves well, then lay them shiny side down on a board. Cut out any coarse stalks. Place a heap of the rice mixture in the centre of each vine leaf. Fold the stem end over, then the sides and pointed end to make neat parcels.

COOK'S TIP

If vine leaves are not available, the leaves of Swiss chard, young spinach or cabbage can be used instead.

Breaded Aubergine with Hot Vinaigrette

Crisp on the outside, beautifully tender within, these aubergine slices taste wonderful with a spicy dressing flavoured with chilli and capers.

Serves 2

INGREDIENTS
1 large aubergine
50 g/2 oz/¹/₂ cup plain flour
2 eggs, beaten
115 g/4 oz/2 cups fresh
  white breadcrumbs
vegetable oil for frying
1 head radicchio
salt and freshly ground black pepper

FOR THE DRESSING
30 ml/2 tbsp olive oil
1 garlic clove, crushed
15 ml/1 tbsp capers, drained
15 ml/1 tbsp white wine vinegar
15 ml/1 tbsp chilli oil

COOK'S TIP
When serving a salad with a warm dressing use robust leaves that will stand up to the heat.

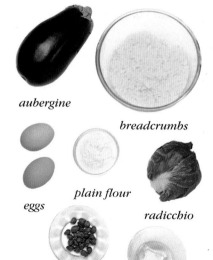

aubergine

breadcrumbs

eggs

plain flour

radicchio

capers

garlic clove

white wine vinegar

1 Top and tail the aubergine. Cut it into 5 mm/¹/₄ in slices. Set aside.

2 Season the flour with a generous amount of salt and black pepper. Spread out in a shallow dish. Pour the beaten eggs into a second dish, and spread out the breadcrumbs in a third.

3 Dip the aubergine slices in the flour, then in the beaten egg and finally in the breadcrumbs, patting them on to make an even coating.

4 Pour vegetable oil into a large frying pan to a depth of about 5 mm/¹/₄ in. Heat the oil, then fry the aubergine slices for 3–4 minutes, turning once. Drain on kitchen paper.

5 Heat the olive oil in a small pan. Add the garlic and the capers and cook over gentle heat for 1 minute. Increase the heat, add the vinegar and cook for 30 seconds. Stir in the chilli oil and remove the pan from the heat.

6 Arrange the radicchio leaves on two plates. Top with the hot aubergine slices. Drizzle over the vinaigrette and serve.

Vegetable Tempura

These deep-fried fritters are based on Kaki-age, a Japanese dish that often incorporates fish and prawns as well as vegetables.

COOK'S TIP
Paring strips of peel from the courgettes and aubergine will avoid too much tough skin in the finished dish.

Makes 8

INGREDIENTS
2 medium courgettes
½ medium aubergine
1 large carrot
½ small Spanish onion
1 egg
120 ml/4 fl oz/½ cup
    iced water
115 g/4 oz/1 cup plain flour
salt and ground black pepper
vegetable oil, for deep-frying
sea salt flakes, lemon slices and
    Japanese soy sauce (*shoyu*),
    to serve

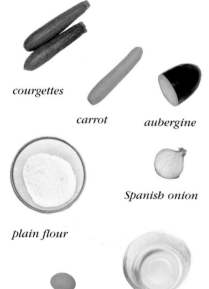

courgettes

carrot *aubergine*

Spanish onion

plain flour

egg *vegetable oil*

1 Using a potato peeler, pare strips of peel from the courgettes and aubergine to give a stripy effect.

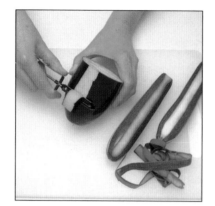

2 Cut the courgettes, aubergine and carrot into strips about 7.5–10 cm/ 3–4 in long and 3 mm/⅛ in wide.

3 Put the courgettes, aubergine and carrot in a colander and sprinkle liberally with salt. Leave for about 30 minutes, then rinse thoroughly under cold running water. Drain well.

4 Thinly slice the onion from top to base, discarding the plump pieces in the middle. Separate the layers so that there are lots of fine long strips. Mix all the vegetables together and season with salt and pepper.

5 Make the batter immediately before frying: mix the egg and iced water in a bowl, then sift in the flour. Mix very briefly using a fork or chopsticks. Do not overmix – the batter should remain lumpy. Add the vegetables to the batter and mix to combine.

6 Meanwhile, half-fill a wok with oil and heat to 180°C/350°F. Scoop up one heaped tablespoon of the mixture at a time and carefully lower into the oil. Deep fry in batches for about 3 minutes until golden brown and crisp. Drain on kitchen paper. Serve each diner with salt, lemon slices and a tiny bowl of Japanese soy sauce for dipping.

Cheese-stuffed Pears

These pears, with their scrumptious creamy topping, make a sublime dish when served with a simple salad.

Serves 4

INGREDIENTS

50 g/2 oz/¼ cup ricotta cheese
50 g/2 oz/¼ cup dolcelatte cheese
15 ml/1 tbsp honey
½ celery stick, finely sliced
8 green olives, pitted and roughly chopped
4 dates, stoned and cut into thin strips
pinch of paprika
4 ripe pears
150 ml/¼ pint/⅔ cup apple juice

honey

pear

apple juice

dates

dolcelatte

celery

olives

1 Preheat the oven to 200°C/400°F/ Gas 6. Place the ricotta in a bowl and crumble in the dolcelatte. Add the rest of the ingredients except for the pears and apple juice and mix well.

2 Halve the pears lengthwise and use a melon baller to remove the cores. Place in a ovenproof dish and divide the filling equally between them.

COOK'S TIP

Choose ripe pears in season such as Conference, William or Comice.

3 Pour in the apple juice and cover the dish with foil. Bake for 20 minutes or until the pears are tender.

4 Remove the foil and place the dish under a hot grill for 3 minutes. Serve immediately.

Nutty Cheese Balls

An extremely quick and simple recipe. Try making a smaller version to serve as canapés at a drinks party.

Serves 4

INGREDIENTS
225 g/8 oz/1 cup low-fat soft cheese
   such as Quark
50 g/2 oz/¼ cup dolcelatte cheese
15 ml/1 tbsp finely chopped onion
15 ml/1 tbsp finely chopped celery
   stick
15 ml/1 tbsp finely chopped parsley
15 ml/1 tbsp finely chopped gherkin
5 ml/1 tsp brandy or port (optional)
pinch of paprika
50 g/2 oz/½ cup walnuts, roughly
   chopped
90 ml/6 tbsp snipped chives
salt and freshly ground black pepper

celery

dolcelatte

gherkins *soft cheese*

onion

walnuts

chives

parsley

paprika

1 Beat the soft cheese and dolcelatte together using a spoon.

2 Mix in all the remaining ingredients, except the snipped chives.

3 Divide the mixture into 12 pieces and roll into balls.

4 Roll each ball gently in the snipped chives. Leave in the fridge to chill for about an hour before serving.

Rice Cakes with Cream and Mixed Mushrooms

Mushroom-topped rice cakes, served with a few spring vegetables, make a memorable starter.

Serves 4

INGREDIENTS

165 g/5½ oz/¾ cup long grain rice
1 egg
15 ml/1 tbsp plain flour
60 ml/4 tbsp freshly grated Parmesan, Fontina or Pecorino cheese
50 g/2 oz/¼ cup unsalted butter, plus extra for frying rice cakes
1 small onion, chopped
175 g/6 oz/1½-2 cups assorted wild and cultivated mushrooms, trimmed and sliced
1 fresh thyme sprig
30 ml/2 tbsp Madeira or sherry
150 ml/¼ pint/⅔ cup soured cream or crème fraîche
salt and freshly ground black pepper
paprika for dusting (optional)

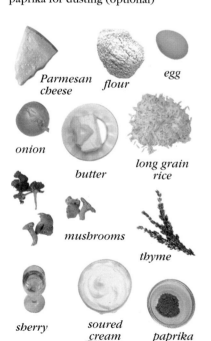

Parmesan cheese   flour   egg

onion   butter   long grain rice

mushrooms   thyme

sherry   soured cream   paprika

1 Bring a saucepan of water to the boil. Add the rice and cook for about 12 minutes. Rinse, drain and cool.

2 Beat the egg, flour and cheese together with a fork, then stir in the cold cooked rice. Mix well and set aside. Melt half the butter and fry the onion until soft but not browned. Add the mushrooms and thyme and cook until the juices run. Add the Madeira or sherry. Increase the heat to reduce the juices and concentrate the flavour. Season to taste, transfer to a bowl, cover and keep hot.

3 Using a dessert spoon, shape the rice mixture into cakes. Melt a knob of butter in a frying pan and fry the rice cakes in batches for 1 minute on each side. Add more butter as needed. Keep the fried rice cakes hot.

4 When all the rice cakes are cooked, arrange on four warmed plates, top with soured cream or crème fraîche and add a spoonful of mushrooms. Dust with paprika, if using. Serve with a selection of cooked vegetables, if you like.

COOK'S TIP

Although the recipe specifies Parmesan, Fontina or Pecorino, you could use mature Cheddar cheese or even a hard goat's cheese.

Oatmeal Tartlets with Minted Hummus

Serve these wholesome little tartlets with a crisp salad of cos lettuce.

Serves 6

INGREDIENTS
225 g/8 oz/1½ cups medium oatmeal
2.5 ml/½ tsp bicarbonate of soda
5 ml/1 tsp salt
25g/1 oz/2 tbsp butter
1 egg yolk
30 ml/2 tbsp skimmed milk
1 × 400 g/14 oz can chick-peas,
    rinsed and drained
juice of 1–2 lemons
350 g/12 oz/1½ cups low-fat fromage
    blanc
60 ml/4 tbsp tahini
freshly ground black pepper
45 ml/3 tbsp chopped fresh mint
25 g/1 oz/2 tbsp pumpkin seeds
paprika, for dusting

tahini

pumpkin seeds

fromage blanc

chick-peas

oatmeal

mint

lemon

1 Preheat the oven to 160°C/325°F/ Gas 3. Mix together the oatmeal, bicarbonate of soda and salt in a large bowl. Rub in the butter until the mixture resembles fine breadcrumbs. Stir in the egg yolk and add the milk if the mixture seems too dry.

2 Press into 6 × 9 cm/3½ in tartlet tins. Bake for 25–30 minutes. Allow to cool.

3 Purée the chick-peas, the juice of 1 lemon, fromage blanc and tahini in a food processor until smooth. Spoon into a bowl and season with black pepper and more lemon juice to taste. Stir in the chopped mint. Divide between the tartlet moulds, sprinkle with pumpkin seeds and dust with paprika.

Parsnip and Pecan Gougères with Watercress and Rocket Sauce

These scrumptious nutty puffs conceal a surprisingly sweet parsnip centre.

Makes 18

INGREDIENTS

115 g/4 oz/½ cup butter
300 ml/½ pint/1¼ cups water
75 g/3 oz/¾ cup plain flour
50 g/2 oz/½ cup wholemeal flour
3 × size 3 eggs, beaten
25 g/1 oz Cheddar cheese, grated
pinch of cayenne pepper or paprika
75 g/3 oz/⅔ cup pecans, chopped
1 medium parsnip, cut into
    18 × 2 cm/¾ in pieces
15 ml/1 tbsp skimmed milk
10 ml/2 tsp sesame seeds

FOR THE SAUCE

150 g/5 oz watercress, trimmed
150 g/5 oz rocket, trimmed
175 ml/6 fl oz/¾ cup low-fat yogurt
salt, grated nutmeg and freshly ground
    black pepper
watercress sprigs, to garnish

1 Preheat the oven to 200°C/400°F/ Gas 6. Place the butter and water in a pan. Bring to the boil and add all the flour in one go. Beat vigorously until the mixture leaves the sides of the pan and forms a ball. Remove from heat and allow the mixture to cool slightly. Beat in the eggs a little at a time until the mixture is shiny and soft enough to fall gently from a spoon.

2 Beat in the Cheddar, cayenne pepper or paprika and the chopped pecans.

3 Lightly grease a baking sheet and drop onto it 18 heaped tablespoons of the mixture. Place a piece of parsnip on each and top with another heaped tablespoon of the mixture.

4 Brush the gougères with a little milk and sprinkle with sesame seeds. Bake in the oven for 25–30 minutes until firm and golden.

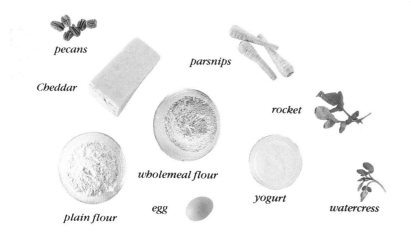

pecans

Cheddar

parsnips

rocket

wholemeal flour

plain flour

egg

yogurt

watercress

5 Meanwhile make the sauce. Bring a pan of water to the boil and blanch the watercress and rocket for 2–3 minutes. Drain and immediately refresh in cold water. Drain well and chop.

6 Purée the watercress and rocket in a blender or food processor with the yogurt until smooth. Season to taste with salt, nutmeg and freshly ground black pepper. To reheat, place the sauce in a bowl over a gently simmering pan of hot water and heat gently, taking care not to let the sauce curdle. Garnish with watercress.

Asparagus Rolls with Herb Butter Sauce

For a taste sensation, try tender asparagus spears wrapped in crisp filo pastry. The buttery herb sauce makes the perfect accompaniment.

Serves 2

INGREDIENTS
4 sheets of filo pastry
50 g/2 oz/¼ cup butter, melted
16 young asparagus spears, trimmed

FOR THE SAUCE
2 shallots, finely chopped
1 bay leaf
150 ml/¼ pint/⅔ cup dry white wine
175 g/6 oz butter, softened
15 ml/1 tbsp chopped fresh herbs
salt and freshly ground black pepper
snipped chives, to garnish

fresh herbs

chives

dry white wine

asparagus spears

filo pastry   *butter*

bay leaf   *shallots*

1 Preheat the oven to 200°C/400°F/ Gas 6. Brush each filo sheet with melted butter. Fold one corner of the sheet down to the bottom edge to give a wedge shape.

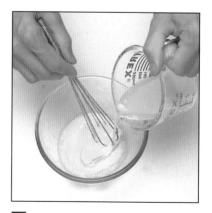

2 Lay 4 asparagus spears on top at the longest edge and roll up towards the shortest edge. Using the remaining filo and asparagus spears make 3 more rolls in the same way.

3 Lay the rolls on a greased baking sheet. Brush with the remaining melted butter. Bake in the oven for 8 minutes until golden.

4 Meanwhile, put the shallots, bay leaf and wine into a pan. Cover and cook over a high heat until the wine is reduced to about 45–60 ml/3–4 tbsp.

5 Strain the wine mixture into a bowl. Whisk in the butter, a little at a time, until the sauce is smooth and glossy.

6 Stir in the herbs and add salt and pepper to taste. Return to the pan and keep the sauce warm. Serve the rolls on individual plates with a salad garnish, if liked. Serve the butter sauce separately, sprinkled with a few snipped chives.

Red Pepper and Watercress Filo Parcels

Peppery watercress combines well with sweet red pepper in these crisp little parcels.

Makes 8

INGREDIENTS
3 red peppers
175 g/6 oz watercress
225 g/8 oz/1 cup ricotta cheese
50 g/2 oz/¼ cup blanched almonds,
   toasted and chopped
salt and freshly ground black pepper
8 sheets of filo pastry
30 ml/2 tbsp olive oil

ricotta

red pepper

watercress

almonds

filo pastry

1 Preheat the oven to 190°C/375°F/
Gas 5. Place the peppers under a hot grill until blistered and charred. Place in a plastic bag. When cool enough to handle peel, seed and pat dry on kitchen paper.

2 Place the peppers and watercress in a food processor and pulse until coarsely chopped. Spoon into a bowl.

3 Mix in the ricotta and almonds, and season to taste.

4 Working with 1 sheet of filo pastry at a time, cut out 2 × 18 cm/7 in and 2 × 5 cm/2 in squares from each sheet. Brush 1 large square with a little olive oil and place a second large square at an angle of 90 degrees to form a star shape.

5 Place 1 of the small squares in the centre of the star shape, brush lightly with oil and top with a second small square.

6 Top with ⅛ of the red pepper mixture. Bring the edges together to form a purse shape and twist to seal. Place on a lightly greased baking sheet and cook for 25–30 minutes until golden.

Ciabatta Rolls with Courgettes and Saffron

Split crunchy ciabatta rolls are filled with courgettes in a creamy tomato sauce flavoured with saffron. Use a mixture of green and yellow courgettes if possible.

Serves 4

INGREDIENTS
675 g/1½ lb small courgettes
15 ml/1 tbsp olive oil
2 shallots, freshly chopped
4 ciabatta rolls
200 g/7 oz can chopped tomatoes
pinch of sugar
a few saffron threads
50 ml/2 fl oz/¼ cup single cream
salt and freshly ground black pepper

courgettes

chopped tomatoes

saffron

shallots

ciabatta rolls   *single cream*

COOK'S TIP
To avoid heating your oven, heat the rolls in a microwave. Put them on a plate, cover with kitchen paper and heat on HIGH for 30–45 seconds.

1 Preheat the oven to 180°C/350°F/ Gas 4. Top and tail the courgettes. Then, using a sharp knife, cut them into 4 cm/1½ in lengths, then cut each piece into quarters lengthways.

2 Heat the oil in a large frying pan. Add the shallots and fry over a moderate heat for 1–2 minutes. Put the rolls into the oven to warm through.

3 Add the courgettes to the shallots, mix well and cook for 6 minutes, stirring frequently, until just beginning to soften.

4 Stir in the tomatoes and sugar. Steep the saffron threads in a little hot water for a few minutes, then add to the pan with the cream. Cook for 4 minutes, stirring occasionally. Season to taste. Split open the rolls and fill with the courgettes and sauce.

Brioche with Mixed Mushrooms

Mushrooms in a rich sherry sauce, served on toasted brioche, make a delectable lunch, but would also serve 6 as a starter.

Serves 4

INGREDIENTS

75 g/3 oz/6 tbsp butter
1 vegetable stock cube
450 g/1 lb shiitake mushrooms,
  caps only, sliced
225 g/8 oz button
  mushrooms, sliced
45 ml/3 tbsp dry sherry
250 ml/8 fl oz/1 cup crème fraîche
10 ml/2 tsp lemon juice
8 thick slices of brioche
salt and freshly ground black pepper

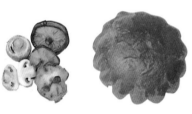

shiitake and button mushrooms

brioche

butter

stock cube

crème fraîche

lemon

COOK'S TIP

If shiitake mushrooms are too expensive or not available, substitute more button or brown cap mushrooms. Wipe the mushrooms with kitchen paper before use.

1 Melt the butter in a large pan. Crumble in the stock cube and stir for about 30 seconds.

2 Add the shiitake and button mushrooms to the pan and cook for 5 minutes over a moderate to high heat, stirring occasionally.

3 Stir in the sherry. Cook for 1 minute, then add the crème fraîche. Cook, stirring, over a gentle heat for 5 minutes. Stir in the lemon juice and add salt and pepper to taste. Preheat the grill.

4 Toast the brioche slices under the grill until just golden on both sides. Spoon the mushrooms on top, flash briefly under the grill, and serve. Fresh thyme may be used to garnish, if liked.

Ciabatta Rolls with Goat's Cheese

The Tomato Relish gives a piquant bite that nicely complements the goat's cheese. If you can't find ciabatta rolls, use a ciabatta loaf instead.

Makes 4

INGREDIENTS
2 ciabatta rolls
60 ml/4 tbsp tomato relish (see below)
30 ml/2 tbsp chopped fresh basil
175 g/6 oz goat's cheese, thinly sliced
6 black olives, stoned

ciabatta rolls

Tomato Relish

goat's cheese

basil

olives

1 Cut the rolls in half and toast on one side only.

2 Spread a little relish over each half and sprinkle with the chopped basil.

3 Arrange the goat's cheese slices over the tomato mixture and scatter a few olives over the top. Place under a hot grill until the goat's cheese begins to melt, then serve garnished with a sprig of basil.

TOMATO RELISH

Makes 450 ml/$^3/_4$ pint/scant 2 cups
45 ml/3 tbsp olive oil
1 onion, chopped
1 red pepper, seeded and chopped
2 garlic cloves, crushed
1.5 ml/$^1/_4$ tsp chilli powder
400 g/14 oz can chopped tomatoes
15 ml/1 tbsp clear honey
10 ml/2 tsp black olive paste
30 ml/2 tbsp red wine vinegar
salt and ground black pepper

Heat the oil and fry the onion and red pepper until softened. Add the garlic and the remaining ingredients and season to taste. Simmer for 15 minutes until thickened.

Ciabatta with Mozzarella and Grilled Onion

Ciabatta is readily available in most supermarkets. It's even more delicious when made with spinach, sun-dried tomatoes or olives, and you'll probably find these in your local delicatessen.

Makes 4

INGREDIENTS
1 ciabatta loaf
60 ml/4 tbsp red pesto
2 small onions
oil, for brushing
225 g/8 oz mozzarella cheese
8 black olives

ciabatta loaf

tomato

onion

mozzarella

olives

red pesto

1 Cut the bread in half horizontally and toast lightly. Spread with the red pesto.

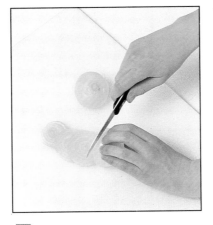

2 Peel the onions and cut horizontally into thick slices. Brush with oil and grill for 3 minutes until lightly browned.

3 Slice the cheese and arrange over the bread. Lay the onion slices on top and scatter some olives over. Cut in half diagonally. Place under a hot grill for 2–3 minutes until the cheese melts and the onion chars.

Welsh Rarebit

This recipe is traditionally made with brown ale (beer) or red wine, which gives it a delicious flavour. You can use other cheeses too, such as Stilton or Red Leicester. If you put a poached or fried egg on top, the dish becomes a Buck Rarebit.

Makes 4

INGREDIENTS
100 g/4 oz/1 cup grated strong
    Cheddar cheese
30 ml/2 tbsp brown ale
5 ml/1 tsp English mustard
cayenne pepper
4 slices bread

bread

brown ale

mustard

Cheddar cheese

cayenne pepper

1 Put the cheese in a saucepan with the brown ale, mustard and cayenne pepper and mix together thoroughly.

2 Heat gently, stirring constantly, until the cheese is just beginning to melt.

3 Meanwhile toast the bread. Spread the cheese mixture over the toast.

4 Grill under a medium heat until lightly tinged with brown.

Fried Mozzarella Sandwich

This sandwich is very popular in southern Italy, where it is known as Mozzarella in Carrozza. Use mozzarella that has been packed in brine for the best flavour. Or, alternatively, try Cheddar or Gruyère cheese.

Makes 2

INGREDIENTS
100 g/4 oz mozzarella cheese, thickly
    sliced
4 thick slices white bread, crusts
    removed
salt and pepper
1 egg
30 ml/2 tbsp milk
oil for shallow-frying

white bread

mozzarella cheese

egg

1 Lay the mozzarella slices on 2 slices of bread, sprinkle with salt and pepper, then top with the remaining bread slices to make 2 cheese sandwiches.

2 Mix the egg and milk together, season and place in a large shallow dish.

3 Lay the sandwiches in the egg mixture, turn over so that they are saturated and leave to soak for a few minutes. Pour enough oil into a frying pan to give 1 cm/½ in depth. Heat the oil and fry the sandwiches for 3–4 minutes until golden brown and crisp, turning them once. Drain well on kitchen paper and serve hot.

VARIATION

Add 2 chopped sun-dried tomatoes or some black olive paste to the sandwich before soaking in egg.

Tostadas with Refried Beans

A tostada is a crisp, fried tortilla used as a base on which to pile the topping of your choice – a variation on a sandwich and a very tasty snack popular in Mexico and South America.

Makes 6

INGREDIENTS

30 ml/2 tbsp vegetable oil
1 onion, chopped
2 garlic cloves, chopped
2.5 ml/½ tsp chilli powder
425 g/15 oz can borlotti or pinto beans, drained
150 ml/¼ pint/⅔ cup vegetable stock
15 ml/1 tbsp tomato purée
30 ml/2 tbsp chopped fresh coriander
6 wheat or corn tortillas
45 ml/3 tbsp tomato salsa (see right)
30 ml/2 tbsp soured cream
50 g/2 oz/½ cup grated Cheddar cheese
salt and ground black pepper
coriander leaves, to garnish

beans

onion

tortillas

garlic

chilli powder

Cheddar cheese

1 Heat the oil in a pan and fry the onion until softened.

2 Add the garlic and chilli powder and fry for 1 minute, stirring.

3 Mix in the beans and mash very roughly with a potato masher.

4 Add the stock, tomato purée, chopped fresh coriander and seasoning to taste. Mix thoroughly and cook for a few minutes.

5 Fry the tortillas in hot oil for 1 minute, turning once, until crisp, then drain on kitchen paper.

TOMATO SALSA

Makes about 300 ml/10 fl oz/1¼ cups

1 small onion, chopped
1 garlic clove, crushed
2 fresh green chillies, seeded and
    finely chopped, or 5 ml/1 tsp
    bottled chopped chillies
450 g/1 lb tomatoes, skinned and
    chopped
salt
30 ml/2 tbsp chopped fresh coriander

Stir all the ingredients together until
well mixed.

6 Put a spoonful of refried beans on
each tostada, spoon over some Tomato
Salsa, then some soured cream, sprinkle
with grated Cheddar cheese and garnish
with coriander.

Courgettes, Carrots and Pecans in Pitta Bread

Chunks of fried courgette served with a tangy salad in pitta pockets.

Serves 2

INGREDIENTS
2 carrots
25 g/1 oz/¼ cup pecan nuts
4 spring onions, sliced
50 ml/2 fl oz/¼ cup Greek yogurt
35 ml/7 tsp olive oil
5 ml/1 tsp lemon juice
15 ml/1 tbsp chopped fresh mint
2 courgettes
25 g/1 oz/¼ cup plain flour
2 pitta breads
salt and freshly ground black pepper
shredded lettuce, to serve

courgettes

spring onions

pecan nuts *lemon*

mint

Greek yogurt

carrots

1 Top and tail the carrots. Grate them coarsely into a bowl.

2 Stir in the pecans and spring onions and toss well.

3 In a clean bowl, whisk the yogurt with 7.5 ml/1½ tsp of the olive oil, the lemon juice and the fresh mint. Stir the dressing into the carrot mixture and mix well. Cover and chill until required.

4 Top and tail the courgettes. Cut them diagonally into slices. Season the flour with salt and pepper. Spread it out on a plate and coat the courgette slices.

COOK'S TIP
Do not fill the pitta breads too soon or the carrot mixture will make the bread soggy.

5 Heat the remaining oil in a large frying pan. Add the coated courgette slices and cook for 3–4 minutes, turning once, until browned. Drain the courgettes on kitchen paper.

6 Make a slit in each pitta bread to form a pocket. Fill the pittas with the carrot mixture and the courgette slices. Serve on a bed of shredded lettuce.

Rice Balls Filled with Manchego Cheese

For a really impressive Spanish tapa-style snack, serve these delicious rice balls.

Serves 6

INGREDIENTS
1 globe artichoke
50 g/2 oz/¼ cup butter
1 small onion, finely chopped
1 garlic clove, crushed
115 g/4 oz/⅔ cup risotto rice
450 ml/¾ pint/scant 2 cups hot
  vegetable stock
50 g/2 oz/⅔ cup freshly grated
  Parmesan cheese
150 g/5 oz Manchego cheese, very
  finely diced
45–60 ml/3–4 tbsp polenta
olive oil, for frying
salt and freshly ground black
  pepper
flat leaf parsley, to garnish

artichoke *onion* *butter*

polenta *risotto rice*

stock *garlic* *Parmesan cheese*

olive oil *Manchego cheese* *flat leaf parsley*

1 Remove the stalk, leaves and choke to leave just the heart of the artichoke. Chop the heart finely.

2 Melt the butter in a saucepan and gently fry the chopped artichoke heart, onion and garlic for 5 minutes until softened. Stir in the rice and cook for about 1 minute.

COOK'S TIP

Manchego cheese is made with sheep's milk from La Mancha in Spain. It is ideal for grating or grilling.

3 Keeping the heat fairly high, gradually add the stock, stirring constantly until all the liquid has been absorbed and the rice is cooked – this should take about 20 minutes. Season well, then stir in the Parmesan. Transfer to a bowl. Leave to cool, then cover and chill for at least 2 hours.

4 Spoon about 15 ml/1 tbsp of the mixture into one hand, flatten slightly, and place a few pieces of diced Manchego cheese in the centre. Shape to make a small ball. Flatten, then lightly roll in the polenta. Make about 12 cakes in total. Shallow fry in hot olive oil for about 4–5 minutes until the rice cakes are crisp and golden brown. Drain on kitchen paper and serve hot, garnished with parsley.

Chick-pea Falafel with Coriander Dip

Little balls of spicy chick-pea purée, deep-fried until crisp, are served together with a coriander-flavoured mayonnaise.

Serves 4

INGREDIENTS
400 g/14 oz can chick-peas, drained
6 spring onions, finely sliced
1 egg
2.5 ml/¹/₂ tsp ground turmeric
1 garlic clove, crushed
5 ml/1 tsp ground cumin
60 ml/4 tbsp chopped
  fresh coriander
oil for deep-frying
1 small red chilli, seeded and
  finely chopped
45 ml/3 tbsp mayonnaise
salt and freshly ground black pepper
coriander sprig, to garnish

spring onions *chick-peas* *coriander*

ground turmeric

ground cumin

egg *garlic clove* *red chilli*

mayonnaise

COOK'S TIP
If you have time, chill the chick-pea purée before making it into balls. It will be easier to shape.

1 Tip the chick-peas into a food processor or blender. Add the spring onions and process to a smooth purée. Add the egg, turmeric, garlic, cumin and 15 ml/1 tbsp of the chopped coriander. Process briefly to mix, then add salt and pepper to taste.

2 Working with clean wet hands, shape the chick-pea mixture into about 16 small balls.

3 Heat the oil for deep-frying to 180°C/350°F or until a cube of bread, when added to the oil, browns in 30–45 seconds. Deep-fry the falafel in batches for 2–3 minutes or until golden. Drain on kitchen paper, then place in a serving bowl.

4 Stir the remaining coriander and the chilli into the mayonnaise. Garnish with the coriander sprig and serve alongside the falafel.

Deep-fried Florets with Tangy Thyme Mayonnaise

Cauliflower and broccoli make a sensational snack when coated in a beer batter and deep-fried. Serve with a tangy mayonnaise.

Serves 2–3

INGREDIENTS
175 g/6 oz cauliflower
175 g/6 oz broccoli
2 eggs, separated
30 ml/2 tbsp olive oil
250 ml/8 fl oz/1 cup beer
150 ml/5 oz/1¼ cups plain flour
pinch of salt
30 ml/2 tbsp shredded fresh basil
vegetable oil for deep-frying
150 ml/¼ pint/⅔ cup good quality
 mayonnaise
10 ml/2 tsp chopped fresh thyme
10 ml/2 tsp grated lemon rind
10 ml/2 tsp lemon juice
sea salt, for sprinkling

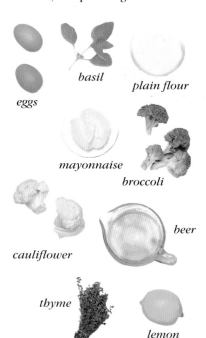

eggs
basil
plain flour
mayonnaise
broccoli
cauliflower
beer
thyme
lemon

1 Break the cauliflower and broccoli into small florets, cutting large florets into smaller pieces. Set aside.

2 Beat the egg yolks, olive oil, beer, flour and salt in a bowl. Strain the batter if necessary, to remove any lumps.

3 Whisk the egg whites until stiff. Fold into the batter with the basil.

4 Heat the oil for deep-frying to 180°C/350°F or until a cube of bread, when added to the oil, browns in 30–45 seconds. Dip the florets in the batter and deep-fry in batches for 2–3 minutes until the coating is golden and crisp. Drain on kitchen paper.

5 Mix the mayonnaise, thyme, lemon rind and juice in a small bowl.

6 Sprinkle the florets with sea salt. Serve with the thyme and lemon mayonnaise.

Cannellini Bean Dip

This soft bean dip or pâté is good spread on wheaten crackers or toasted muffins. Alternatively, it can be served with wedges of tomato and a crisp green salad.

Serves 4

INGREDIENTS
400 g/14 oz can cannellini beans
grated rind and juice of 1 lemon
30 ml/2 tbsp olive oil
1 garlic clove, finely chopped
30 ml/2 tbsp chopped fresh parsley
red Tabasco sauce, to taste
cayenne pepper
salt and pepper

cannellini beans

olive oil

lemon juice and rind

garlic

parsley

red Tabasco sauce

cayenne pepper

1 Drain the beans in a sieve and rinse them well under cold water. Transfer to a shallow bowl.

2 Use a potato masher to roughly purée the beans, then stir in the lemon and olive oil.

3 Stir in the chopped garlic and parsley. Add Tabasco sauce and salt and pepper to taste.

4 Spoon the mixture into a small bowl and dust lightly with cayenne pepper. Chill until ready to serve.

VARIATION
Other beans can be used for this dip, for example butter beans or kidney beans.

Hummus

This nutritious dip can be served with vegetable crudités or packed into salad-filled pitta, but it is best spread thickly on hot buttered toast.

Serves 4

INGREDIENTS
400 g/14 oz can chick-peas,
    drained
2 garlic cloves
30 ml/2 tbsp tahini or smooth
    peanut butter
60 ml/4 tbsp olive oil
juice of 1 lemon
2.5 ml/½ tsp cayenne pepper
15 ml/1 tbsp sesame seeds
sea salt

garlic

sea salt

chick-peas

olive oil

tahini

lemon
juice

cayenne pepper

sesame
seeds

COOK'S TIP
Tahini is a thick smooth and oily paste made from sesame seeds. It is available from health-food shops and large supermarkets. Tahini is a classic ingredient in hummus, this Middle-Eastern dip; peanut butter would not be used in a traditional recipe but it is a useful substitute.

1 Rinse the chick-peas well and place in a blender or food processor with the garlic and a good pinch of sea salt. Process until very finely chopped.

2 Add the tahini or peanut butter and process until fairly smooth. With the motor still running, slowly pour in the oil and lemon juice.

3 Stir in the cayenne pepper and add more salt, to taste. If the mixture is too thick, stir in a little cold water. Transfer the purée to a serving bowl.

4 Heat a small non-stick pan and add the sesame seeds. Cook for 2–3 minutes, shaking the pan, until the seeds are golden. Allow to cool, then sprinkle over the purée.

Creamy Aubergine Dip

Spread this velvet-textured dip thickly on to toasted rounds of bread, then top them with slivers of sun-dried tomato to make wonderful, Italian-style crostini.

Serves 4

INGREDIENTS
1 large aubergine
1 small onion
2 garlic cloves
30 ml/2 tbsp olive oil
60 ml/4 tbsp chopped fresh parsley
75 ml/5 tbsp crème fraîche
red Tabasco sauce, to taste
juice of 1 lemon, to taste
salt and pepper

aubergine

garlic

onion

olive oil

parsley

crème fraîche

red Tabasco sauce

lemon juice

1 Preheat the grill to medium. Place the whole aubergine on a baking sheet and grill it for 20–30 minutes, turning occasionally, until the skin is blackened and wrinkled, and the aubergine feels soft when squeezed.

2 Cover the aubergine with a clean dish towel and leave it to cool for about 5 minutes.

3 Finely chop the onion and garlic. Heat the oil in a frying pan and cook the onion and garlic for 5 minutes, until softened, but not browned.

4 Peel the skin from the aubergine. Mash the flesh with a large fork or potato masher to make a pulpy purée.

5 Stir in the onion and garlic, parsley and crème fraîche. Add Tabasco, lemon juice and salt and pepper to taste.

6 Transfer the dip to a serving bowl and serve warm or leave to cool and serve at room temperature.

COOK'S TIP
The aubergine can be roasted in the oven at 200°C/400°F/Gas 6 for 20 minutes, if preferred.

Blue Cheese Dip

This dip can be mixed up in next-to-no-time and is delicious served with pears. Add more yogurt to make a great dressing.

Serves 4

INGREDIENTS
150 g/5 oz blue cheese, such as
  Stilton or Danish Blue
150 g/5oz/⅔ cup soft cheese
75 ml/5 tbsp Greek-style yogurt
salt and pepper

*blue
cheese*

*soft
cheese*

*Greek-style
yogurt*

1 Crumble the blue cheese into a bowl. Using a wooden spoon, beat the cheese to soften it.

2 Add the soft cheese and beat well to blend the two cheeses together.

3 Gradually beat in the Greek-style yogurt, adding enough to give you the consistency you prefer.

4 Season with lots of black pepper and a little salt. Chill until ready to serve.

COOK'S TIP
This is a very thick dip to which you can add a little more Greek-style yogurt, or stir in a little milk, for a softer consistency.

Red Onion Raita

Raita is a traditional Indian accompaniment for hot curries. It is also delicious served with poppadoms as a dip.

Serves 4

INGREDIENTS
5 ml/1 tsp cumin seeds
1 small garlic clove
1 small green chilli, seeded
1 large red onion
150 ml/¼ pint/⅔ cup natural
   yogurt
30 ml/2 tbsp chopped fresh
   coriander, plus extra, to garnish
2.5 ml/½ tsp sugar
salt

cumin   *garlic*   *green chilli*

red onion   *coriander*

yogurt   *sugar*

COOK'S TIP

For an extra tangy raita stir in 15 ml/1 tbsp lemon juice. To make a pretty garnish, reserve a few thin wedges of onion, before chopping the rest.

1 Heat a small pan and dry-fry the cumin seeds for 1–2 minutes, until they release their aroma and begin to pop.

2 Lightly crush the seeds in a pestle and mortar or flatten them with the heel of a heavy-bladed knife.

3 Finely chop the garlic, chilli and red onion. Stir into the yogurt with the crushed cumin seeds and coriander.

4 Add sugar and salt to taste. Spoon the raita into a small bowl and chill until ready to serve. Garnish with extra coriander before serving.

Mellow Garlic Dip

Two whole heads of garlic may seem like a lot but, once cooked, it becomes sweet and mellow. Serve with crunchy bread sticks and crisps.

Serves 4

INGREDIENTS
2 whole garlic heads
15 ml/1 tbsp olive oil
60 ml/4 tbsp mayonnaise
75 ml/5 tbsp Greek-style yogurt
5 ml/1 tsp wholegrain mustard
salt and pepper

garlic

olive oil

mayonnaise

Greek-style yogurt

wholegrain mustard

1 Preheat the oven to 200°C/400°F/ Gas 6. Separate the garlic cloves and place them in a small roasting tin.

2 Pour the olive oil over the garlic cloves and turn them with a spoon to coat them evenly. Roast for 20–30 minutes, until the garlic is tender and softened. Leave to cool for 5 minutes.

3 Trim off the root end of each roasted garlic clove. Peel the cloves and discard the skins.

4 Place the roasted garlic on a chopping board and sprinkle with salt. Mash with a fork until puréed.

5 Place the garlic in a small bowl and stir in the mayonnaise, yogurt and wholegrain mustard.

COOK'S TIP
If you are already cooking on a barbecue, leave the garlic heads whole and cook them on the hot barbecue until tender, then peel and mash.

VARIATION
For a low fat version of this dip, use reduced-fat mayonnaise and low fat natural yogurt.

6 Check and adjust the seasoning, then spoon the dip into a bowl. Cover and chill until ready to serve.

Tsatziki

Serve this classic Greek dip with strips of toasted pitta bread.

Serves 4

INGREDIENTS
1 mini cucumber
4 spring onions
1 garlic clove
200 ml/7 fl oz/scant 1 cup Greek-
  style yogurt
45 ml/3 tbsp chopped fresh mint
fresh mint sprig, to garnish (optional)
salt and pepper

*mini
cucumber*

*spring
onions*

garlic

*Greek-style
yogurt*

mint

1 Trim the ends from the cucumber, then cut it into 5 mm/¼ in dice.

2 Trim the spring onions and garlic, then chop both very finely.

3 Beat the yogurt until smooth, if necessary, then gently stir in the cucumber, onions, garlic and mint.

4 Transfer the mixture to a serving bowl and add salt and plenty of freshly ground black pepper to taste. Chill until ready to serve and then garnish with a small mint sprig, if you like.

COOK'S TIP
Choose Greek-style yogurt for this dip – it has a higher fat content than most yogurts, which gives it a deliciously rich, creamy texture.

Guacamole

Nachos or tortilla chips are the perfect accompaniment for this classic Mexican dip.

Serves 4

INGREDIENTS
2 ripe avocados
2 red chillies, seeded
1 garlic clove
1 shallot
30 ml/2 tbsp olive oil, plus extra
   to serve
juice of 1 lemon
salt
flat-leaf parsley leaves, to garnish

avocados

red
chillies

shallot

olive oil

garlic

flat-leaf
parsley

lemon juice

VARIATION

Make a completely smooth guacamole by whizzing the ingredients in a blender or food processor. For a chunkier version, add a diced tomato or red pepper.

1 Halve the avocados, remove their stones and, using a spoon, scoop out their flesh into a bowl.

2 Mash the flesh well with a potato masher or a large fork.

3 Finely chop the chillies, garlic and shallot, then stir into the mashed avocado with the olive oil and lemon juice. Add salt to taste.

4 Spoon the mixture into a small serving bowl. Drizzle over a little olive oil and scatter with a few flat-leaf parsley leaves. Serve immediately.

Ratatouille Pancakes

These pancakes are made slightly thicker than usual to hold the juicy vegetable filling.

Serves 4

INGREDIENTS
75 g/3 oz/¾ cup plain flour
25 g/1 oz/¼ cup medium oatmeal
1 egg
300 ml/½ pint/1¼ cups
    skimmed milk
mixed salad, to serve

FOR THE FILLING
1 large aubergine, cut into 2.5 cm/1 in
    cubes
1 garlic clove, crushed
2 medium courgettes, sliced
1 green pepper, seeded and sliced
1 red pepper, seeded and sliced
75 ml/5 tbsp vegetable stock
200 g/7 oz can chopped tomatoes
5 ml/1 tsp cornflour
salt and freshly ground black pepper

courgettes

oatmeal

pepper

cornflour

chopped tomatoes

aubergine

flour

egg

1 Sift the flour and a pinch of salt into a bowl. Stir in the oatmeal. Make a well in the centre, add the egg and half the milk and mix to a smooth batter. Gradually beat in the remaining milk. Cover the bowl and leave to stand for 30 minutes.

2 Spray a 18 cm/7 in pancake pan or heavy-based frying pan with non-stick cooking spray. Heat the pan, then pour in just enough batter to cover the base of the pan thinly. Cook for 2-3 minutes, until the underside is golden brown. Flip over and cook for a further 1-2 minutes.

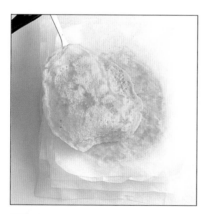

3 Slide the pancake out onto a plate lined with non-stick baking paper. Stack the other pancakes on top as they are made, interleaving each with non-stick baking paper. Keep warm.

4 For the filling, put the aubergine in a colander and sprinkle well with salt. Leave to stand on a plate for 30 minutes. Rinse thoroughly and drain well.

5 Put the garlic clove, courgettes, peppers, stock and tomatoes into a large saucepan. Simmer uncovered and stir occasionally for 10 minutes. Add the aubergine and cook for a further 15 minutes. Blend the cornflour with 10 ml/2 tsp water and add to the saucepan. Simmer for 2 minutes. Season to taste.

6 Spoon the ratatouille mixture into the middle of each pancake. Fold each one in half, then in half again to make a cone shape. Serve hot with a mixed salad.

Cucumber and Alfalfa Tortillas

Wheat tortillas are extremely simple to prepare at home. Served with a crisp, fresh salsa, they make a marvellous light lunch or supper dish.

Serves 4

INGREDIENTS
225 g/8 oz/2 cups plain flour
pinch of salt
45 ml/3 tbsp olive oil
100 ml–150 ml/4–5 fl oz/½–⅔ cup
    warm water
lime wedges, to garnish

FOR THE SALSA
1 red onion, finely chopped
1 fresh red chilli, seeded and finely
    chopped
30 ml/2 tbsp chopped fresh dill or
    coriander
½ cucumber, peeled and chopped
175 g/6 oz alfalfa sprouts

FOR THE SAUCE
1 large avocado, peeled and stoned
juice of 1 lime
25 g/1 oz/2 tbsp soft goat's cheese
pinch of paprika

avocado

goat's cheese

red chilli

cucumber

dill

alfalfa sprouts

1 Mix all the salsa ingredients together in a bowl and set aside.

2 To make the sauce, place the avocado, lime juice and goat's cheese in a food processor or blender and blend until smooth. Place in a bowl and cover with clear film. Dust with paprika just before serving.

3 To make the tortillas, place the flour and salt in a food processor, add the oil and blend. Gradually add the water (the amount will vary depending on the type of flour). Stop adding water when a stiff dough has formed. Turn out onto a floured board and knead until smooth. Cover with a damp cloth.

4 Divide the mixture into 8 pieces. Knead each piece for a couple of minutes and form into a ball. Flatten and roll out each ball to a 23 cm/9 in circle.

5 Heat an ungreased heavy-based pan. Cook 1 tortilla at a time for about 30 seconds on each side. Place the cooked tortillas in a clean tea-towel and repeat until you have 8 tortillas.

6 To serve, spread each tortilla with a spoonful of avocado sauce, top with salsa and roll up. Garnish with lime wedges.

Baked Herb Crêpes

These mouth-watering, light herb crêpes make a striking starter at a dinner party, but are equally splendid served with a crisp salad for lunch.

Serves 4

INGREDIENTS
25 g/1 oz chopped fresh herbs
   (e.g. parsley, thyme, and chervil)
15 ml/1 tbsp sunflower oil, plus extra
   for frying
100 ml/4 fl oz/½ cup skimmed milk
3 eggs
25 g/1 oz/¼ cup plain flour
pinch of salt

FOR THE SAUCE
30 ml/ 2 tbsp olive oil
1 small onion, chopped
2 garlic cloves, crushed
15 ml/1 tbsp grated fresh ginger root
1 × 400 g/14 oz can chopped
   tomatoes

FOR THE FILLING
450 g/1 lb fresh spinach
175 g/6 oz/¾ cup ricotta cheese
25 g/1 oz/2 tbsp pine nuts, toasted
5 halves sun-dried tomatoes in olive
   oil, drained and chopped
30 ml/2 tbsp shredded fresh basil
salt, nutmeg and freshly ground black
   pepper
4 egg whites

2 Heat a small non-stick crêpe or frying pan and add a very small amount of oil. Pour out any excess oil and pour in a ladleful of the batter. Swirl around to cover the base. Cook for 1–2 minutes, turn over and cook the other side. Repeat to make 8 crêpes.

3 To make the sauce, heat the oil in a small pan. Add the onion, garlic and ginger and cook gently for 5 minutes until softened. Add the tomatoes and cook for a further 10–15 minutes until the mixture thickens. Purée , sieve and set aside.

1 To make the crêpes, place the herbs and oil in a blender and blend until smooth, pushing down any whole pieces with a spatula. Add the milk, eggs, flour and salt and process again until smooth and pale green. Leave to rest for 30 minutes.

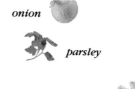
onion

parsley

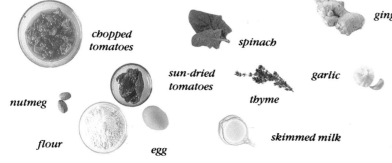
chopped tomatoes

ginger

spinach

sun-dried tomatoes

garlic

thyme

nutmeg

flour

egg

skimmed milk

4 To make the filling, wash the spinach, removing any large stalks, and place in a large pan with only the water that clings to the leaves. Cover and cook, stirring once, until the spinach has just wilted. Remove from the heat and refresh in cold water. Place in a sieve or colander, squeeze out the excess water and chop finely. Mix the spinach with the ricotta, pine nuts, sun-dried tomatoes and basil. Season with salt, nutmeg and freshly ground black pepper.

5 Preheat the oven to 190°C/375°F/ Gas 5. Whisk the 4 egg whites until stiff but not dry. Fold ⅓ into the spinach and ricotta to lighten the mixture, then gently fold in the rest.

6 Taking each crêpe at a time, place on a lightly oiled baking sheet. Place a large spoonful of filling on each one and fold into quarters. Repeat until all the filling and crêpes are used up. Bake in the oven for 10–15 minutes or until set. Reheat the tomato sauce to serve with the crêpes.

COOK'S TIP

If preferred, use plain sun-dried tomatoes without any oil, and soak them in warm water for 20 minutes before using.

Buckwheat Blinis

These delectable light pancakes originated in Russia. For a special occasion, serve with a small glass of chilled vodka.

Serves 4

INGREDIENTS

5 ml/1 tsp easy-blend dry yeast
250 ml/8 fl oz/1 cup skimmed milk, warmed
40 g/1½ oz/⅓ cup buckwheat flour
40 g/1½ oz/⅓ cup plain flour
10ml/2 tsp caster sugar
pinch of salt
1 egg, separated
oil, for frying

FOR THE AVOCADO CREAM
1 large avocado
75 g/3 oz/⅓ cup low-fat fromage blanc
juice of 1 lime

FOR THE PICKLED BEETROOT
225 g/8 oz beetroot
45 ml/3 tbsp lime juice
snipped chives, to garnish
cracked black peppercorns, to garnish

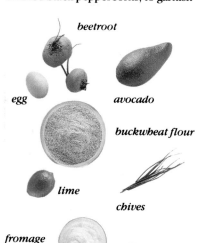

beetroot
egg
avocado
buckwheat flour
lime
chives
fromage blanc
skimmed milk

1 Mix the dry yeast with the milk, then mix with the next 4 ingredients and the egg yolk. Cover with a cloth and leave to prove for about 40 minutes. Whisk the egg white until stiff but not dry and fold into the blini mixture.

2 Heat a little oil in a non-stick pan and add a ladleful of batter to make a 10 cm/ 4 in pancake. Cook for 2–3 minutes on each side. Repeat with the remaining batter mixture to make 8 blinis.

3 Cut the avocado in half and remove the stone. Peel and place the flesh in a blender with the fromage blanc and lime juice. Blend until smooth.

4 Peel the beetroot and shred finely. Mix with the lime juice. To serve, top each blini with a spoonful of avocado cream. Serve with the pickled beetroot and garnish with snipped chives and cracked black peppercorns.

Vegetable Fajita

A colourful medley of mushrooms and peppers in a spicy sauce, wrapped in tortillas and served with creamy guacamole.

Serves 2

INGREDIENTS
1 onion
1 red pepper
1 green pepper
1 yellow pepper
1 garlic clove, crushed
225 g/8 oz mushrooms
90 ml/6 tbsp vegetable oil
30 ml/2 tbsp medium chilli powder
salt and freshly ground black pepper
coriander sprigs and 1 lime, cut into
    wedges, to garnish

FOR THE GUACAMOLE
1 ripe avocado
1 shallot, roughly chopped
1 green chilli, seeded and
    roughly chopped
juice of 1 lime

TO SERVE
4–6 flour tortillas, warmed

green pepper　　*yellow pepper*　　*red pepper*

mushrooms　　*green chilli*

shallot　　*garlic clove*

avocado

lime　　*chilli powder*　　*onion*

1 Slice the onion. Cut the peppers in half, remove the seeds and cut the flesh into strips. Combine the onion and peppers in a bowl. Add the crushed garlic and mix lightly.

2 Remove the mushroom stalks. Save for making stock, or discard. Slice the mushroom caps and add to the pepper mixture in the bowl. Mix the oil and chilli powder in a cup, pour over the vegetable mixture and stir well. Set aside.

3 Make the guacamole. Cut the avocado in half and remove the stone and the peel. Put the flesh into a food processor or blender with the shallot, green chilli and lime juice. Process for 1 minute until smooth. Scrape into a small bowl, cover closely and put in the fridge to chill until required.

4 Heat a frying pan or wok until very hot. Add the marinated vegetables and stir-fry over high heat for 5–6 minutes until the mushrooms and pepper are just tender. Season well. Spoon a little of the filling on to each tortilla and roll up. Garnish with fresh coriander and lime wedges and serve with the guacamole.

Egg and Lentil Curry

A few Indian spices can transform eggs and lentils into a tasty, economical curry.

Serves 4

INGREDIENTS

75 g/3 oz green lentils
750 ml/1¼ pints/3 cups
    vegetable stock
6 eggs
30 ml/2 tbsp oil
3 cloves
1.5 ml/¼ tsp black peppercorns
1 onion, finely chopped
2 green chillies, finely chopped
2 garlic cloves, crushed
2.5 cm/1 in root ginger,
    finely chopped
30 ml/2 tbsp curry paste
400 g/14 oz can chopped tomatoes
2.5 ml/½ tsp sugar
2.5 ml/½ tsp garam masala

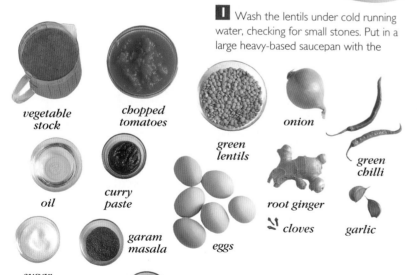

vegetable stock

chopped tomatoes

green lentils

onion

oil

curry paste

root ginger

green chilli

garlic

sugar

garam masala

eggs

cloves

black peppercorns

1 Wash the lentils under cold running water, checking for small stones. Put in a large heavy-based saucepan with the stock. Cover and simmer gently for about 15 minutes or until the lentils are soft. Drain and set aside.

2 Cook the eggs in boiling water for 10 minutes. When cool enough to handle, peel and cut in half lengthways.

3 Heat the oil in a large saucepan and fry the cloves and peppercorns for about 2 minutes. Add the onion, chillies, garlic and ginger and fry the mixture for a further 5–6 minutes.

4 Stir in the curry paste and fry for 2 minutes.

5 Stir in the tomatoes and sugar with 175 ml/6 fl oz/³/₄ cup water

6 Simmer for 5 minutes until the sauce thickens. Add the eggs, drained lentils and garam masala. Cover and simmer for about 10 minutes, then serve.

Sweet Potato Roulade

Sweet potato works particularly well as the base for this roulade. Serve in thin slices for a truly impressive dinner party dish.

Serves 6

INGREDIENTS

225 g/8 oz/1 cup low-fat soft cheese
    such as Quark
75 ml/5 tbsp low-fat yogurt
6–8 spring onions, finely sliced
30 ml/2 tbsp chopped brazil nuts,
    roasted
450 g/1 lb sweet potatoes, peeled and
    cubed
12 allspice berries, crushed
4 eggs, separated
50 g/2 oz/¼ cup Edam cheese, finely
    grated
salt and freshly ground black pepper
15 ml/1 tbsp sesame seeds

soft cheese

sesame seeds

sweet potato

yogurt

Edam

brazil nuts

spring onions

peppercorns

egg

1 Preheat the oven to 200°C/400°F/ Gas 6. Grease and line a 33 × 25 cm/ 13 × 10 in Swiss roll tin with non-stick baking paper, snipping the corners with scissors to fit.

2 In a small bowl, mix together the soft cheese, yogurt, spring onions and brazil nuts. Set aside.

3 Boil or steam the sweet potato until tender. Drain well. Place in a food processor with the allspice and blend until smooth. Spoon into a bowl and stir in the egg yolks and Edam. Season to taste.

4 Whisk the egg whites until stiff but not dry. Fold ⅓ of the egg whites into the sweet potatoes to lighten the mixture before gently folding in the rest.

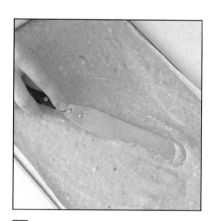

5 Pour into the prepared tin, tipping it to get the mixture right into the corners. Smooth gently with a palette knife and cook in the oven for 10–15 minutes.

COOK'S TIP

Choose the orange-fleshed variety of sweet potato for the most striking colour.

6 Meanwhile, lay a large sheet of greaseproof paper on a clean tea-towel and sprinkle with the sesame seeds. When the roulade is cooked, tip it onto the paper, trim the edges and roll it up. Leave to cool. When cool carefully unroll, spread with the filling and roll up again. Cut into slices to serve.

Spanish Omelette

Spanish omelette belongs in every cook's repertoire and can vary according to what you have in store. This version includes soft white beans and is finished with a layer of toasted sesame seeds.

VARIATION

You can also use sliced cooked potatoes, any seasonal vegetables, baby artichoke hearts and chick-peas in a Spanish omelette.

Serves 4

INGREDIENTS

30 ml/2 tbsp olive oil
5 ml/1 tsp sesame oil
1 Spanish onion, chopped
1 small red pepper, deseeded and diced
2 celery sticks, chopped
1 × 400 g/14 oz can soft white beans, drained
8 eggs
45 ml/3 tbsp sesame seeds
salt and freshly ground black pepper
115 g/4 oz green salad, to serve

celery

red pepper

white beans

sesame oil

sesame seeds

eggs

1 Heat the olive and sesame oils in a 30 cm/12 in paella or frying pan. Add the onion, pepper and celery and cook to soften without colouring.

2 Add the beans and continue to cook for several minutes to heat through.

3 In a small bowl beat the eggs with a fork, season well and pour over the ingredients in the pan.

4 Stir the egg mixture with a flat wooden spoon until it begins to stiffen, then allow to firm over a low heat for about 6–8 minutes.

5 Preheat a moderate grill. Sprinkle the omelette with sesame seeds and brown evenly under the grill.

6 Cut the omelette into thick wedges and serve warm with a green salad.

Omelette aux Fines Herbs

Eggs respond well to fast cooking and combine beautifully with a handful of fresh herbs. Serve with oven-ready chips and a green salad.

Serves 1

INGREDIENTS
3 eggs
30 ml/2 tbsp chopped fresh parsley
30 ml/2 tbsp chopped fresh chervil
30 ml/2 tbsp chopped fresh tarragon
15 ml/1 tbsp chopped fresh chives
15 ml/½ oz/1 tbsp butter
salt and freshly ground black pepper
350 g/12 oz oven-ready chips,
   to serve
115 g/4 oz green salad, to serve
1 tomato, to serve

eggs

tarragon

chives

chervil

butter

parsley

1 Break the eggs into a bowl, season to taste and beat with a fork, then add the chopped herbs.

2 Heat an omelette or frying pan over a fierce heat, add the butter and cook until it foams and browns. Quickly pour in the beaten egg and stir briskly with the back of the fork. When the egg is two-thirds scrambled, let the omelette finish cooking for 10–15 seconds more.

3 Tap the handle of the omelette or frying pan sharply with your fist to make the omelette jump up the sides of the pan, fold and turn onto a plate. Serve with oven-ready chips, green salad and a halved tomato.

COOK'S TIP

From start to finish, an omelette should be cooked and on the table in less than a minute. For best results use free-range eggs at room temperature.

Soufflé Omelette

This delectable soufflé omlette is light and delicate enough to melt in the mouth.

Serves 1

INGREDIENTS
2 eggs, separated
30 ml/2 tbsp cold water
15 ml/1 tbsp chopped fresh coriander
salt and freshly ground black pepper
7.5 ml/½ tbsp olive oil
30 ml/2 tbsp mango chutney
25 g/1 oz/¼ cup Jarlsberg cheese, grated

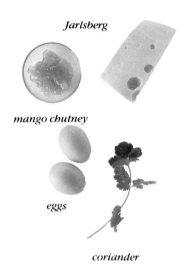

Jarlsberg

mango chutney

eggs

coriander

COOK'S TIP

A light hand is essential to the success of this dish. Do not overmix the egg whites into the yolks or the mixture will be heavy.

1 Beat the egg yolks together with the cold water, coriander and seasoning.

2 Whisk the egg whites until stiff but not dry and gently fold into the egg yolk mixture.

3 Heat the oil in a frying pan, pour in the egg mixture and reduce the heat. Do not stir. Cook until the omelette becomes puffy and golden brown on the underside (carefully lift one edge with a palette knife to check).

4 Spoon on the chutney and sprinkle on the Jarlsberg. Fold over and slide onto a warm plate. Eat immediately. (If preferred, before adding the chutney and cheese, place the pan under a hot grill to set the top.)

Tomato Omelette Envelopes

Delicious chive omelettes, folded and filled with tomato and melting Camembert cheese.

Serves 2

INGREDIENTS
1 small onion
4 tomatoes
30 ml/2 tbsp vegetable oil
4 eggs
30 ml/2 tbsp snipped fresh chives
115 g/4 oz Camembert cheese,
  rinded and diced
salt and freshly ground black pepper

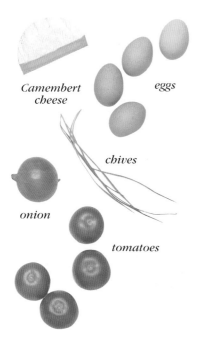

Camembert cheese

eggs

chives

onion

tomatoes

1 Cut the onion in half. Cut each half into thin wedges. Cut the tomatoes into wedges of similar size.

2 Heat 15 ml/1 tbsp of the oil in a frying pan. Cook the onion for 2 minutes over a moderate heat, then raise the heat and add the tomatoes. Cook for a further 2 minutes, then remove the pan from the heat.

3 Beat the eggs with the chives in a bowl. Add salt and pepper to taste. Heat the remaining oil in an omelette pan. Add half the egg mixture and tilt the pan to spread thinly. Cook for 1 minute.

4 Flip the omelette over and cook for 1 minute more. Remove from the pan and keep hot. Make a second omelette with the remaining egg mixture.

5 Return the tomato mixture to a high heat. Add the cheese and toss the mixture over the heat for 1 minute.

6 Divide the mixture between the omelettes and fold them over. Serve at once. Add crisp lettuce leaves and chunks of Granary bread, if liked.

COOK'S TIP
You may need to wipe the pan clean between the omelettes and reheat a little more oil.

Stir-fried Vegetables with Coriander Omelette

This is a great supper dish for vegetarians. The glaze is added here only to make the mixture shine, it is not intended as a sauce.

Serves 3-4

INGREDIENTS
FOR THE OMELETTE
2 eggs
30 ml/2 tbsp water
45 ml/3 tbsp chopped
    fresh coriander
salt and ground black pepper
15 ml/1 tbsp groundnut oil

FOR THE GLAZED VEGETABLES
15 ml/1 tbsp cornflour
30 ml/2 tbsp dry sherry
15 ml/1 tbsp sweet chilli sauce
120 ml/4 fl oz/½ cup
    vegetable stock
30 ml/2 tbsp groundnut oil
5 ml/1 tsp grated fresh
    root ginger
6-8 spring onions, sliced
115 g/4 oz mange-touts
1 yellow pepper, seeded
    and sliced
115 g/4 oz fresh shiitake or
    button mushrooms
75 g/3 oz (drained weight)
    canned water chestnuts, rinsed
115 g/4 oz beansprouts
½ small Chinese cabbage,
    coarsely shredded

egg

coriander

groundnut oil

mange-touts

spring onion

mushrooms

yellow pepper

stock

*sweet chilli
sauce*

Chinese cabbage

beansprouts

1 Make the omelette: whisk the eggs, water, coriander and seasoning in a small bowl. Heat the oil in a wok. Pour in the eggs, then tilt the wok so that the mixture spreads to an even layer. Cook over a high heat until the edges are slightly crisp.

2 With a wok spatula or palette knife, flip the omelette over and cook the other side for about 30 seconds until lightly browned. Turn the omelette on to a board and leave to cool. When cold, roll up loosely and cut into thin slices. Wipe the wok clean.

3 In a bowl, blend together the cornflour, soy sauce, chilli sauce and stock. Set aside.

4 Heat the wok until hot, add the oil and swirl it around, add the ginger and spring onions and stir-fry for a few seconds to flavour the oil. Add the mange-touts, pepper, mushrooms and water chestnuts and stir-fry for 3 minutes.

VARIATION

Vary the combination of vegetables used according to availability and taste.

5 Add the beansprouts and Chinese cabbage and stir-fry for 2 minutes.

6 Pour in the glaze ingredients and cook, stirring, for about 1 minute until the glaze thickens and coats the vegetables. Turn the vegetables on to a warmed serving plate and top with the omelette shreds. Serve at once.

Pumpkin and Pistachio Risotto

This elegant combination of creamy golden rice and orange pumpkin can be as pale or bright as you like by adding different quantities of saffron.

Serves 4

INGREDIENTS

1.1 litres/2 pints/5 cups vegetable
  stock or water
generous pinch of saffron threads
30 ml/2 tbsp olive oil
1 medium onion, chopped
2 garlic cloves, crushed
450 g/1 lb arborio rice
900 g/2 lb pumpkin, peeled, seeded
  and cut into 2 cm/¾ in cubes
200 ml/7 fl oz/¾ cup dry white wine
15 g/½ oz Parmesan cheese, finely
  grated
50 g/2 oz/½ cup pistachios
45 ml/3 tbsp chopped fresh marjoram
  or oregano, plus extra leaves, to
  garnish
salt, freshly grated nutmeg and ground
  black pepper

saffron

pumpkin

white wine

onion

garlic

marjoram

Parmesan

arborio rice

pistachios

1 Bring the stock or water to the boil and reduce to a low simmer. Ladle a little stock into a small bowl. Add the saffron threads and leave to infuse.

4 Gradually add the stock or water, a ladleful at a time, allowing the rice to absorb the liquid before adding more and stirring all the time. After 20–30 minutes the rice should be golden yellow and creamy, and *al dente* when tested.

2 Heat the oil in a large saucepan. Add the onion and garlic and cook gently for about 5 minutes until softened. Add the rice and pumpkin and cook for a few more minutes until the rice looks transparent.

3 Pour in the wine and allow it to bubble hard. When it is absorbed add ¼ of the stock and the infused saffron and liquid. Stir constantly until all the liquid is absorbed.

5 Stir in the Parmesan cheese, cover the pan and leave to stand for 5 minutes.

6 To finish, stir in the pistachios and marjoram or oregano. Season to taste with a little salt, nutmeg and pepper, and scatter over a few extra marjoram or oregano leaves.

COOK'S TIP
Italian arborio rice must be used to make an authentic risotto. Choose unpolished white arborio as it contains more starch.

Wild Rice Rösti with Carrot and Orange Purée

Rösti is a traditional dish from Switzerland. This variation has the extra nuttiness of wild rice and a bright simple sauce as a fresh accompaniment.

Serves 6

INGREDIENTS
50 g/2 oz/½ cup wild rice
900 g/2 lb large potatoes
45 ml/3 tbsp walnut oil
5 ml/1 tsp yellow mustard seeds
1 onion, coarsely grated and drained
    in a sieve
30 ml/2 tbsp fresh thyme leaves
salt and freshly ground black pepper

FOR THE PURÉE
350 g/12 oz carrots, peeled and
    roughly chopped
rind and juice of 1 large orange

onion

thyme

carrot

wild rice

potatoes

yellow mustard seeds

orange

1 For the purée, place the carrots in a pan, cover with cold water and add 2 pieces of orange rind. Bring to the boil and cook for 10 minutes or until tender. Drain well and discard the rind.

2 Purée the mixture in a blender with 60 ml/4 tbsp of the orange juice. Return to the pan to reheat.

3 Place the wild rice in a clean pan and cover with water. Bring to the boil and cook for 30–40 minutes, until the rice is just starting to split, but still crunchy. Drain the rice.

4 Scrub the potatoes, place in a large pan and cover with cold water. Bring to the boil and cook for 10–15 minutes until just tender. Drain well and leave to cool slightly. When the potatoes are cool, peel and coarsely grate them into a large bowl. Add the cooked rice.

5 Heat 30 ml/2 tbsp of the walnut oil in a non-stick frying pan and add the mustard seeds. When they start to pop, add the onion and cook gently for 5 minutes until softened. Add to the bowl of potato and rice, together with the thyme, and mix thoroughly. Season to taste with salt and pepper.

6 Heat the remaining oil in the frying pan and add the potato mixture. Press down well and cook for 10 minutes or until golden brown. Cover the pan with a plate and flip over, then slide the rösti back into the pan for another 10 minutes to cook the other side. Serve with the reheated carrot and orange purée.

Thai Fragrant Rice

A lovely, soft, fluffy rice dish, perfumed with fresh lemon grass.

Serves 4

INGREDIENTS
1 piece of lemon grass
2 limes
225 g/8 oz/1 cup brown basmati rice
15 ml/1 tbsp olive oil
1 onion, chopped
2.5 cm/1 in piece of fresh ginger root, peeled and finely chopped
7.5 ml/1½ tsp coriander seeds
7.5 ml/1½ tsp cumin seeds
700 ml/1¼ pints/3 cups vegetable stock
60 ml/4 tbsp chopped fresh coriander
lime wedges, to serve

onion
lime
ginger
lemon grass
coriander seeds
basmati rice
cumin seeds
coriander

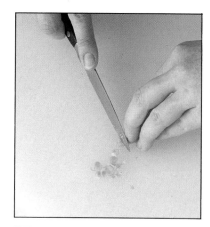

1 Finely chop the lemon grass.

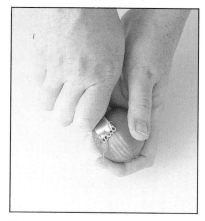

2 Remove the zest from the limes using a zester or fine grater.

3 Rinse the rice in plenty of cold water until the water runs clear. Drain through a sieve.

4 Heat the oil in a large pan and add the onion, spices, lemon grass and lime zest and cook gently for 2–3 minutes.

5 Add the rice and cook for another minute, then add the stock and bring to the boil. Reduce the heat to very low and cover the pan. Cook gently for 30 minutes then check the rice. If it is still crunchy, cover the pan again and leave for a further 3–5 minutes. Remove from the heat.

6 Stir in the fresh coriander, fluff up the grains, cover and leave for 10 minutes. Serve with lime wedges.

COOK'S TIP

Other varieties of rice, such as white basmati or long grain, can be used for this dish but you will need to adjust the cooking times accordingly.

Red Fried Rice

This vibrant rice dish owes its appeal as much to the bright colours of red onion, red pepper and cherry tomatoes as it does to their distinctive flavours.

Serves 2

INGREDIENTS
115 g/4 oz/³/₄ cup basmati rice
30 ml/2 tbsp groundnut oil
1 small red onion, chopped
1 red pepper, seeded and chopped
225 g/8 oz cherry tomatoes, halved
2 eggs, beaten
salt and freshly ground black pepper

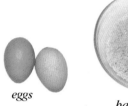

eggs

basmati rice

cherry tomatoes

red onion

red pepper

2 Meanwhile, heat the oil in a wok until very hot. Add the onion and red pepper and stir-fry for 2–3 minutes. Add the cherry tomatoes and stir-fry for a further 2 minutes.

3 Pour in the beaten eggs all at once. Cook for 30 seconds without stirring, then stir to break up the egg as it sets.

4 Drain the cooked rice thoroughly, add to the wok and toss it over the heat with the vegetable and egg mixture for 3 minutes. Season the fried rice with salt and pepper to taste.

Rice and Vegetable Stir-fry

If you have some left-over cooked rice and a few vegetables to spare, then you've got the basis for this quick and tasty side dish.

Serves 4

INGREDIENTS
1/2 cucumber
1 small red or yellow pepper
2 carrots
45 ml/3 tbsp sunflower or groundnut oil
2 spring onions, sliced
1 garlic clove, crushed
1/4 small green cabbage, shredded
75 g/3 oz/scant 1/2 cup cup long grain rice, cooked
30 ml/2 tbsp light soy sauce
15 ml/1 tbsp sesame oil
fresh parsley or coriander, chopped (optional)
115 g/4 oz/1 cup unsalted cashew nuts, almonds or peanuts
salt and freshly ground black pepper

cucumber

spring onions

carrots

garlic

pepper

green cabbage

soy sauce

long grain rice

sunflower oil

parsley

sesame oil

cashew nuts

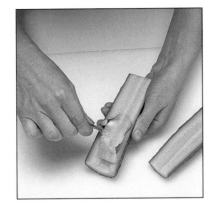

I Halve the cucumber lengthways and scoop out the seeds with a teaspoon. Slice the flesh diagonally. Set aside.

2 Cut the red or yellow pepper in half and remove the core and seeds. Slice the pepper thinly.

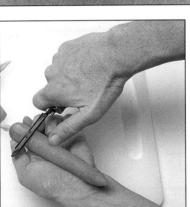

3 Peel the carrots and cut in thin slices. Heat the oil in a wok or large frying pan and stir-fry the sliced spring onions, garlic, carrots and pepper for 3 minutes until the vegetables are crisp but still tender.

4 Add the cabbage and cucumber and fry for another minute or two until the leaves begin to wilt. Mix in the rice, soy sauce, sesame oil and seasoning. Reheat the mixture thoroughly, stirring and tossing all the time. Add the herbs, if using, and nuts. Check the seasoning and adjust if necessary. Serve piping hot.

Stuffed Vegetables

Vegetables such as peppers make wonderful containers for savoury fillings. Instead of sticking to one type of vegetable serve a selection. Thick, creamy Greek yogurt is the ideal accompaniment.

Serves 3-6

INGREDIENTS
1 aubergine
1 large green pepper
2 large tomatoes
1 large onion, chopped
2 garlic cloves, crushed
45 ml/3 tbsp olive oil
200 g/7 oz/1 cup brown rice
600 ml/1 pint/2½ cups vegetable
    stock
75 g/3 oz/1 cup pine nuts
50 g/2 oz/⅓ cup currants
45 ml/3 tbsp chopped fresh dill
45 ml/3 tbsp chopped fresh parsley
15 ml/1 tbsp chopped fresh mint
extra olive oil, to sprinkle
salt and freshly ground black pepper
Greek yogurt and fresh dill sprigs,
    to serve

garlic *tomatoes*

yogurt

aubergine *green pepper* *onion*

olive oil *brown rice* *pine nuts* *vegetable stock*

dill *parsley* *mint* *currants*

1 Halve the aubergine, scoop out the flesh with a sharp knife and chop finely. Salt the insides and leave to drain upside down for 20 minutes while you prepare the other ingredients. Halve the pepper, seed and core.

2 Cut the tops from the tomatoes, scoop out the insides and chop roughly along with the tomato tops. Set the tomato shells aside. Fry the onion, garlic and chopped aubergine in the oil for 10 minutes, then stir in the rice and cook for 2 minutes. Add the tomato flesh, stock, pine nuts, currants and seasoning. Bring to the boil, cover and lower the heat. Simmer for 15 minutes then stir in the herbs.

3 Preheat the oven to 190°C/375°F/ Gas 5. Blanch the aubergine and green pepper halves in boiling water for about 3 minutes, then drain them upside down on kitchen paper.

4 Spoon the rice filling into all six vegetable containers and place on a lightly greased shallow baking dish. Drizzle some olive oil over the stuffed vegetables and bake for 25–30 minutes. Serve hot, topped with spoonfuls of yogurt and the dill sprigs.

Pigeon Peas Cook-up Rice

This Guyanese-style rice dish is made with the country's most commonly used peas. It is flavoured with creamed coconut, another popular West Indian ingredient.

Serves 4-6

INGREDIENTS

25 g/1 oz/2 tbsp butter or margarine
1 onion, chopped
1 garlic clove, crushed
25 g/1 oz/2 tbsp chopped spring onions
1 large carrot, diced
175 g/6 oz/about 1 cup pigeon peas
1 fresh thyme sprig or 5 ml/1 tsp dried thyme
1 cinnamon stick
600 ml/1 pint/2½ cups vegetable stock
65 g/2½ oz/4 tbsp creamed coconut
1 red chilli, chopped
450 g/1 lb/2¼ cups long grain rice
salt and freshly ground black pepper

butter   onion
cinnamon   spring onion

garlic   carrot   chilli

vegetable stock   long grain rice

creamed coconut   thyme

COOK'S TIP

Pigeon peas are also known as gunga peas. The fresh peas can be difficult to obtain, but you will find them in specialist shops. The frozen peas are green and the canned variety are brown. Drain the salted water from canned peas and rinse before using them in this recipe.

1 Melt the butter or margarine in a large heavy saucepan, add the chopped onion and crushed garlic and sauté over a medium heat for about 5 minutes, stirring occasionally.

2 Add the spring onions, carrot, pigeon peas, thyme, cinnamon, stock, creamed coconut, chilli and seasoning. Bring to the boil.

3 Reduce the heat and then stir in the rice. Cover and simmer over a low heat for about 10–15 minutes, or until all the liquid has been absorbed and the rice is tender. Stir with a fork to fluff up the rice before serving.

Nut Pilaff with Omelette Rolls

A wonderful mixture of textures – soft fluffy rice with crunchy nuts and omelette rolls.

Serves 2

INGREDIENTS
175 g/6 oz/1 cup basmati rice
15 ml/1 tbsp sunflower oil
1 small onion, chopped
1 red pepper, finely diced
350 ml/12 fl oz/1½ cups hot
  vegetable stock
2 eggs
25 g/1 oz/¼ cup salted peanuts
15 ml/1 tbsp soy sauce
salt and freshly ground black pepper
parsley sprigs, to garnish

salted peanuts *parsley* *onion*

stock cube *eggs*

basmati rice *red pepper*

soy sauce

1 Wash the rice several times under cold running water. Drain thoroughly. Heat half the oil in a large frying pan. Fry the onion and pepper for 2–3 minutes then stir in the rice and stock. Bring to the boil and cook for 10 minutes until the rice is tender.

2 Meanwhile, beat the eggs lightly with salt and pepper to taste. Heat the remaining oil in a second large frying pan. Pour in the eggs and tilt the pan to cover the base thinly. Cook the omelette for 1 minute, then flip it over and cook the other side for 1 minute.

3 Slide the omelette on to a clean board and roll it up tightly. Cut the omelette roll into 8 slices.

4 Stir the peanuts and the soy sauce into the pilaff and add black pepper to taste. Turn the pilaff into a serving dish, arrange the omelette rolls on top and garnish with the parsley. Serve at once.

Kedgeree with French Beans and Mushrooms

Crunchy French beans and mushrooms are the star ingredients in this vegetarian version of an old favourite.

Serves 2

INGREDIENTS
115 g/4 oz/³/₄ cup basmati rice
3 eggs
175 g/6 oz French beans, trimmed
50 g/2 oz/¹/₄ cup butter
1 onion, finely chopped
225 g/8 oz brown cap mushrooms, quartered
30 ml/2 tbsp single cream
15 ml/1 tbsp chopped fresh parsley
salt and freshly ground black pepper

single cream

brown cap mushrooms

parsley

onion

butter

French beans

eggs

basmati rice

1 Wash the rice several times under cold running water. Drain thoroughly. Bring a pan of water to the boil, add the rice and cook for 10–12 minutes until tender. Drain thoroughly.

2 Half fill a second pan with water, add the eggs and bring to the boil. Lower the heat and simmer for 8 minutes. Drain the eggs, cool them under cold water, then remove the shells.

3 Bring another pan of water to the boil and cook the French beans for 5 minutes. Drain, refresh under cold running water, then drain again.

4 Melt the butter in a large frying pan. Add the onion and mushrooms. Cook for 2–3 minutes over a moderate heat.

5 Add the French beans and rice to the onion mixture. Stir lightly to mix. Cook for 2 minutes. Cut the hard-boiled eggs in wedges and add them to the pan.

6 Stir in the cream and parsley, taking care not to break up the eggs. Reheat the kedgeree, but do not allow it to boil. Serve at once.

Nutty Rice and Mushroom Stir-fry

This delicious and substantial supper dish can be eaten hot or cold with salads.

Serves 4–6

INGREDIENTS
350 g/12 oz long grain rice
45 ml/3 tbsp sunflower oil
1 small onion, roughly chopped
225 g/8 oz field mushrooms, sliced
50 g/2 oz/½ cup hazelnuts,
  roughly chopped
50 g/2 oz/½ cup pecan nuts,
  roughly chopped
50 g/2 oz/½ cup almonds,
  roughly chopped
60 ml/4 tbsp fresh parsley, chopped
salt and freshly ground black pepper

rice

almonds

field mushroom

hazelnuts

pecan nuts

1 Rinse the rice, then cook for 10–12 minutes in 700–850 ml/1¼–1½ pints water in a saucepan with a tight-fitting lid. When cooked, refresh under cold water. Heat the wok, then add half the oil. When the oil is hot, stir-fry the rice for 2–3 minutes. Remove and set aside.

2 Add the remaining oil and stir-fry the onion for 2 minutes until softened.

3 Mix in the field mushrooms and stir-fry for 2 minutes.

4 Add all the nuts and stir-fry for 1 minute. Return the rice to the wok and stir-fry for 3 minutes. Season with salt and pepper. Stir in the parsley and serve.

Pilau Rice Flavoured with Whole Spices

This fragrant rice dish will make a perfect accompaniment to any Indian meal.

Serves 4-6

INGREDIENTS
generous pinch saffron strands
600ml/1 pint/2½ cups hot vegetable
    stock
50 g/2 oz/¼ cup butter
1 onion, chopped
1 garlic clove, crushed
½ cinnamon stick
6 green cardamom pods
1 bay leaf
50 g/2 oz/⅓ cup sultanas
250g/9oz/1⅓ cups basmati rice,
    rinsed and drained
15 ml/1 tbsp vegetable oil
50 g/2 oz/½ cup cashew nuts

1 Add the saffron strands to the hot stock and set aside. Heat the butter in a large saucepan and fry the onion and garlic for 5 minutes. Stir in the cinnamon stick, cardamoms and bay leaf and cook for 2 minutes.

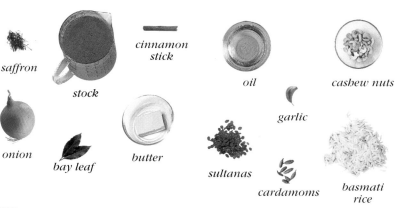

saffron

stock

cinnamon stick

oil

cashew nuts

onion

bay leaf

butter

garlic

sultanas

cardamoms

basmati rice

2 Add the rice and cook, stirring, for 2 minutes more. Pour in the stock and saffron mixture and add the sultanas. Bring to the boil, stir, then lower the heat. Cover the pan and leave to cook gently for about 15 minutes or until the rice is tender and all the liquid has been absorbed.

3 Meanwhile, heat the oil in a wok or frying pan and fry the cashew nuts until browned. Drain on kitchen paper. Scatter over the rice and serve.

VARIATION

You can add a mixture of nuts to this recipe, if you like, such as almonds, peanuts or hazelnuts. Some nuts may be bought complete with their brown, papery skins, which should be removed before use. The flavour of all nuts is improved by toasting.

COOK'S TIP

Remember to keep all spices stored in separate airtight containers. This helps them to retain their flavour as well as preventing their aromas from spreading to other ingredients in your store cupboard.

Vegetable Biryani

Aromatic, spicy rice cooked with fresh vegetables makes a delicious vegetarian main course.

Serves 4–6

INGREDIENTS

175 g/6 oz/1 cup long-grain rice
2 whole cloves
seeds of 2 cardamom pods
450 ml/¾ pint/scant 2 cups
  vegetable stock
2 garlic cloves
1 small onion, roughly chopped
5 ml/1 tsp cumin seeds
5 ml/1 tsp ground coriander
2.5 ml/½ tsp ground turmeric
2.5 ml/½ tsp chilli powder
1 large potato, peeled and cut into
  2.5 cm/1 in cubes
2 carrots, sliced
½ cauliflower, broken into florets
50 g/2 oz French beans, cut into
  2.5 cm/1 in lengths
30 ml/2 tbsp chopped fresh coriander
30 ml/2 tbsp lime juice
salt and freshly ground black pepper
sprig of fresh coriander, to garnish

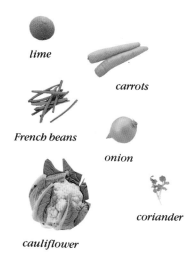

lime

carrots

French beans

onion

coriander

cauliflower

1 Put the rice, cloves and cardamom seeds into a large, heavy-based saucepan. Pour over the stock and bring to the boil.

2 Reduce the heat, cover and simmer for 20 minutes, or until all the stock has been absorbed.

3 Meanwhile put the garlic cloves, onion, cumin seeds, coriander, turmeric, chilli powder and seasoning into a blender or coffee grinder together with 30 ml/ 2 tbsp water. Blend to a paste.

4 Preheat the oven to 180°C/350°F/ Gas 4. Spoon the spicy paste into a flameproof casserole and cook over a low heat for 2 minutes, stirring occasionally.

5 Add the potato, carrots, cauliflower, beans and 90 ml/6 tbsp water. Cover and cook over a low heat for a further 12 minutes, stirring occasionally. Add the chopped coriander.

6 Spoon the rice over the vegetables. Sprinkle over the lime juice. Cover and cook in the oven for 25 minutes, or until the vegetables are tender. Fluff up the rice with a fork before serving and garnish with a sprig of fresh coriander.

Vegetable Pilau

Cashew nuts, sweetcorn and peas flavour this delicious rice accompaniment.

Serves 4–6

INGREDIENTS

225 g/8 oz/1 cup basmati rice
30 ml/2 tbsp oil
2.5 ml/½ tsp cumin seeds
2 bay leaves
4 green cardamom pods
4 cloves
1 onion, finely chopped
1 carrot, finely diced
50 g/2 oz/½ cup frozen
    peas, thawed
50 g/2 oz/⅓ cup frozen sweetcorn,
    thawed
25 g/1 oz/¼ cup cashew nuts,
    lightly fried
475 ml/16 fl oz/2 cups water
1.5 ml/¼ tsp ground cumin

basmati rice

peas

ground
coriander

cumin seeds

sweetcorn

carrot

ground
cumin

oil

bay
leaves

onion

cashew
nuts

cardamom
pods

cloves

salt

1 Wash the basmati rice in several changes of cold water. Put into a bowl and cover with water. Leave to soak for 30 minutes.

2 Heat the oil in a large frying pan and fry the cumin seeds for 2 minutes. Add the bay leaves, cardamoms and cloves and fry for 2 minutes.

3 Add the onion and fry for 5 minutes until lightly browned.

4 Stir in the carrot and cook for 3–4 minutes.

5 Drain the rice and add to the pan with the peas, sweetcorn and cashew nuts. Fry for 4–5 minutes.

6 Add the water, remaining spices and salt. Bring to the boil, cover, and simmer for 15 minutes over a low heat until all the water is absorbed. Leave to stand, covered, for 10 minutes before serving.

Mexican-style Rice

This side dish is the perfect accompaniment to spicy dishes, such as vegetable fajitas. It is garnished with a stunning but dangerous display of flowers made from red chillies.

Serves 6

INGREDIENTS
350 g/12 oz/1¾ cups long grain rice
1 onion, chopped
2 garlic cloves, chopped
450 g/1 lb tomatoes, peeled, seeded
    and chopped
60 ml/4 tbsp vegetable oil
900 ml/1½ pints/3¾ cups vegetable
    stock
175 g/6 oz/1½ cups peas, thawed
    if frozen
salt and freshly ground black
    pepper
fresh coriander and 4–6 chilli
    flowers, to garnish

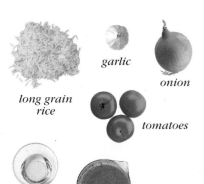

long grain rice *garlic* *onion* *tomatoes*

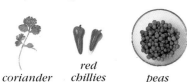

corn oil *stock* *coriander* *red chillies* *peas*

1 Soak the rice in a bowl of hot water for 15 minutes. Drain, rinse well under cold running water, drain again and set aside. Combine the onion, garlic and tomatoes in a food processor and process to a purée.

2 Heat the oil in a large frying pan. Add the drained rice and sauté until it becomes golden brown. Using a slotted spoon, to leave behind as much oil as possible, transfer the rice to a saucepan.

COOK'S TIP
To make chilli flowers, it is a good idea to wear rubber gloves and avoid touching your face or eyes, as the essential oils will cause a painful reaction. Slice the red chillies from tip to stem end into four or five sections. Place in a bowl of iced water until they curl back to form flowers, then drain. Wash hands or gloves thoroughly.

3 Reheat the oil remaining in the pan and cook the tomato, garlic and onion purée for 2–3 minutes. Tip it into the saucepan of rice and pour in the stock. Season to taste. Bring to the boil, reduce the heat to the lowest possible setting, cover the pan and cook for about 15–20 minutes until almost all the liquid has been absorbed.

4 Stir the peas into the rice mixture and cook, without a lid, until all the liquid has been absorbed and the rice is tender. Stir the mixture from time to time. Transfer the rice to a serving dish and garnish with the drained chilli flowers and sprigs of coriander. Warn the diners that the chilli flowers are hot and should be approached with caution.

Leek, Mushroom and Lemon Risotto

A delicious risotto, packed full of flavour makes a marvellous treat for friends or family.

Serves 4

INGREDIENTS
225 g/8 oz trimmed leeks
225 g/8 oz/2-3 cups brown cap
  mushrooms
30 ml/2 tbsp olive oil
3 garlic cloves, crushed
75 g/3 oz/6 tbsp butter
1 large onion, roughly chopped
350 g/12 oz/1¾ cups risotto rice
1.2 litres/2 pints/5 cups simmering
  vegetable stock
grated rind of 1 lemon
45 ml/3 tbsp lemon juice
50 g/2 oz/⅔ cup freshly grated
  Parmesan cheese
60 ml/4 tbsp mixed chopped fresh
  chives and flat leaf parsley
salt and freshly ground black pepper
lemon wedges, to serve

leeks

olive oil

mushrooms

lemon

butter

risotto rice

Parmesan cheese

onion

garlic

vegetable stock

parsley

chives

1 Wash the leeks well. Slice them in half lengthways and chop them roughly. Wipe the mushrooms with kitchen paper and chop them roughly.

2 Heat the oil in a large saucepan and cook the garlic for 1 minute. Add the leeks, mushrooms and plenty of seasoning and cook over a medium heat for about 10 minutes, or until softened and browned. Remove from the pan and set aside.

3 Add 25 g/1 oz of the butter to the pan. As soon as it has melted, add the onion and cook over a medium heat for 5 minutes until softened and golden.

4 Stir in the rice and cook for about 1 minute until the grains begin to look translucent and are coated in the fat. Add a ladleful of stock to the pan and cook gently, stirring occasionally, until the liquid has been absorbed.

5 Continue to add stock, a ladleful at a time, until all the stock has been absorbed. This should take about 25–30 minutes. The risotto will turn thick and creamy and the rice should be tender but not sticky.

6 Just before serving, stir in the leeks, mushrooms, remaining butter, grated lemon rind and juice. Add half the grated Parmesan and herbs. Adjust the seasoning and serve, sprinkled with the remaining Parmesan, herbs and lemon wedges. Garnish with parsley, if you like.

Risotto-stuffed Aubergines with Spicy Tomato Sauce

Aubergines are a challenge to the creative cook and allow for some unusual recipe ideas. Here, they are stuffed and baked with a cheese and pine nut topping.

Serves 4

INGREDIENTS
4 small aubergines
105 ml/7 tbsp olive oil
1 small onion, chopped
175 g/6 oz/scant 1 cup arborio rice
750 ml/1¼ pints/3⅔ cups
    vegetable stock
15 ml/1 tbsp white wine vinegar
8 fresh basil sprigs, to garnish

FOR THE TOPPING
25 g/1 oz/¼ cup freshly grated
    Parmesan cheese
15 g/½ oz/1 tbsp pine nuts

FOR THE TOMATO SAUCE
300 ml/½ pint/1¼ cups thick passata
    or tomato pulp
5 ml/1 tsp mild curry paste
pinch of salt

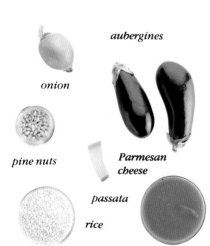

onion

aubergines

pine nuts

Parmesan cheese

passata

rice

COOK'S TIP

Don't be put off by the amount of oil aubergines absorb when cooking. Use olive oil and remember that good oils are low in saturated fat and are believed to fight against heart disease.

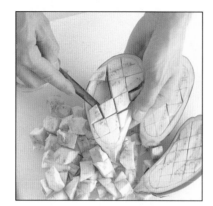

1 Preheat the oven to 200°C/400°F/Gas 6. Cut the aubergines in half lengthways and take out their flesh with a small knife. Brush with 30 ml/2 tbsp of the oil, place on a baking sheet and cook in the preheated oven for 6–8 minutes.

2 Chop the reserved aubergine flesh and heat the remainder of the olive oil in a medium saucepan. Add the aubergine flesh and the onion and cook over a gentle heat for 3–4 minutes until soft.

3 Add the rice, stir in the stock and simmer uncovered for a further 15 minutes. Stir in the vinegar.

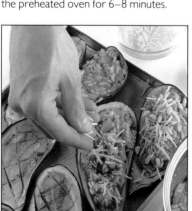

4 Increase the oven temperature to 230°C/450°F/Gas 8. Spoon the rice into the aubergine skins, top with cheese and pine nuts, return to the oven and brown for 5 minutes.

5 To make the sauce, combine the passata or tomato pulp with the curry paste, heat through and add salt to taste.

6 Spoon the sauce onto four large serving plates and position two aubergine halves on each. Garnish with basil sprigs.

Sweet Vegetable Couscous

A wonderful combination of sweet vegetables and spices, this makes a substantial winter dish.

Serves 4–6

INGREDIENTS

1 generous pinch of saffron threads
45 ml/3 tbsp boiling water
15 ml/1 tbsp olive oil
1 red onion, sliced
2 garlic cloves crushed
1–2 fresh red chillies, seeded and finely chopped
2.5 ml/½ tsp ground ginger
2.5 ml/½ tsp ground cinnamon
1 × 400 g/14 oz can chopped tomatoes
300 ml/½ pint/1¼ cups vegetable stock or water
4 medium carrots, peeled and cut into 5 mm/¼ in slices
2 medium turnips, peeled and cut into 2 cm/¾ in cubes
450 g/1 lb sweet potatoes, peeled and cut into 2 cm/¾ in cubes
75 g/3 oz/⅓ cup raisins
2 medium courgettes, cut into 5 mm/¼ in slices
1 × 400 g/14 oz can chick-peas, drained and rinsed
45 ml/3 tbsp chopped fresh parsley
45 ml/3 tbsp chopped fresh coriander
450 g/1 lb quick-cook couscous

1 Leave the saffron to infuse in the boiling water.

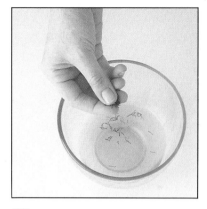

2 Heat the oil in a large saucepan. Add the onion, garlic and chillies and cook gently for 5 minutes.

3 Add the ground ginger and cinnamon and cook for a further 1–2 minutes.

4 Add the tomatoes, stock or water, infused saffron and liquid, carrots, turnips, sweet potatoes and raisins, cover and simmer for 25 minutes.

red onion

chick-peas

couscous

chopped tomatoes

courgette

carrot

red chilli

garlic

turnip

raisins

sweet potato

5 Add the courgettes, chick-peas, parsley and coriander and cook for another 10 minutes.

6 Meanwhile prepare the couscous following the packet instructions and serve with the vegetables.

Aubergine Pilaff

This hearty dish is made with bulgur wheat and aubergine, flavoured with fresh mint.

Serves 2

INGREDIENTS
2 medium aubergines
60-90 ml/4-6 tbsp sunflower oil
1 small onion, finely chopped
175 g/6 oz/1 cup bulgur wheat
450 ml/16 fl oz/scant 2 cups
  vegetable stock
30 ml/2 tbsp pine nuts, toasted
15 ml/1 tbsp chopped fresh mint
salt and freshly ground black pepper

FOR THE GARNISH
lime wedges
lemon wedges
torn mint leaves

mint

pine nuts

stock cube

onion

bulgur wheat

aubergines

1 Trim the ends from the aubergines. Using a sharp knife, cut them into neat sticks and then into 1 cm/½ in dice.

COOK'S TIP
To cut down on the cooking time, soak the bulgur wheat in water to cover by 2.5 cm/1 in for up to 8 hours. Drain and continue as described in the recipe, reducing the cooking time to 8 minutes.

2 Heat 60 ml/4 tbsp of the oil in a large frying pan. Add the onion and sauté for 1 minute.

3 Add the diced aubergine. Cook over a high heat, stirring frequently, for about 4 minutes until just tender. Add the remaining oil if needed.

4 Stir in the bulgur wheat, mixing well, then pour in the vegetable stock. Bring to the boil, then lower the heat and simmer for 10 minutes or until all the liquid has evaporated. Season to taste.

5 Add the pine nuts, stir gently with a wooden spoon, then stir in the mint.

6 Spoon the pilaff on to individual plates and garnish each portion with lime and lemon wedges. Sprinkle with torn mint leaves for extra colour.

Buckwheat Couscous with Goat's Cheese and Celery

Couscous is made from cracked, partially cooked wheat, which is dried and then reconstituted in water or stock. It tastes of very little by itself, but carries the flavour of other ingredients very well.

Serves 4

INGREDIENTS
1 egg
30 ml/2 tbsp olive oil
1 small bunch spring onions, chopped
2 celery sticks, sliced
175 g/6 oz/1 cup couscous
75 g/3 oz/½ cup buckwheat
45 ml/3 tbsp chopped fresh parsley
finely grated zest of ½ lemon
25 g/1 oz/¼ cup chopped walnuts, toasted
150 g/5 oz strongly flavoured goat's cheese
salt and freshly ground black pepper
Cos lettuce leaves, to serve

1 Boil the egg for 10 minutes, cool, peel and set aside. Heat the oil in a saucepan and add the spring onions and celery. Cook for 2–3 minutes until soft.

buckwheat

celery

egg

goat's cheese

parsley

walnuts

2 Add the couscous and buckwheat and cover with 600 ml/1 pint/2½ cups of boiling salted water. Cover and return to a simmer. Remove from the heat and allow the couscous to soften and absorb the water for about 3 minutes. Transfer the mixture to a large bowl.

3 Grate the hard-boiled egg finely into a small bowl and add the chopped parsley, lemon zest and walnuts. Fold into the couscous, season, and crumble in the goat's cheese. Mix well and then turn out into a shallow dish. Serve warm with a salad of Cos lettuce.

VARIATION

Couscous is ideal as a filling for pitta breads when accompanied with crisp salad leaves.

Lentil Stir-fry

Mushrooms, artichokes, sugar snap peas and lentils make a satisfying stir-fry supper.

Serves 2–3

INGREDIENTS
115 g/4 oz sugar snap peas
25 g/1 oz butter
1 small onion, chopped
115 g/4 oz cup or brown cap
  mushrooms, sliced
400 g/14 oz can artichoke hearts,
  drained and halved
400 g/14 oz can green
  lentils, drained
60 ml/4 tbsp single cream
25 g/1 oz/¼ cup flaked
  almonds, toasted
salt and freshly ground black pepper
French bread, to serve

single cream

green lentils

cup mushrooms

sugar snap peas

flaked almonds

artichoke hearts

onion

1 Bring a pan of salted water to the boil, add the sugar snap peas and cook for about 4 minutes until just tender. Drain, refresh under cold running water, then drain again. Pat dry the peas with kitchen paper and set aside.

2 Melt the butter in a frying pan. Cook the chopped onion for 2–3 minutes, stirring occasionally.

3 Add the sliced mushrooms to the onion. Stir until combined, then cook for 2–3 minutes until just tender. Add the artichokes, sugar snap peas and lentils to the pan. Stir-fry for 2 minutes.

4 Stir in the cream and almonds and cook for 1 minute. Season to taste. Serve at once, with chunks of French bread.

COOK'S TIP
Use Greek yogurt instead of the cream, if preferred.

Lentils and Rice

Lentils are cooked with whole and ground spices, potatoes, rice and onions to produce an authentic Indian-style risotto.

Serves 4

INGREDIENTS
150 g/5 oz/³⁄₄ cup toovar dhal or red
  split lentils
115 g/4 oz basmati rice
1 large potato
1 large onion
30 ml/2 tbsp oil
4 whole cloves
1.5 ml/¹⁄₄ tsp cumin seeds
1.5 ml/¹⁄₄ tsp ground turmeric
10 ml/2 tsp salt
300 ml/¹⁄₂ pints/1¹⁄₄ cups water

basmati rice

oil

cumin seeds

ground turmeric

red split lentils

potato

salt

onion

cloves

1 Wash the toovar dhal or lentils and rice in several changes of cold water. Put into a bowl and cover with water. Leave to soak for 15 minutes then drain.

2 Peel then cut the potato into 2.5 cm/1 in chunks.

3 Thinly slice the onion.

4 Heat the oil in a large heavy-based saucepan and fry the cloves and cumin seeds for 2 minutes until the seeds are beginning to splutter.

5 Add the onion and potatoes and fry for 5 minutes. Add the lentils, rice, turmeric and salt and fry for 3 minutes.

6 Add the water. Bring to the boil, cover and simmer for 15–20 minutes until all the water has been absorbed and the potatoes are tender. Leave to stand, covered, for about 10 minutes before serving.

Mung Beans with Potatoes

Mung beans are one of the quicker-cooking pulses which do not require soaking and are therefore very easy to use. In this recipe they are cooked with potatoes and traditional Indian spices to give a tasty nutritious dish.

Serves 4

INGREDIENTS
175 g/6 oz/1 cup mung beans
750 ml/1¼ pints/3 cups water
225 g/8 oz potatoes, cut into
    2 cm/¾ in chunks
30 ml/2 tbsp oil
2.5 ml/½ tsp cumin seeds
1 green chilli, finely chopped
1 garlic clove, crushed
2.5 cm/1 in piece root ginger,
    finely chopped
1.5 ml/¼ tsp ground turmeric
2.5 ml/½ tsp chilli powder
5 ml/1 tsp salt
5 ml/1 tsp sugar
4 curry leaves
5 tomatoes, skinned and
    finely chopped
15 ml/1 tbsp tomato purée
curry leaves, to garnish
plain rice, to serve

potatoes

mung beans

tomatoes

oil

chilli powder

tomato purée

sugar

root ginger

garlic

cumin seeds

ground turmeric

green chilli

curry leaves

salt

1 Wash the beans. Bring to the boil in the water, cover and simmer until soft, about 30 minutes. Par-boil the potatoes for 10 minutes in another saucepan, then drain well.

2 Heat the oil and fry the cumin seeds until they splutter. Add the chilli, garlic and ginger and fry for 3–4 minutes.

3 Add the turmeric, chilli powder, salt and sugar and cook for 2 minutes, stirring to prevent the mixture from sticking to the saucepan.

4 Add the curry leaves, tomatoes and tomato purée and simmer for 5 minutes until the sauce thickens. Add the tomato sauce and potatoes to the mung beans and mix together. Serve with plain boiled rice, and garnish with curry leaves.

Spicy Bean and Lentil Loaf

An appetizing meat-free and high fibre savoury loaf, ideal for picnics or a packed lunch.

Serves 12

INGREDIENTS
10 ml/2 tsp olive oil
1 onion, finely chopped
1 garlic clove, crushed
2 sticks celery, finely chopped
400 g/14 oz can red kidney beans
400 g/14 oz can lentils
1 egg
1 carrot, coarsely grated
50 g/2 oz/½ cup hazelnuts,
    finely chopped
50 g/2 oz/½ cup reduced-fat mature
    Cheddar cheese, finely grated
50 g/2 oz/1 cup fresh
    wholemeal breadcrumbs
15 ml/1 tbsp tomato purée
15 ml/1 tbsp tomato ketchup
5 ml/1 tsp each ground cumin,
    ground coriander and hot
    chilli powder
salt and ground black pepper

olive oil *onion* *garlic* *celery*

red kidney beans *lentils* *egg*

carrot *hazelnuts* *reduced-fat mature Cheddar cheese*

fresh wholemeal breadcrumbs *tomato purée*

tomato ketchup *ground coriander* *ground cumin* *hot chilli powder*

1 Preheat the oven to 180°C/350°F/ Gas 4. Lightly grease a 900 g/2 lb loaf tin. Heat the oil in a saucepan, add the onion, garlic and celery and cook gently for 5 minutes, stirring occasionally. Remove the pan from the heat and cool slightly.

2 Rinse and drain the beans and lentils. Put in a blender or food processor with the onion mixture and egg and process until smooth.

3 Transfer the mixture to a bowl, add all the remaining ingredients and mix well. Season to taste.

4 Spoon the mixture into the pre-pared tin and level the surface. Bake for about 1 hour then remove from the tin and serve hot or cold in slices.

Chilli Mixed Bean Sauce

Serves 6

INGREDIENTS
1 onion, finely chopped
1–2 garlic cloves, crushed
1 large green chilli, seeded
   and chopped
150 ml/¼ pint/⅔ cup
   vegetable stock
400 g/14 oz can chopped tomatoes
30 ml/2 tbsp concentrated
   tomato purée
120 ml/4 fl oz/½ cup red wine
5 ml/1 tsp dried oregano
200 g/7 oz French beans, sliced
400 g/14 oz can red kidney
   beans, drained
400 g/14 oz can cannellini
   beans, drained
400 g/14 oz can chick-peas, drained
450 g/1 lb spaghetti
salt and ground black pepper

spaghetti

onion

green chilli   *garlic*   *French beans*

tomato purée   *red kidney beans*   *cannellini beans*

red wine   *chopped tomatoes*

vegetable stock   *chick-peas*

1 To make the sauce, put the chopped onion, garlic and chilli into a non-stick pan with the stock. Bring to the boil and cook for 5 minutes until tender.

2 Add the tomatoes, tomato purée, wine, seasoning and oregano. Bring to the boil, cover and simmer the sauce for 20 minutes.

3 Cook the beans in boiling, salted water for about 5–6 minutes until tender. Drain thoroughly.

4 Add all the beans to the sauce and simmer for a further 10 minutes. Cook the spaghetti in a large pan of boiling, salted water until *al dente*. Drain thoroughly. Transfer to a serving dish and top with the chilli beans.

Chilli Bean Bake

The contrasting textures of saucy beans, vegetables and crunchy cornbread topping make this a memorable meal.

Serves 4

INGREDIENTS
225 g/8 oz/1⅓ cups red kidney beans
1 bay leaf
1 large onion, finely chopped
1 garlic clove, crushed
2 celery sticks, sliced
5 ml/1 tsp ground cumin
5 ml/1 tsp chilli powder
400 g/14 oz can chopped tomatoes
15 ml/1 tbsp tomato purée
5 ml/1 tsp dried mixed herbs
15 ml/1 tbsp lemon juice
1 yellow pepper, seeded and diced
salt and freshly ground black pepper
mixed salad, to serve

FOR THE CORNBREAD TOPPING
175 g/6 oz/1½ cups corn meal
15 ml/1 tbsp wholemeal flour
5 ml/1 tsp baking powder
1 egg, beaten
175 ml/6 fl oz/¾ cup skimmed milk

kidney beans

celery

tomato purée

pepper

1 Soak the beans overnight in cold water. Drain and rinse well. Pour 1 litre/ 1¾ pints/4 cups of water into a large, heavy-based saucepan together with the beans and bay leaf and boil rapidly for 10 minutes. Lower the heat, cover and simmer for 35–40 minutes, or until the beans are tender.

2 Add the onion, garlic clove, celery, cumin, chilli powder, chopped tomatoes, tomato purée and dried mixed herbs. Half-cover the pan with a lid and simmer for a further 10 minutes.

3 Stir in the lemon juice, yellow pepper and seasoning. Simmer for a further 8-10 minutes, stirring occasionally, until the vegetables are just tender. Discard the bay leaf and spoon the mixture into a large casserole.

4 Pre-heat the oven to 220°C/425°F/ Gas 7. For the topping, put the corn meal, flour, baking powder and a pinch of salt into a bowl and mix together. Make a well in the centre and add the egg and milk. Mix and pour over the bean mixture. Bake in the pre-heated oven for 20 minutes, or until brown.

Lemon and Ginger Spicy Beans

An extremely quick delicious meal, made with canned beans for speed. You probably won't need extra salt as canned beans tend to be already salted.

Serves 4

INGREDIENTS

5 cm/2 in piece fresh ginger root, peeled and roughly chopped
3 garlic cloves, roughly chopped
250 ml/8 fl oz/1 cup cold water
15 ml/1 tbsp sunflower oil
1 large onion, thinly sliced
1 fresh red chilli, seeded and finely chopped
¼ tsp cayenne pepper
10 ml/2 tsp ground cumin
5 ml/1 tsp ground coriander
½ tsp ground turmeric
30 ml/2 tbsp lemon juice
75 g/3 oz/⅓ cup chopped fresh coriander
1 × 400 g/14 oz can black-eyed beans, drained and rinsed
1 × 400 g/14 oz can aduki beans, drained and rinsed
1 × 400 g/14 oz can haricot beans, drained and rinsed
freshly ground black pepper

garlic
red chilli
aduki beans
ginger
ground coriander
black-eyed beans
ground turmeric
ground cumin
haricot beans
onion

1 Place the ginger, garlic and 60 ml/4 tbsp of the cold water in a blender and mix until smooth.

2 Heat the oil in a pan. Add the onion and chilli and cook gently for 5 minutes until softened.

3 Add the cayenne pepper, cumin, ground coriander and turmeric and stir-fry for 1 minute.

4 Stir in the ginger and garlic paste from the blender and cook for another minute.

5 Add the remaining water, lemon juice and fresh coriander, stir well and bring to the boil. Cover the pan tightly and cook for 5 minutes.

6 Add all the beans and cook for a further 5–10 minutes. Season with pepper and serve.

Creamy Cannellini Beans with Asparagus

Cannellini beans in a creamy sauce contrast with tender asparagus in this tasty toast topper.

Serves 2

INGREDIENTS

10 ml/2 tsp butter
1 small onion, finely chopped
1 small carrot, grated
5 ml/1 tsp fresh thyme leaves
400 g/14 oz can cannellini
  beans, drained
150 ml/¼ pint/⅔ cup single cream
115 g/4 oz young asparagus
  spears, trimmed
2 slices of fresh cut Granary bread
salt and freshly ground black pepper

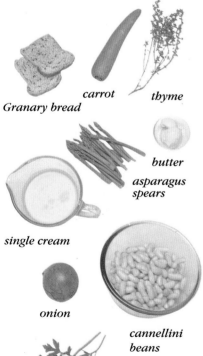

Granary bread   *carrot*   *thyme*

butter
asparagus spears

single cream

onion

cannellini beans

parsley

1 Melt the butter in a pan. Add the onion and carrot and fry over a moderate heat for 4 minutes until soft. Add the thyme leaves.

2 Rinse the cannellini beans under cold running water. Drain thoroughly, then add to the onion and carrot. Mix lightly.

3 Pour in the cream and heat slowly to just below boiling point, stirring occasionally. Remove the pan from the heat and add salt and pepper to taste. Preheat the grill.

4 Place the asparagus spears in a saucepan. Pour over just enough boiling water to cover. Poach for 3–4 minutes until the spears are just tender.

5 Meanwhile, toast the bread under the grill until both sides are golden.

6 Place the toast on individual plates. Drain the asparagus and divide the spears between the slices of toast. Spoon the bean mixture over each portion and serve.

COOK'S TIP
Use your favourite variety of canned beans such as borlotti, haricot or flageolets.

Mixed Bean Curry

You can use any combination of beans that you
have in the storecupboard for this recipe.

Serves 4

INGREDIENTS
50 g/2 oz/¹/₃ cup red kidney beans
50 g/2 oz/¹/₃ cup black-eyed beans
50 g/2 oz/¹/₃ cup haricot beans
50 g/2 oz/¹/₃ cup flageolet beans
30 ml/2 tbsp oil
5 ml/1 tsp cumin seeds
5 ml/1 tsp black mustard seeds
1 onion, finely chopped
2 garlic cloves, crushed
2.5 cm/1 in piece root ginger, grated
2 green chillies, finely chopped
30 ml/2 tbsp curry paste
2.5 ml/¹/₂ tsp salt
400 g/14 oz can chopped tomatoes
30 ml/2 tbsp tomato purée
250 ml/8 fl oz/1 cup water
30 ml/2 tbsp chopped
    fresh coriander
chopped fresh coriander, to garnish

black
mustard
seeds

chopped
tomatoes

cumin
seeds

curry
paste

red
kidney
beans

oil

black-eyed
beans

tomato
purée

haricot
beans

onion
flageolet
beans

root
ginger

green
chillies

fresh
coriander   garlic

1 Put the beans in a large bowl and cover with plenty of cold water. Leave to soak overnight, mixing occasionally.

2 Drain the beans and put into a large heavy-based saucepan with double the volume of cold water. Boil vigorously for 10 minutes. Skim off any scum. Cover and simmer for 1¹/₂ hours or until the beans are soft.

3 Heat the oil in a large saucepan and fry the cumin seeds and mustard seeds for 2 minutes until the seeds begin to splutter. Add the onion, garlic, ginger and chilli and fry for 5 minutes.

4 Add the curry paste and fry for a further 2–3 minutes, stirring, then add the salt.

5 Add the tomatoes, tomato purée and the water and simmer for 5 minutes.

6 Add the drained beans and the fresh coriander. Cover and simmer for about 30–40 minutes until the sauce thickens and the beans are cooked. Garnish with chopped fresh coriander.

COOK'S TIP
Depending on the types of beans you use, you may need to adjust the cooking time.

Vegetarian Cassoulet

Every town in south-west France has its own version of this popular classic. Warm French bread is all that is needed to complete this hearty vegetable version.

Serves 4–6

INGREDIENTS
400 g/14 oz/2 cups dried
    haricot beans
1 bay leaf
2 onions
3 whole cloves
2 garlic cloves, crushed
5 ml/1 tsp olive oil
2 leeks, thickly sliced
12 baby carrots
115 g/4 oz button mushrooms
400 g/14 oz can chopped tomatoes
15 ml/1 tbsp tomato purée
5 ml/1 tsp paprika
15 ml/1 tbsp chopped fresh thyme
30 ml/2 tbsp chopped fresh parsley
115 g/4 oz/2 cups fresh white
    breadcrumbs
salt and freshly ground black pepper

chopped tomatoes

bay leaf

leek

breadcrumbs

carrots

mushrooms

COOK'S TIP

If you're short of time use canned haricot beans – you'll need two 400 g/14 oz cans. Drain, reserving the bean juices and make up to 400 ml/14 fl oz/1⅔ cups with vegetable stock.

1 Soak the beans overnight in plenty of cold water. Drain and rinse under cold running water. Put them in a saucepan together with 1.75 litres/3 pints/7½ cups of cold water and the bay leaf. Bring to the boil and cook rapidly for 10 minutes.

2 Peel one of the onions and spike with cloves. Add to the beans and reduce the heat. Cover and simmer gently for 1 hour, until the beans are almost tender. Drain, reserving the stock but discarding the bay leaf and onion.

3 Chop the remaining onion and put it into a large flameproof casserole together with the garlic cloves and olive oil. Cook gently for 5 minutes, or until softened.

4 Pre-heat the oven to 160°C/325°F/Gas 3. Add the leeks, carrots, mushrooms, chopped tomatoes, tomato purée, paprika, thyme and 400 ml/14 fl oz/1⅔ cups of the reserved stock to the casserole.

5 Bring to the boil, cover and simmer gently for 10 minutes. Stir in the cooked beans and parsley. Season to taste.

6 Sprinkle with the breadcrumbs and bake uncovered in the pre-heated oven for 35 minutes, or until the topping is golden brown and crisp.

Three Bean Salad with Yogurt Dressing

This tangy bean and pasta salad is great on its own or can be served as a side dish.

Serves 3–4

INGREDIENTS
75 g/3 oz penne or other dried
  pasta shapes
2 tomatoes
200 g/7 oz can red kidney
  beans, drained
200 g/7 oz can cannellini
  beans, drained
200 g/7 oz can chick-peas, drained
1 green pepper, seeded and diced
75 ml/3 tbsp natural yogurt
30 ml/2 tbsp sunflower oil
grated rind of ¹/₂ lemon
10 ml/2 tsp wholegrain mustard
5 ml/1 tsp chopped fresh oregano
salt and freshly ground black pepper

oregano
penne
green pepper
red kidney beans
cannellini beans
natural yogurt
chick-peas
lemon
wholegrain mustard
tomatoes

1 Bring a large pan of salted water to the boil. Add the pasta and cook for 10–12 minutes until just tender. Drain, cool under cold water and drain again.

2 Make a cross with the tip of a sharp knife in each of the tomatoes. Plunge them into a bowl of boiling water for 30 seconds. Remove with a slotted spoon or spatula, run under cold water and peel away the skins. Cut the tomatoes into segments.

3 Drain the canned beans and chick-peas in a colander, rinse them under cold water and drain again. Tip into a bowl. Add the tomato segments, green pepper and pasta.

4 Whisk the yogurt until smooth. Gradually whisk in the oil, lemon rind and mustard. Stir in the oregano and salt and pepper to taste. Pour the dressing over the salad and toss well.

Polenta and Baked Tomatoes

A staple of northern Italy, polenta is a nourishing, filling food, served here with a delicious fresh tomato and olive topping.

Serves 4–6

INGREDIENTS
2 litres/3½ pints/9 cups water
500 g/1¼ lb quick-cook polenta
12 large ripe plum tomatoes, sliced
4 garlic cloves, thinly sliced
30 ml/2 tbsp chopped fresh oregano
   or marjoram
115 g/4 oz/½ cup black olives, pitted
salt and freshly ground black pepper
30 ml/2 tbsp olive oil

black olives

marjoram

plum tomatoes

garlic

oregano

polenta

1 Place the water in a large saucepan and bring to the boil. Whisk in the polenta and simmer for 5 minutes.

2 Remove the pan from the heat and pour the polenta into a 23 cm × 33 cm/ 9 in × 13 in Swiss roll tin. Smooth out the surface with a palette knife until level, and leave to cool.

3 Preheat the oven to 180°C/350°F/ Gas 4. With a 7.5 cm/3 in round pastry cutter, stamp out 12 rounds of polenta. Lay them so that they slightly overlap in a lightly oiled ovenproof dish.

4 Layer the tomatoes, garlic, oregano or marjoram and olives on top of the polenta, seasoning the layers as you go. Sprinkle with the olive oil, and bake uncovered for 30–35 minutes. Serve immediately.

Red Pepper Polenta with Sunflower Salsa

This recipe is inspired by Italian and Mexican cookery. Cornmeal polenta is a staple food in Italy, served with brightly coloured vegetables. Mexican *Pipian* is made from sunflower seeds, chilli and lime.

Serves 4

INGREDIENTS
3 young courgettes
oil, for greasing
1.2 litres/2 pints/5 cups light
   vegetable stock
250 g/9 oz/2 cups fine polenta or
   cornmeal
1 × 200 g/7 oz can red peppers,
   drained and sliced
115 g/4 oz green salad, to serve

FOR THE SUNFLOWER SALSA
75 g/3 oz sunflower seeds, toasted
50 g/2 oz/1 cup crustless
   white bread
200 ml/7 fl oz/scant 1 cup
   vegetable stock
1 garlic clove, crushed
½ red chilli, deseeded and chopped
30 ml/2 tbsp chopped fresh coriander
5 ml/1 tsp sugar
15 ml/1 tbsp lime juice
pinch of salt

1 Bring a saucepan of salted water to the boil. Add the courgettes and simmer over a low heat for 2–3 minutes. Refresh under cold running water and drain. When they are cool, cut into strips.

2 Lightly oil a 23 cm/9 in loaf tin and line with a single sheet of greaseproof paper.

polenta

sunflower seeds

courgettes

limes

red chillies

red peppers

coriander

white bread

3 Bring the vegetable stock to a simmer in a heavy saucepan. Add the polenta in a steady stream, stirring continuously for about 2–3 minutes until thickened.

4 Partly fill the lined tin with the polenta mixture. Layer the sliced courgettes and peppers over the polenta. Fill the tin with the remaining polenta and leave to set for about 10–15 minutes. Polenta should be served warm or at room temperature.

COOK'S TIP
Sunflower salsa will keep for up to 10 days in the refrigerator. It is delicious poured over a simple dish of pasta.

5 To make the salsa, reduce the sunflower seeds to a thick paste in a food processor. Add the remaining ingredients and combine thoroughly.

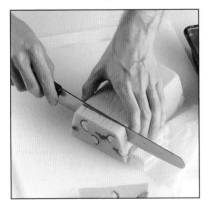

6 Turn the warm polenta out onto a board, remove the paper and cut into thick slices with a large wet knife. Serve with the salsa and a green salad.

Basic Pasta Dough

Serves 3–4

INGREDIENTS
200 g/7 oz/1¾ cups plain flour
pinch of salt
2 eggs
10 ml/2 tsp cold water

Making pasta on a work surface

1 Sift the flour and salt on to a clean work surface and make a well in the centre with your hand.

2 Put the eggs and water into the well. Using a fork, beat the eggs gently together, then gradually draw in the flour from the sides, to make a thick paste.

3 When the mixture becomes too stiff to use a fork, use your hands to mix to a firm dough. Knead the dough for about 5 minutes, until smooth. (This can be done in an electric food mixer fitted with a dough hook). Wrap in clear film to prevent it drying out and leave to rest for 20–30 minutes.

Making pasta in a bowl

1 Sift the flour and salt into a glass bowl and make a well in the centre. Add the eggs and water.

2 Using a fork, beat the eggs gently together, then gradually draw in the flour from the sides, to make a thick paste.

3 When the mixture becomes too stiff to use a fork, use your hands to mix to a firm dough. Knead the dough for 5 minutes until smooth. (This can be done in an electric food mixer fitted with a dough hook). Wrap in clear film to prevent it drying out and leave to rest for 20–30 minutes.

VARIATIONS

TOMATO: add 20 ml/4 tsp concentrated tomato purée to the eggs before mixing.
SPINACH: add 115 g/4 oz frozen spinach, thawed and squeezed of excess moisture. Liquidize with the eggs, before adding to the flour.
HERB: add 45 ml/3 tbsp finely chopped fresh herbs to the eggs before mixing the dough.
WHOLEMEAL: use 150 g/5 oz wholemeal flour and 50 g/2 oz plain flour. Add an extra 10 ml/2 tsp cold water (wholemeal flour will absorb more liquid than plain flour).
PAPRIKA: use 5 ml/1 tsp ground paprika sifted with the flour.

Rolling out pasta dough by hand

Rolling out dough using a pasta machine

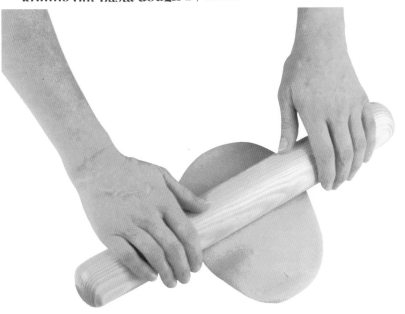

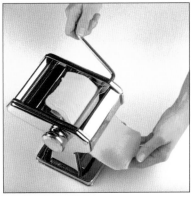

1 Cut the basic dough into quarters. Use one quarter at a time and re-wrap the rest in clear film, so it does not dry out. Flatten the dough and dust liberally with flour. Start with the machine set to roll at the thickest setting. Pass the dough through the rollers several times, dusting the dough from time to time with flour until it is smooth.

2 Fold the strip of dough into three press the joins well together and pass through the machine again. Repeat the folding and rolling several times on each setting.

1 Cut the basic dough in quarters. Use one quarter at a time and re-wrap the rest in clear film, so it does not dry out. Flatten the dough and dust liberally with flour. Start rolling out the dough, making sure you roll it evenly.

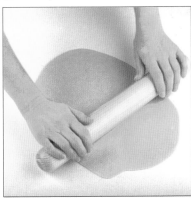

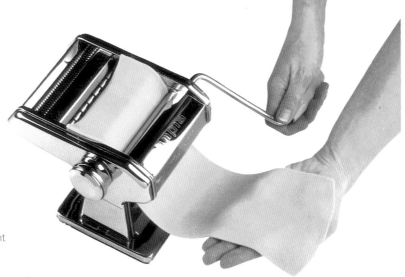

2 As the dough becomes thinner, keep on rotating it on the work surface by gently lifting the edges with your fingers and supporting it over the rolling pin. Make sure you don't tear the dough.

3 Carry on rolling out the dough unt it has reached the desired thickness, about 3 mm/⅛ in thick.

3 Guide the dough through the machine but do not pull or stretch it or the dough will tear. As the dough is worked through all the settings, it will become thinner and longer. Guide the dough over the back of your hand, as the dough is rolled out to a thin sheet. Pasta used for stuffing, such as ravioli or tortellini, should be used straight away. Otherwise lay the rolled sheets on a clean dish towel, lightly dusted with sifted flour, and leave to dry for 10 minutes before cutting. This makes it easier to cut and prevents the strands of pasta sticking together.

Cutting pasta shapes

Until you are confident at handling and shaping pasta dough, it is easier to work with small quantities. Always keep the dough well wrapped in clear film to prevent it drying out, until you are ready to work with it.

Cutting out spaghetti
To cut spaghetti, fit the appropriate attachment to the machine or move the handle to the appropriate slot. Cut the pasta sheets into 25 cm/10 in lengths and pass these through the machine. Guide the strands over the back of your hand as they appear out of the machine.

Cutting out tagliatelle
To cut tagliatelle, fit the appropriate attachment to the machine or move the handle to the appropriate slot. Cut the pasta sheets into 25 cm/10 in lengths and pass these through the machine as for spaghetti.

Cutting out lasagne
Take a sheet of pasta dough and cut out neat rectangles about 18 x 7.5 cm/7 x 3 in to make sheets of lasagne. Lay on a clean dish towel to dry.

Shaping ravioli

1 To make square ravioli, place spoonfuls of filling on a sheet of dough at intervals of 5–7.5 cm/2–3 in, leaving a 2.5 cm/1 in border. Brush the dough between the spoonfuls of filling with egg white.

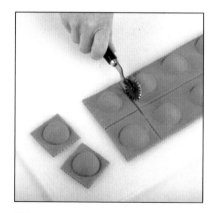

2 Lay a second sheet of pasta carefully over the top. Press around each mound of filling, excluding any air pockets.

3 Using a fluted pastry wheel or a sharp knife, cut between the stuffing.

Making pasta bows (farfalle)

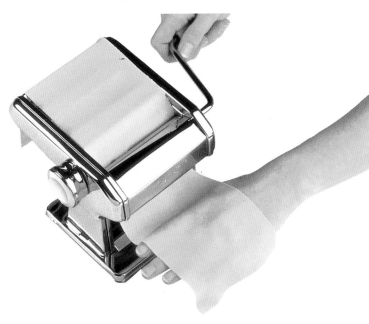

1 Roll the pasta dough through a pasta machine until the sheets are very thin. Then cut into long strips 4 cm/1½ in wide.

2 Cut the strips into small rectangles. Run a pastry wheel along the two shorter edges of the little rectangles – this will give the bows a decorative edge.

3 Moisten the centre of the strips and using a finger and thumb, gently pinch each rectangle together in the middle to make little pasta bows.

Making tagliatelle

1 Lightly flour some spinach-flavoured pasta dough and roll it up into a strip 30 x 10 cm/12 x 4 in.

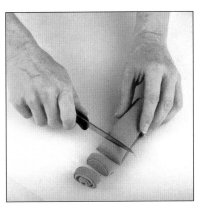

2 Using a sharp knife, cut straight across the roll.

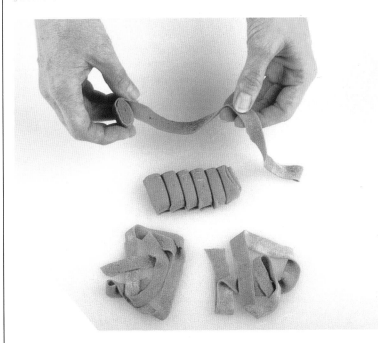

3 Carefully unravel each little roll as you cut it to make ribbons of fresh tagliatelle.

Penne with Aubergine and Mint Pesto

This splendid variation on the classic Italian pesto uses fresh mint rather than basil for a different flavour.

Serves 4

INGREDIENTS
2 large aubergines
salt
450 g/1 lb penne
50 g/2 oz walnut halves

FOR THE PESTO
25 g/1 oz fresh mint
15 g/½ oz flat-leaf parsley
40 g/1½ oz walnuts
40 g/1½ oz Parmesan cheese, finely
   grated
2 garlic cloves
90 ml/6 tbsp olive oil
salt and freshly ground black pepper

penne

garlic

walnuts

aubergine

olive oil

parsley

mint

Parmesan

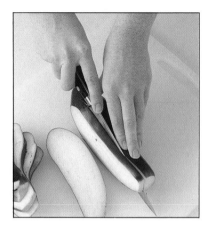

1 Cut the aubergines lengthwise into 1 cm/½ in slices.

2 Cut the slices again crossways to give short strips.

3 Layer the strips in a colander with salt and leave to stand for 30 minutes over a plate to catch any juices. Rinse well in cool water and drain.

4 Place all the pesto ingredients, except the oil in a blender or food processor, blend until smooth, then gradually add the oil in a thin stream until the mixture amalgamates. Season to taste.

5 Cook the penne following the instructions on the side of the packet for about 8 minutes or until nearly cooked. Add the aubergine and cook for a further 3 minutes.

6 Drain well and mix in the mint pesto and walnut halves. Serve immediately.

Campanelle with Yellow Pepper Sauce

Roasted yellow peppers make a deliciously sweet and creamy sauce to serve with pasta.

Serves 4

INGREDIENTS
2 yellow peppers
50 g/2 oz/¼ cup soft goat's cheese
115 g/4 oz/½ cup low-fat fromage blanc
salt and freshly ground black pepper
450 g/1 lb short pasta such as campanelle or fusilli
50 g/2 oz/¼ cup flaked almonds, toasted, to serve

pepper

fromage blanc

flaked almonds

goat's cheese

campanelle

1. Place the whole yellow peppers under a preheated grill until charred and blistered. Place in a plastic bag to cool. Peel and remove the seeds.

2 Place the pepper flesh in a blender with the goat's cheese and fromage blanc. Blend until smooth. Season with salt and lots of black pepper.

3 Cook the pasta following the instructions on the side of the packet until *al dente*. Drain well.

4 Toss with the sauce and serve sprinkled with the toasted flaked almonds.

Spaghetti with Black Olive and Mushroom Sauce

A rich pungent sauce topped with sweet cherry tomatoes.

Serves 4

INGREDIENTS
15 ml/1 tbsp olive oil
1 garlic clove, chopped
225 g/8 oz mushrooms, chopped
150 g/5 oz/generous ½ cup black
   olives, pitted
30 ml/2 tbsp chopped fresh parsley
1 fresh red chilli, seeded and chopped
450 g/1 lb spaghetti
225 g/8 oz cherry tomatoes
slivers of Parmesan cheese, to serve
   (optional)

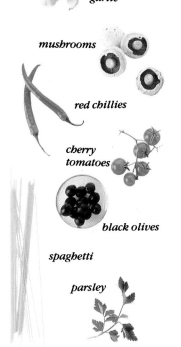

garlic

mushrooms

red chillies

cherry tomatoes

black olives

spaghetti

parsley

1 Heat the oil in a large pan. Add the garlic and cook for 1 minute. Add the mushrooms, cover, and cook over a medium heat for 5 minutes.

2 Place the mushrooms in a blender or food processor with the olives, parsley and red chilli. Blend until smooth.

3 Cook the pasta following the instructions on the side of the packet until *al dente*. Drain well and return to the pan. Add the olive mixture and toss together until the pasta is well coated. Cover and keep warm.

4 Heat an ungreased frying pan and shake the cherry tomatoes around until they start to split (about 2–3 minutes). Serve the pasta topped with the tomatoes and garnished with slivers of Parmesan, if liked.

Tagliatelle with Pea Sauce, Asparagus and Broad Beans

A creamy pea sauce makes a wonderful combination with the crunchy young vegetables.

Serves 4

INGREDIENTS
15 ml/1 tbsp olive oil
1 garlic clove, crushed
6 spring onions, sliced
225 g/8 oz/1 cup frozen peas,
   defrosted
350 g/12 oz fresh young asparagus
30 ml/2 tbsp chopped fresh sage, plus
extra leaves to garnish
finely grated rind of 2 lemons
450 ml/¾ pint/1¾ cups vegetable
   stock or water
225 g/8 oz frozen broad beans,
   defrosted
450 g/1 lb tagliatelle
60 ml/4 tbsp low-fat yogurt

lemon

garlic

asparagus

broad beans

peas

yogurt

tagliatelle

sage

spring onion

1 Heat the oil in a pan. Add the garlic and spring onions and cook gently for 2–3 minutes until softened.

2 Add the peas and ⅓ of the asparagus, together with the sage, lemon rind and stock or water. Bring to the boil, reduce the heat and simmer for 10 minutes until tender. Purée in a blender until smooth.

3 Meanwhile remove the outer skins from the broad beans and discard.

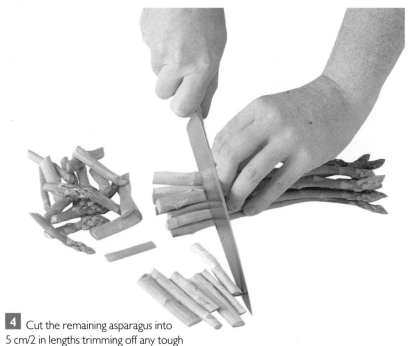

4 Cut the remaining asparagus into 5 cm/2 in lengths trimming off any tough fibrous stems, and blanch in boiling water for 2 minutes.

5 Cook the tagliatelle following the instructions on the side of the packet until *al dente*. Drain well.

COOK'S TIP

Frozen peas and beans have been used here to cut down the preparation time, but the dish tastes even better if you use fresh young vegetables when in season.

6 Add the cooked asparagus and shelled beans to the sauce and reheat. Stir in the yogurt and toss into the tagliatelle. Garnish with a few extra sage leaves and serve.

Capellini with Rocket, Mange-tout and Pine Nuts

A light but filling pasta dish with the added pepperiness of fresh rocket.

Serves 4

INGREDIENTS

250 g/9 oz capellini or angel-hair pasta
225 g/8 oz mange-tout
175 g/6 oz rocket
50 g/2 oz/¼ cup pine nuts, roasted
30 ml/2 tbsp Parmesan cheese, finely grated (optional)
30 ml/2 tbsp olive oil (optional)

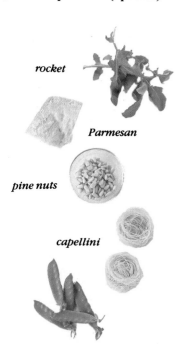

rocket

Parmesan

pine nuts

capellini

mange-tout

1 Cook the capellini or angel-hair pasta following the instructions on the side of the packet until *al dente*.

2 Meanwhile, carefully top and tail the mange-tout.

3 As soon as the pasta is cooked, drop in the rocket and mange-tout. Drain immediately.

4 Toss the pasta with the roasted pine nuts, and Parmesan and olive oil if using. Serve at once.

COOK'S TIP

Olive oil and Parmesan are optional as they obviously raise the fat content.

Pasta Bows with Fennel and Walnut Sauce

A scrumptious blend of walnuts and crisp steamed fennel.

Serves 4

INGREDIENTS
75 g/3 oz/½ cup walnuts, roughly
  chopped
1 garlic clove
25 g/1 oz fresh flat-leaf parsley, picked
  from the stalks
115 g/4 oz/½ cup ricotta cheese
450 g/1 lb pasta bows
450 g/1 lb fennel bulbs
chopped walnuts, to garnish

garlic

pasta bows

ricotta

fennel

parsley

walnut halves

chopped walnuts

1 Place the chopped walnuts, garlic and parsley in a food processor. Pulse until roughly chopped. Transfer to a bowl and stir in the ricotta.

2 Cook the pasta following the instructions on the side of the packet until *al dente*. Drain well.

3 Slice the fennel thinly and steam for 4–5 minutes until just tender but still crisp.

4 Return the pasta to the pan and add the walnut mixture and the fennel. Toss well and sprinkle with the chopped walnuts. Serve immediately.

Pasta with Spring Vegetables

This delicious vegetarian dish is perfect for a light lunch or supper.

Serves 4

INGREDIENTS
115 g/4 oz broccoli florets
115 g/4 oz baby leeks
225 g/8 oz asparagus
1 small fennel bulb
115 g/4 oz fresh or frozen peas
40 g/1½ oz/3 tbsp butter
1 shallot, chopped
45 ml/3 tbsp chopped fresh mixed
    herbs, such as parsley, thyme
    and sage
300 ml/½ pint/1¼ cups
    double cream
350 g/12 oz dried penne pasta
salt and ground black pepper
freshly grated Parmesan cheese,
    to serve

peas

broccoli

butter

penne

double
cream

Parmesan
cheese

mixed herbs

shallot

baby leeks

asparagus

fennel

1 Divide the broccoli florets into tiny sprigs. Cut the leeks and asparagus diagonally into 5 cm/2 in lengths. Trim the fennel bulb and remove any tough outer leaves. Cut into wedges, leaving the layers attached at the root ends so that the pieces stay intact.

2 Cook each prepared vegetable, including the peas, separately in boiling salted water until just tender – use the same water for each vegetable. Drain well and keep warm.

3 Melt the butter in a separate pan, add the chopped shallot and cook, stirring occasionally, until softened but not browned. Stir in the herbs and cream and cook for a few minutes until slightly thickened. Meanwhile, bring a large pan of salted water to the boil.

4 Add the pasta to the boiling water and cook according to the packet instructions until it is just *al dente*. Drain well and add to the sauce with the vegetables. Toss gently and season with plenty of pepper. Serve hot with a sprinkling of freshly grated Parmesan.

Tagliatelle with Mushrooms

The mushroom sauce is quick to make and the pasta cooks very quickly; both need to be cooked as near to serving as possible, so careful co-ordination is required.

Serves 4

INGREDIENTS
about 50 g/2 oz/4 tbsp butter
225–350 g/8–12 oz chanterelles
15 ml/1 tbsp plain flour
150 ml/¼ pint/⅔ cup milk
90 ml/6 tbsp crème fraîche
15 ml/1 tbsp chopped fresh parsley
275 g/10 oz fresh or dried tagliatelle
olive oil, for tossing
salt and ground black pepper

butter
flour
chanterelles
milk
crème fraîche
parsley
olive oil
tagliatelle

1 Melt 40 g/1½ oz/3 tbsp of the butter in a frying pan and fry the mushrooms for about 2–3 minutes over a gentle heat until the juices begin to run, then increase the heat and cook until the liquid has almost evaporated. Transfer the cooked mushrooms to a bowl using a slotted spoon.

COOK'S TIP
Chanterelles are a little tricky to wash, as they are so delicate. However, since these are woodland mushrooms, it's important to clean them thoroughly. Hold each one by the stalk and let cold water run under the gills to dislodge hidden dirt. Shake gently to dry.

2 Stir in the flour, adding a little more butter if necessary, and cook for about 1 minute, then gradually stir in the milk to make a smooth sauce.

3 Add the crème fraîche, mushrooms and parsley and seasoning and stir well. Cook very gently to heat through and then keep warm while cooking the pasta.

4 Bring a large pan of salted water to the boil. Add the pasta and cook according to the packet instructions until it is just *al dente*. Drain well, toss in a little olive oil and then turn on to a warmed serving plate. Pour the mushroom sauce over and serve immediately whilst it is hot.

VARIATION
If chanterelles are unavailable, use other wild mushrooms of your choice.

Double Tomato Tagliatelle

Sun-dried tomatoes add pungency to this dish, while the grilled fresh tomatoes add bite.

Serves 4

INGREDIENTS

45 ml/3 tbsp olive oil
1 garlic clove, crushed
1 small onion, chopped
50 ml/2 fl oz/¼ cup dry white wine
6 sun-dried tomatoes, chopped
30 ml/2 tbsp chopped fresh parsley
50 g/2 oz/½ cup stoned black
  olives, halved
450 g/1 lb fresh tagliatelle
4 tomatoes, halved
Parmesan cheese, to serve
salt and freshly ground black pepper

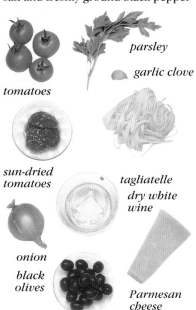

tomatoes

parsley

garlic clove

sun-dried tomatoes

tagliatelle

dry white wine

onion

black olives

Parmesan cheese

COOK'S TIP

It is essential to buy Parmesan in a piece for this dish. Find a good source – fresh Parmesan should not be unacceptably hard – and shave or grate it yourself. The flavour will be much more intense than that of the ready-grated product.

1 Heat 30 ml/2 tbsp of the oil in a pan. Add the garlic and onion and cook for 2–3 minutes, stirring occasionally. Add the wine, sun-dried tomatoes and the parsley. Cook for 2 minutes. Stir in the black olives.

2 Bring a large pan of salted water to the boil. Add the fresh tagliatelle and cook for 2–3 minutes until just tender. Preheat the grill.

3 Put the tomatoes on a tray and brush with the remaining oil. Grill for 3–4 minutes.

4 Drain the pasta, return it to the pan and toss with the sauce. Serve with the grilled tomatoes, freshly ground black pepper and shavings of Parmesan.

Pasta with Coriander and Grilled Aubergines

Pasta with a piquant sauce of coriander and lime – a variation on the classic pesto – is superb served with grilled aubergines.

Serves 2

INGREDIENTS

15 g/¹/₂ oz coriander leaves
30 ml/2 tbsp pine nuts
30 ml/2 tbsp freshly grated
  Parmesan cheese
3 garlic cloves
juice of ¹/₂ lime
105 ml/7 tbsp olive oil
225 g/8 oz dried cellentani or other
  pasta shapes
1 large aubergine
salt and freshly ground black pepper

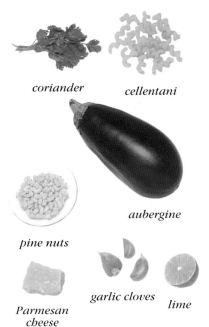

coriander   *cellentani*

aubergine

pine nuts

Parmesan cheese   *garlic cloves*   *lime*

1 Process the coriander leaves, pine nuts, Parmesan, garlic, lime juice and 60 ml/4 tbsp of the olive oil in a food processor or blender for 30 seconds until almost smooth. Bring a pan of salted water to the boil, add the pasta and cook for 10–12 minutes until cooked but firm to the bite.

2 Meanwhile, cut the aubergine in half lengthways, then cut each half into 5 mm/¹/₄ in slices. Spread out on a baking sheet, brush with the remaining oil and season well with salt and black pepper.

3 Grill the aubergine slices for about 4 minutes. Turn them over and brush with the remaining oil. Season as before. Grill for 4 minutes more.

4 Drain the pasta, tip it into a bowl and toss with the coriander sauce. Serve with the grilled aubergine slices.

Pasta Primavera

Serves 4

INGREDIENTS

225 g/8 oz thin asparagus spears,
cut in half
115 g/4 oz mange-tout, topped
and tailed
115 g/4 oz whole baby corn-on-
the-cob
225 g/8 oz whole baby
carrots, trimmed
1 small red pepper, seeded
and chopped
8 spring onions, sliced
225 g/8 oz torchietti
150 ml/¼ pint/⅔ cup low-fat
cottage cheese
150 ml/¼ pint/⅔ cup low-fat yogurt
15 ml/1 tbsp lemon juice
15 ml/1 tbsp chopped parsley
15 ml/1 tbsp snipped chives
skimmed milk (optional)
salt and ground black pepper
sun-dried tomato bread, to serve

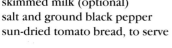

red
pepper

parsley

baby corn-
on-the-cob

spring
onions

baby
carrots

lemon

chives

torchietti

mange-tout

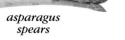

asparagus
spears

1 Cook the asparagus spears in a pan of boiling, salted water for 3–4 minutes. Add the mange-tout halfway through the cooking time. Drain and rinse both under cold water.

2 Cook the baby corn, carrots, red pepper and spring onions in the same way until tender. Drain and rinse.

low-fat
yogurt

low-fat
cottage cheese

3 Cook the pasta in a large pan of boiling, salted water until *al dente*. Drain thoroughly.

4 Put the cottage cheese, yogurt, lemon juice, parsley, chives and seasoning into a food processor or blender and process until smooth. Thin the sauce with skimmed milk, if necessary. Put into a large pan with the pasta and vegetables, heat gently and toss carefully. Transfer to a serving plate and serve with sun-dried tomato bread.

Tagliatelle with Sun-dried Tomatoes

Sun-dried tomatoes give this sauce a deliciously intense flavour – use drained sun-dried tomatoes in oil if you prefer.

Serves 4

INGREDIENTS

1 garlic clove, crushed
1 celery stick, finely sliced
115 g/4 oz/1 cup sun-dried tomatoes,
  finely chopped
90 ml/3½ fl oz/scant ½ cup red wine
8 plum tomatoes
350 g/12 oz dried tagliatelle
salt and freshly ground black pepper

celery

sun-dried tomatoes

tagliatelle

plum tomatoes

1 Put the garlic, celery, sun-dried tomatoes and wine into a large saucepan. Gently cook for 15 minutes.

2 Plunge the plum tomatoes into a saucepan of boiling water for 1 minute, then into a saucepan of cold water. Slip off their skins. Halve, remove the seeds and cores and roughly chop the flesh.

3 Add the plum tomatoes to the saucepan and simmer for a further 5 minutes. Season to taste.

4 Meanwhile, cook the tagliatelle in plenty of lightly salted rapidly boiling water for 8-10 minutes, or until *al dente*. Drain well. Toss with half the sauce and serve on warmed plates, topped with the remaining sauce.

Tagliatelle with Spinach Gnocchi

Serves 4–6

INGREDIENTS
450 g/1 lb mixed flavoured
    tagliatelle
flour, for dusting
shavings of Parmesan cheese,
    to garnish

SPINACH GNOCCHI
450 g/1 lb frozen chopped spinach
1 small onion, finely chopped
1 garlic clove, crushed
1.5 ml/¼ tsp ground nutmeg
400 g/14 oz low-fat cottage cheese
115 g/4 oz dried white breadcrumbs
75 g/3 oz semolina or plain flour
50 g/2 oz grated Parmesan cheese
3 egg whites
salt and pepper

TOMATO SAUCE
1 onion, finely chopped
1 stick celery, finely chopped
1 red pepper, seeded and diced
1 garlic clove, crushed
150 ml/¼ pint/⅔ cup
    vegetable stock
400 g/14 oz can tomatoes
15 ml/1 tbsp tomato purée
10 ml/2 tsp caster sugar
5 ml/1 tsp dried oregano

1 To make the tomato sauce, put the chopped onion, celery, pepper and garlic into a non-stick pan. Add the stock, bring to the boil and cook for 5 minutes or until tender.

2 Add the tomatoes, tomato purée, sugar and oregano. Season to taste, bring to the boil and simmer for 30 minutes until thick, stirring occasionally.

3 Meanwhile, put the frozen spinach, onion and garlic into a saucepan, cover and cook until the spinach is defrosted. Remove the lid and increase the heat to drive off any moisture. Season with salt, pepper and nutmeg. Cool the spinach in a bowl, add the remaining ingredients and mix thoroughly.

celery

garlic

egg

nutmeg

onion

low-fat cottage cheese

flavoured tagliatelle

red pepper

grated Parmesan cheese

spinach

dried white breadcrumbs

vegetable stock

tomato purée

tomatoes

semolina

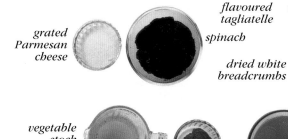

4 Shape the mixture into about 24 ovals with two dessertspoons and place them on a lightly floured tray. Place in the fridge for 30 minutes.

5 Have a large shallow pan of boiling, salted water ready. Cook the gnocchi in batches, for about 5 minutes (the water should simmer gently and not boil). As soon as the gnocchi rise to the surface, remove them with a slotted spoon and drain thoroughly.

6 Cook the tagliatelle in a large pan of boiling, salted water until *al dente*. Drain thoroughly. Transfer to warmed serving plates, top with gnocchi and spoon over the tomato sauce. Scatter with shavings of Parmesan cheese and serve at once.

Pasta Rapido with Parsley Pesto

Pasta suppers can often be dull. Here's a fresh, lively sauce that will stir the appetite.

Serves 4

INGREDIENTS
450 g/1 lb dried pasta
75 g/3 oz/¾ cup whole almonds
50 g/2 oz/½ cup flaked almonds, toasted
25 g/1 oz/¼ cup freshly grated Parmesan cheese
pinch of salt

FOR THE SAUCE
35 g/1½ oz fresh parsley
2 garlic cloves, crushed
45 ml/3 tbsp olive oil
45 ml/3 tbsp lemon juice
5 ml/1 tsp sugar
250 ml/8 fl oz/1 cup boiling water

pasta

lemon

parsley

garlic

Parmesan cheese

flaked almonds

almonds

1 Bring a large saucepan of salted water to the boil. Toss in the pasta and cook according to the instructions on the packet. Toast the whole and flaked almonds separately under a moderate grill until golden brown. Put the flaked almonds aside until required.

2 For the sauce, chop the parsley finely in a food processor. Add the whole almonds and reduce to a fine consistency. Add the garlic, olive oil, lemon juice, sugar and water. Combine to make a sauce.

3 Drain the pasta and combine with half of the sauce. (The remainder of the sauce will keep in a screw-topped jar in the refrigerator for up to ten days.) Top with Parmesan and flaked almonds.

COOK'S TIP
To prevent pasta from sticking together during cooking, use plenty of water and stir well before the water returns to the boil.

Penne with Fennel Concassé and Blue Cheese

The aniseed flavour of the fennel makes it the perfect partner for tomato, especially when topped with blue cheese.

Serves 2

INGREDIENTS

1 fennel bulb
225 g/8 oz penne or other dried
  pasta shapes
30 ml/2 tbsp extra virgin olive oil
1 shallot, finely chopped
300 ml/½ pint/1¼ cups passata
pinch of sugar
5 ml/1 tsp chopped fresh oregano
115 g/4 oz blue cheese
salt and freshly ground black pepper

oregano

shallot

fennel bulb

penne

passata

sugar

blue cheese

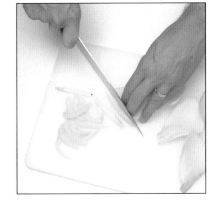

1 Cut the fennel bulb in half. Cut away the hard core and root. Slice the fennel thinly, then cut the slices into strips.

2 Bring a large pan of salted water to the boil. Add the pasta and cook for 10–12 minutes until just tender.

3 Meanwhile, heat the oil in a small saucepan. Add the fennel and shallot and cook for 2–3 minutes over a high heat, stirring occasionally.

4 Add the passata, sugar and oregano. Cover the pan and simmer gently for 10–12 minutes, until the fennel is tender. Add salt and pepper to taste. Drain the pasta and return it to the pan and toss with the sauce. Serve in bowls, with the blue cheese crumbled over the top.

Lemon and Parmesan Capellini with Herb Bread

Cream is thickened with Parmesan and flavoured with lemon to make a superb sauce for pasta.

Serves 2

INGREDIENTS
¹/₂ Granary baguette
50 g/2 oz/¹/₄ cup butter, softened
1 garlic clove, crushed
30 ml/2 tbsp chopped fresh herbs
225 g/8 oz dried or fresh capellini
250 ml/8 fl oz/1 cup single cream
75 g/3 oz Parmesan cheese, grated
finely grated rind of 1 lemon
salt and freshly ground black pepper

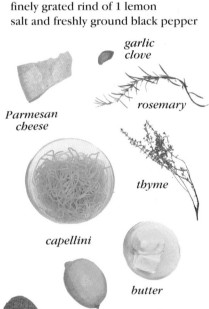

garlic clove

rosemary

Parmesan cheese

thyme

capellini

butter

lemon

single cream

Granary baguette   *parsley*   *oregano*

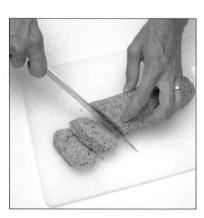

1 Preheat the oven to 200°C/400°F/ Gas 6. Cut the baguette into thick slices.

2 Put the butter in a bowl and beat with the garlic and herbs. Spread thickly over each slice of bread.

3 Reassemble the baguette. Wrap in foil, support on a baking sheet and bake for 10 minutes.

4 Meanwhile, bring a large pan of water to the boil and cook the pasta until just tender. Dried pasta will take 10–12 minutes; fresh pasta will be ready in 2–3 minutes.

5 Pour the cream into another pan and bring to the boil. Stir in the Parmesan and lemon rind. The sauce should thicken in about 30 seconds.

6 Drain the pasta, return it to the pan and toss with the sauce. Season to taste and sprinkle with a little chopped fresh parsley and grated lemon rind, if liked. Serve with the hot herb bread.

Macaroni Cheese with Mushrooms

Macaroni cheese is an all-time classic from the mid-week menu. Here it is served in a light creamy sauce with mushrooms and topped with pine nuts.

Serves 4

INGREDIENTS

450 g/1 lb quick-cooking elbow
   macaroni
45 ml/3 tbsp olive oil
225 g/8 oz button mushrooms, sliced
2 fresh thyme sprigs
60 ml/4 tbsp plain flour
1 vegetable stock cube
600 ml/1 pint/2½ cups milk
2.5 ml/½ tsp celery salt
5 ml/1 tsp Dijon mustard
175 g/6 oz/1½ cups grated
   Cheddar cheese
25 g/1 oz/¼ cup freshly grated
   Parmesan cheese
25 g/1 oz/2 tbsp pine nuts
salt and freshly ground black pepper

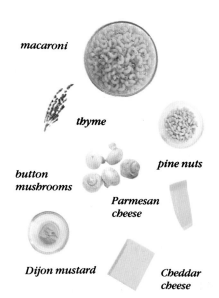

macaroni

thyme

pine nuts

button
mushrooms

Parmesan
cheese

Dijon mustard

Cheddar
cheese

1 Bring a pan of salted water to the boil. Add the macaroni and cook according to the packet instructions.

2 Heat the oil in a heavy saucepan. Add the mushrooms and thyme, cover and cook over a gentle heat for 2–3 minutes. Stir in the flour and draw from the heat, add the stock cube and stir continuously until evenly blended. Add the milk a little at a time, stirring after each addition. Add the celery salt, mustard and Cheddar cheese and season. Stir and simmer briefly for 1–2 minutes until thickened.

3 Preheat a moderate grill. Drain the macaroni well, toss into the sauce and turn out into four individual dishes or one large flameproof gratin dish. Scatter with grated Parmesan cheese and pine nuts, then grill until brown and bubbly.

COOK'S TIP

Closed button mushrooms are best for white cream sauces. Open varieties can darken a pale sauce to an unattractive sludgy grey.

Ratatouille Penne Bake

Serves 6

INGREDIENTS
1 small aubergine
2 courgettes, thickly sliced
200 g/7 oz firm tofu, cubed
45 ml/3 tbsp dark soy sauce
1 garlic clove, crushed
10 ml/2 tsp sesame seeds
1 small red pepper, seeded
    and sliced
1 onion, finely chopped
1–2 garlic cloves, crushed
150 ml/¼ pint/⅔ cup
    vegetable stock
3 firm ripe tomatoes, skinned,
    seeded and quartered
15 ml/1 tbsp chopped mixed herbs
225 g/8 oz penne
salt and ground black pepper
crusty bread, to serve

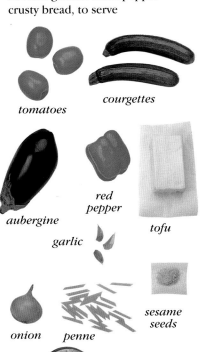

tomatoes

courgettes

aubergine

red pepper

tofu

garlic

onion

penne

sesame seeds

vegetable stock

soy sauce

1 Wash and cut the aubergine into 2.5 cm/1 in cubes. Put into a colander with the courgettes, sprinkle with salt and leave to drain for 30 minutes.

2 Mix the tofu with the soy sauce, garlic and sesame seeds. Cover and marinate for 30 minutes.

3 Put the pepper, onion and garlic into a saucepan, with the stock. Bring to the boil, cover and cook for 5 minutes until tender. Remove the lid and boil until all the stock has evaporated. Add the tomatoes and herbs and cook for a further 3 minutes. Season to taste.

4 Meanwhile cook the pasta in a large pan of boiling, salted water until *al dente*. Drain thoroughly. Toss the pasta with the vegetables and tofu. Transfer to a shallow 25 cm/10 in square ovenproof dish and grill until lightly toasted. Transfer to a serving dish and serve with fresh crusty bread.

Vegetarian Lasagne

Serves 6–8

INGREDIENTS
1 small aubergine
1 large onion, finely chopped
2 garlic cloves, crushed
150 ml/¹/₄ pint/²/₃ cup
    vegetable stock
225 g/8 oz mushrooms, sliced
400 g/14 oz can chopped tomatoes
30 ml/2 tbsp tomato purée
150 ml/¹/₄ pint/²/₃ cup red wine
1.5 ml/¹/₄ tsp ground ginger
5 ml/1 tsp mixed dried herbs
10–12 sheets lasagne
salt and pepper
25 g/1 oz low-fat margarine
25 g/1 oz plain flour
300 ml/¹/₂ pint/1¹/₄ cups
    skimmed milk
large pinch of grated nutmeg
200 g/7 oz low-fat cottage cheese
1 egg, beaten
15 g/¹/₂ oz grated Parmesan cheese
25 g/1 oz reduced-fat Cheddar
    cheese, grated
salt and ground black pepper

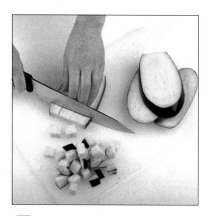

1 Wash the aubergine and cut it into 2.5 cm/1 in cubes. Put the onion and garlic into a saucepan with the stock, cover and cook for about 5 minutes or until tender.

2 Add the diced aubergine, sliced mushrooms, tomatoes, tomato purée, wine, ginger, seasoning and herbs. Bring to the boil, cover and cook for 15–20 minutes. Remove the lid and cook rapidly to evaporate the liquid by half.

3 To make the sauce, put the margarine, flour, skimmed milk and nutmeg into a pan. Whisk together over the heat until thickened and smooth. Season to taste.

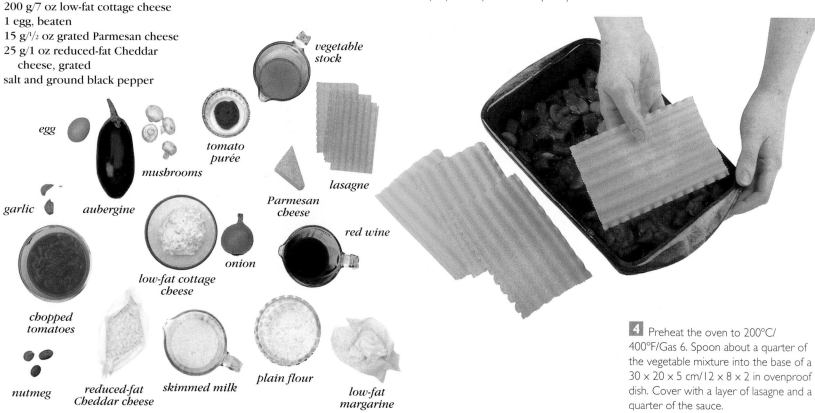

egg

mushrooms

tomato
purée

vegetable
stock

garlic   aubergine

Parmesan
cheese

lasagne

low-fat cottage
cheese

onion

red wine

chopped
tomatoes

nutmeg   reduced-fat
Cheddar cheese

skimmed milk

plain flour

low-fat
margarine

4 Preheat the oven to 200°C/ 400°F/Gas 6. Spoon about a quarter of the vegetable mixture into the base of a 30 x 20 x 5 cm/12 x 8 x 2 in ovenproof dish. Cover with a layer of lasagne and a quarter of the sauce.

5 Repeat with two more layers, then cover with the cottage.cheese. Beat the egg into the remaining sauce and pour over the top. Sprinkle with the two grated cheeses.

6 Bake for 25–30 minutes or until the top is golden brown.

Vegetarian Cannelloni

Serves 4–6

INGREDIENTS

1 onion, finely chopped
2 garlic cloves, crushed
2 carrots, coarsely grated
2 sticks celery, finely chopped
150 g/¹/₄ pint/²/₃ cup vegetable stock
115 g/4 oz red or green lentils
400 g/14 oz can chopped tomatoes
30 ml/2 tbsp tomato purée
2.5 ml/¹/₂ tsp ground ginger
5 ml/1 tsp fresh thyme
5 ml/1 tsp chopped fresh rosemary
40 g/1¹/₂ oz low-fat margarine
40 g/1¹/₂ oz plain flour
600 ml/1 pint/2¹/₂ cups
   skimmed milk
1 bay leaf
large pinch grated nutmeg
16–18 cannelloni
25 g/1 oz reduced-fat Cheddar
   cheese, grated
25 g/1 oz grated Parmesan cheese
25 g/1 oz fresh white breadcrumbs
salt and ground black pepper
flat leaf parsley, to garnish

1 To make the filling put the onion, garlic, carrots and celery into a large saucepan, add half the stock, cover and cook for 5 minutes or until tender.

2 Add the lentils, chopped tomatoes, tomato purée, ginger, thyme, rosemary and seasoning. Bring to the boil, cover and cook for 20 minutes. Remove the lid and cook for about 10 minutes until thick and soft. Leave to cool.

3 To make the sauce, put the margarine, flour; skimmed milk and bay leaf into a pan and whisk over the heat until thick and smooth. Season with salt, pepper and nutmeg. Discard the bay leaf.

plain flour

low-fat margarine

white breadcrumbs

reduced-fat Cheddar cheese

onion   *garlic*   *celery*
          rosemary

bay leaf   *thyme*

red lentils   *Parmesan cheese*   *skimmed milk*

carrots

nutmeg

chopped tomatoes   *vegetable stock*   *tomato purée*

cannelloni tubes

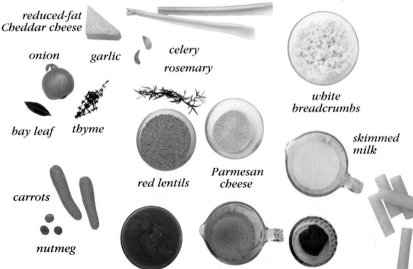

4 Fill the uncooked cannelloni by piping the filling into each tube. (It is easiest to hold them upright with one end flat on a board, while piping into the other end.)

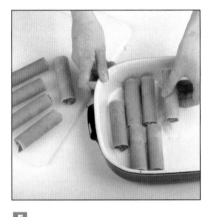

5 Preheat the oven to 180°C/350°F/ Gas 4. Spoon half the sauce into the bottom of a 20 cm/8 in square ovenproof dish. Lay two rows of filled cannelloni on top and spoon over the remaining sauce.

6 Scatter over the cheeses and breadcrumbs. Bake in the preheated oven for 30–40 minutes. Grill to brown the top, if necessary. Garnish with flat leaf parsley.

Spinach and Ricotta Conchiglie

Large pasta shells are designed to hold a variety of delicious stuffings. Few are more pleasing than this mixture of chopped spinach and ricotta cheese.

Serves 4

INGREDIENTS
350 g/12 oz large conchiglie
450 ml/¾ pint/scant 2 cups passata or tomato pulp
275 g/10 oz frozen chopped spinach, defrosted
50 g/2 oz crustless white bread, crumbled
120 ml/4 fl oz/½ cup milk
45 ml/3 tbsp olive oil
250 g/8 oz/2¼ cups Ricotta cheese
pinch of nutmeg
1 garlic clove, crushed
15 ml/1 tbsp olive oil
2.5 ml/½ tsp black olive paste (optional)
25 g/1 oz/¼ cup freshly grated Parmesan cheese
25 g/1 oz/2 tbsp pine nuts
salt and freshly ground black pepper

olive paste
Ricotta cheese
pine nuts
garlic
spinach
conchiglie

1 Bring a large saucepan of salted water to the boil. Toss in the pasta and cook according to the directions on the packet. Refresh under cold water, drain and reserve until needed.

2 Pour the passata or tomato pulp into a nylon sieve over a bowl and strain to thicken. Place the spinach in another sieve and press out any excess liquid with the back of a spoon.

3 Place the bread, milk and oil in a food processor and combine. Add the spinach and Ricotta and season with salt, pepper and nutmeg.

COOK'S TIP
Choose a large saucepan when cooking pasta and give it an occasional stir to prevent shapes from sticking together. If passata is not available, use a can of chopped tomatoes, sieved and puréed.

4 Combine the passata with the garlic, olive oil and olive paste if using. Spread the sauce evenly over the bottom of an ovenproof dish.

5 Spoon the spinach mixture into a piping bag fitted with a large plain nozzle and fill the pasta shapes (alternatively fill with a spoon). Arrange the pasta shapes over the sauce.

6 Preheat a moderate grill. Heat the pasta through in a microwave oven at high power (100%) for 4 minutes. Scatter with Parmesan cheese and pine nuts, and finish under the grill to brown the cheese.

Coriander Ravioli with Pumpkin filling

A stunning herb pasta with a superb creamy pumpkin and roast garlic filling.

Serves 4–6

INGREDIENTS
200 g/7 oz/scant 1 cup strong
   unbleached white flour
2 eggs
pinch of salt
45 ml/3 tbsp chopped fresh coriander
coriander sprigs, to garnish

FOR THE FILLING
4 garlic cloves in their skins
450 g/1 lb pumpkin, peeled and seeds
   removed
115 g/4 oz/½ cup ricotta
4 halves sun-dried tomatoes in olive
   oil, drained and finely chopped, but
   reserve 30 ml/2 tbsp of the oil
freshly ground black pepper

coriander

egg

pumpkin

garlic

flour

ricotta

sun-dried tomatoes

1 Place the flour, eggs, salt and coriander into a food processor. Pulse until combined.

2 Place the dough on a lightly floured board and knead well for 5 minutes, until smooth. Wrap in clear film and leave to rest in the fridge for 20 minutes.

3 Preheat the oven to 200°C/400°F/ Gas 6. Place the garlic cloves on a baking sheet and bake for 10 minutes until softened. Steam the pumpkin for 5–8 minutes until tender and drain well. Peel the garlic cloves and mash into the pumpkin together with the ricotta and drained sun-dried tomatoes. Season with black pepper.

4 Divide the pasta into 4 pieces and flatten slightly. Using a pasta machine, on its thinnest setting, roll out each piece. Leave the sheets of pasta on a clean tea-towel until slightly dried.

5 Using a 7.5 cm/3 in crinkle-edged round cutter, stamp out 36 rounds.

6 Top 18 of the rounds with a teaspoonful of mixture, brush the edges with water and place another round of pasta on top. Press firmly around the edges to seal. Bring a large pan of water to the boil, add the ravioli and cook for 3–4 minutes. Drain well and toss into the reserved tomato oil. Serve garnished with coriander sprigs.

Crescent Spinach Ravioli

Serves 4–6

INGREDIENTS
bunch of spring onions,
    finely chopped
1 carrot, coarsely grated
2 garlic cloves, crushed
200 g/7 oz low-fat cottage cheese
15 ml/1 tbsp chopped dill
4 halves sun-dried tomatoes,
    finely chopped
25 g/1 oz grated Parmesan cheese
1 quantity of basic pasta dough,
    with 115 g/4 oz frozen chopped
    spinach added
egg white, beaten, for brushing
flour, for dusting
salt and ground black pepper
2 halves sun-dried tomatoes, finely
    chopped, and fresh dill,
    to garnish

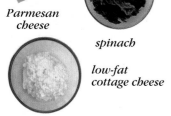

carrot

dill

sun-dried
tomatoes

garlic

spring onions

Parmesan
cheese

spinach

low-fat
cottage cheese

1 Put the spring onions, carrot, garlic and cottage cheese into a bowl. Add the chopped dill, tomatoes, seasoning and Parmesan cheese.

2 Roll the spinach pasta into thin sheets, cut into 7.5 cm/3 in rounds with a fluted pastry cutter.

3 Place a dessertspoon of filling in the centre of each circle. Brush the edges with egg white.

4 Fold each in half to make crescents. Press the edges together to seal. Transfer to a floured dish towel to rest for 1 hour before cooking. Makes about 80 crescents.

5 Cook the pasta in a large pan of boiling, salted water for 5 minutes (cook in batches to stop them sticking together). Drain well.

6 Put the crescents on to warmed serving plates and garnish with sun-dried tomatoes and dill.

Herb Pasta Crescents

Serves 4–6

INGREDIENTS

1 quantity of basic pasta dough,
    with 45 ml/3 tbsp chopped fresh
    herbs added
egg white, beaten, for brushing
flour, for dusting
basil leaves, to garnish

FILLING

225 g/8 oz frozen chopped spinach
1 small onion, finely chopped
pinch of ground nutmeg
115 g/4 oz low-fat cottage cheese
1 egg, beaten
25 g/1 oz Parmesan cheese
salt and ground black pepper

SAUCE

300 ml/½ pint/1¼ cups
    skimmed milk
25 g/1 oz sunflower margarine
45 ml/3 tbsp plain flour
1.5 ml/¼ tsp ground nutmeg
30 ml/2 tbsp chopped fresh herbs
    (chives, basil and parsley)

egg   low-fat   spinach
cottage cheese

chives

onion   Parmesan
cheese

nutmeg

parsley

basil   skimmed milk   basic pasta
dough   margarine

1 To make the filling, put the spinach and onion into a pan, cover and cook slowly to defrost. Remove the lid, increase the heat to drive off any water Season with salt, pepper and nutmeg. Turn the spinach into a bowl and cool slightly. Add the cottage cheese, beaten egg and Parmesan cheese.

2 Roll the herb pasta into thin sheets. Cut into 7.5 cm/3 in rounds with a fluted pastry cutter.

3 Place a dessertspoon of filling in the centre of each round. Brush the edges with egg white. Fold each in half (to make crescents). Press the edges together to seal. Transfer to a floured dish towel and rest for 1 hour before cooking the pasta.

4 Put all the sauce ingredients (except the herbs) into a pan. With a sauce whisk, thicken over a medium heat until smooth. Season with salt, pepper and nutmeg to taste. Stir in the herbs.

5 Cook the pasta in a large pan of boiling, salted water for 3 minutes (cook in batches to stop them sticking together). Drain thoroughly.

6 Put the crescents on to warmed serving plates and pour over the herb sauce. Garnish with basil leaves and serve at once.

Fried Noodles with Beansprouts and Asparagus

Soft fried noodles contrast beautifully with crisp beansprouts and asparagus.

Serves 2

INGREDIENTS
115 g/4 oz dried egg noodles
60 ml/4 tbsp vegetable oil
1 small onion, chopped
2.5 cm/1 in piece of fresh root
  ginger, peeled and grated
2 garlic cloves, crushed
175 g/6 oz young asparagus
  spears, trimmed
115 g/4 oz beansprouts
4 spring onions, sliced
45 ml/3 tbsp soy sauce
salt and freshly ground black pepper

onion

spring onions

garlic cloves

root ginger

soy sauce

egg noodles

beansprouts

asparagus spears

1 Bring a pan of salted water to the boil. Add the noodles and cook for 2–3 minutes, until just tender. Drain and toss in 30 ml/2 tbsp of the oil.

2 Heat the remaining oil in a wok or frying pan until very hot. Add the onion, ginger and garlic and stir-fry for 2–3 minutes. Add the asparagus and stir-fry for a further 2–3 minutes.

3 Add the noodles and beansprouts and stir-fry for 2 minutes.

4 Stir in the spring onions and soy sauce. Season to taste, adding salt sparingly as the soy sauce will add quite a salty flavour. Stir-fry for 1 minute, then serve at once.

Five-spice Vegetable Noodles

Vary this vegetable stir-fry by substituting mushrooms, bamboo shoots, beansprouts, mange-touts or water chestnuts for some or all of the vegetables suggested below.

Serves 2–3

INGREDIENTS

225 g/8 oz dried egg noodles
30 ml/2 tbsp sesame oil
2 carrots
1 celery stick
1 small fennel bulb
2 courgettes, halved and sliced
1 red chilli, seeded and chopped
2.5 cm/1 in piece of fresh root
  ginger, peeled and grated
1 garlic clove, crushed
7.5 ml/1½ tsp Chinese five-spice
  powder
2.5 ml/½ tsp ground cinnamon
4 spring onions, sliced
50 ml/2 fl oz/¼ cup warm water

celery stick
carrots
garlic clove
fennel bulb
egg noodles
courgettes
five-spice powder
spring onions
cinnamon
root ginger

1 Bring a large pan of salted water to the boil. Add the noodles and cook for 2–3 minutes until just tender. Drain the noodles, return them to the pan and toss in a little of the oil. Set aside.

2 Cut the carrot and celery into julienne. Cut the fennel bulb in half and cut out the hard core. Cut into slices, then cut the slices into julienne.

3 Heat the remaining oil in a wok or frying pan until very hot. Add all the vegetables, including the chilli, and stir-fry for 7–8 minutes.

4 Add the ginger and garlic and stir-fry for 2 minutes, then add the spices. Cook for 1 minute. Add the spring onions and stir-fry for 1 minute. Pour in the warm water and cook for 1 minute. Stir in the noodles and toss well together. Serve sprinkled with sliced red chilli, if liked.

Noodles with Asparagus and Saffron Sauce

The asparagus, wine and cream give a distinctly French flavour to this elegant and delicious noodle dish.

Serves 4

INGREDIENTS

450 g/1 lb young asparagus
25 g/1 oz/2 tbsp butter
2 shallots, finely chopped
30 ml/2 tbsp white wine
250 ml/8 fl oz/1 cup double cream
pinch of saffron threads
grated rind and juice of ½ lemon
115 g/4 oz/1 cup garden peas
350 g/12 oz somen noodles
½ bunch chervil, roughly chopped
salt and freshly ground black pepper
grated Parmesan cheese (optional)

asparagus

saffron

shallots

butter

double cream

white wine

lemon

peas

somen noodles

1 Cut off the asparagus tips (about 5 cm/2 in length), then slice the remaining spears into short rounds. Soak the saffron in 30 ml/2 tbsp boiling water for a few minutes until softened.

Melt the butter in a saucepan, add the shallots and cook over a low heat for 3 minutes, until soft. Add the white wine, cream and saffron infusion. Bring to the boil, reduce the heat and simmer gently for 5 minutes or until the sauce thickens to a coating consistency. Add the lemon rind and juice, with salt and pepper to taste.

2 Bring a large saucepan of lightly salted water to the boil. Blanch the asparagus tips, scoop them out and add them to the sauce, then cook the peas and short asparagus rounds in the boiling water until just tender. Scoop them out and add to the sauce.

3 Cook the somen noodles in the same water until just tender, following the directions on the packet. Drain, place in a wide pan and pour the sauce over the top.

4 Toss the noodles with the sauce and vegetables, adding the chervil and more salt and pepper if needed. Finally, sprinkle with the grated Parmesan, if using, and serve hot.

COOK'S TIP

Frozen peas can easily be used instead of fresh peas. Add to the asparagus after 3–4 minutes and cook until tender.

Egg Noodle Stir-fry

The thick egg noodles and potatoes, along with the vegetables, make this a satisfying and healthy main dish. If possible, use fresh egg noodles, which are available from most large supermarkets.

Serves 4

INGREDIENTS

2 eggs
5 ml/1 tsp chilli powder
5 ml/1 tsp ground turmeric
60 ml/4 tbsp oil
1 large onion, finely sliced
2 red chillies, seeded and finely sliced
15 ml/1 tbsp light soy sauce
2 large cooked potatoes, cut into small cubes
6 pieces fried beancurd, sliced
225 g/8 oz/1 cup beansprouts
115 g/4 oz green beans, blanched
350 g/12 oz fresh thick egg noodles
salt and freshly ground black pepper
sliced spring onions, to garnish

 eggs   chilli powder   ground turmeric

 onion   red chillies   light soy sauce

 potatoes   fried beancurd   bean sprouts

green beans   fresh thick egg noodles    spring onions

COOK'S TIP
Ideally wear gloves when preparing chillies; if you don't, certainly wash your hands thoroughly afterwards. Keep your hands away from your eyes as chillies will sting them.

1 Beat the eggs lightly, then strain them into a bowl. Heat a lightly greased omelette pan. Pour in half of the beaten egg to just thinly cover the bottom of the pan. When the egg is set, carefully turn the omelette over and fry the other side briefly.

2 Slide the omelette on to a plate, blot with kitchen paper, roll up and cut into narrow strips. Make a second omelette in the same way and slice. Set the omelette strips aside for the garnish.

3 In a cup, mix together the chilli powder and turmeric. Form a paste by stirring in a little water. Heat the oil in a wok or large frying pan. Fry the onion until soft. Reduce the heat and add the chilli paste, sliced chillies and soy sauce. Fry for 2–3 minutes.

4 Add the potatoes and fry for about 2 minutes, mixing well with the chillies. Add the beancurd, then the beansprouts, green beans and noodles.

5 Gently stir-fry until the noodles are evenly coated and heated through. Take care not to break up the potatoes or the beancurd. Season with salt and pepper. Serve hot, garnished with the reserved omelette strips and spring onion slices.

Stir-fried Beancurd with Noodles

This is a satisfying dish, which is both tasty and easy to make.

Serves 4

INGREDIENTS

225 g/8 oz firm beancurd
groundnut oil, for deep-frying
175 g/6 oz medium egg noodles
15 ml/1 tbsp sesame oil
5 ml/1 tsp cornflour
10 ml/2 tsp dark soy sauce
30 ml/2 tbsp Chinese rice wine
5 ml/1 tsp sugar
6–8 spring onions, cut diagonally
    into 2.5-cm/1-in lengths
3 garlic cloves, sliced
1 green chilli, seeded and sliced
115 g/4 oz Chinese cabbage leaves,
    coarsely shredded
50 g/2 oz/¼ cup beansprouts
50 g/2 oz/½ cup cashew nuts,
    toasted

beancurd

egg noodles

sesame oil

dark soy sauce

garlic

Chinese cabbage

spring onions

green chilli

beansprouts

cashew nuts

1 If in water, drain the beancurd and pat dry with kitchen paper. Cut it into 2.5-cm/1-in cubes. Half-fill a wok with groundnut oil and heat to 180°C/350°F. Deep-fry the beancurd in batches for 1–2 minutes, until golden and crisp. Drain on kitchen paper. Carefully pour all but 30 ml/2 tbsp of the oil from the wok.

2 Cook the noodles. Rinse them thoroughly under cold running water and drain well. Toss in 10ml/2 tsp of the sesame oil and set aside. In a bowl, blend together the cornflour, soy sauce, rice wine, sugar and remaining sesame oil.

3 Reheat the 30 ml/2 tbsp of groundnut oil and, when hot, add the spring onions, garlic, chilli, Chinese cabbage and beansprouts. Stir-fry for 1–2 minutes.

4 Add the beancurd, noodles and cornflour sauce. Cook, stirring, for about 1 minute, until well mixed. Sprinkle over the cashew nuts. Serve at once.

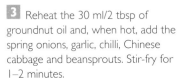

Noodles with Ginger and Coriander

Here is a simple noodle dish that goes well with most oriental dishes. It can also be served as a snack for 2–3 people.

Serves 4

INGREDIENTS
handful of fresh coriander
225 g/8 oz dried egg noodles
45 ml/3 tbsp oil
5 cm/2 in fresh root ginger, cut into fine shreds
6–8 spring onions, cut into shreds
30 ml/2 tbsp light soy sauce
salt and freshly ground black pepper

fresh coriander

dried egg noodles

fresh root ginger

spring onions

light soy sauce

1 Strip the leaves from the coriander stalks. Pile them on to a chopping board and coarsely chop them using a cleaver or large, sharp knife.

2 Cook the noodles according to the packet instructions. Rinse under cold water, drain well and then toss in 15 ml/1 tbsp of the oil.

3 Heat a wok until hot, add the remaining oil and swirl it around. Add the ginger and stir-fry for a few seconds, then add the noodles and spring onions. Stir-fry for 3–4 minutes, until hot.

4 Sprinkle over the soy sauce, coriander and seasoning. Toss well and serve at once.

COOK'S TIP

As with many Thai, Singapore or Malaysian dishes, for best results use groundnut oil. Alternatively fry vegetables in sunflower oil, but toss noodles in sesame oil.

Deep-fried Courgettes with Chilli Sauce

Crunchy coated courgettes are great served with a fiery tomato sauce.

Serves 2

INGREDIENTS
15 ml/1 tbsp olive oil
1 onion, finely chopped
1 red chilli, seeded and finely diced
10 ml/2 tsp hot chilli powder
400 g/14 oz can chopped tomatoes
1 vegetable stock cube
50 ml/2 fl oz/¼ cup hot water
450 g/1 lb courgettes
150 ml/¼ pint/⅔ cup milk
50 g/2 oz/½ cup plain flour
oil for deep-frying
salt and freshly ground black pepper
thyme sprigs, to garnish

TO SERVE
lettuce leaves
watercress sprigs
slices of seeded bread

courgettes

chopped tomatoes

onion

red chilli

plain flour

stock cube

milk

chilli powder

1 Heat the oil in a pan. Add the onion and cook for 2–3 minutes. Add the chilli. Stir in the chilli powder and cook for 30 seconds.

2 Add the tomatoes. Crumble in the stock cube and stir in the water. Cover and cook for 10 minutes.

3 Meanwhile, top and tail the courgettes. Cut into 5 mm/¼ in slices.

4 Pour the milk into one shallow dish and spread out the flour in another. Dip the courgettes first in the milk, then into the flour, until well-coated.

5 Heat the oil for deep-frying to 180°C/350°F or until a cube of bread, when added to the oil, browns in 30–45 seconds. Add the courgettes in batches and deep-fry for 3–4 minutes until crisp. Drain on kitchen paper.

6 Place two or three lettuce leaves on each serving plate. Add a few sprigs of watercress and fan out the bread slices to one side. Season the sauce, spoon some on to each plate, top with the crisp courgettes and garnish with the thyme sprigs. Serve at once with salad and bread.

Cumin-spiced Marrow and Spinach

Tender chunks of marrow with spinach in a creamy, cumin-flavoured sauce.

Serves 2

INGREDIENTS
½ marrow, about 450 g/1 lb
30 ml/2 tbsp vegetable oil
10 ml/2 tsp cumin seeds
1 small red chilli, seeded and
  finely chopped
30 ml/2 tbsp water
50 g/2 oz tender young
  spinach leaves
90 ml/6 tbsp single cream
salt and freshly ground black pepper

spinach leaves

cumin seeds

marrow

single cream

red chilli

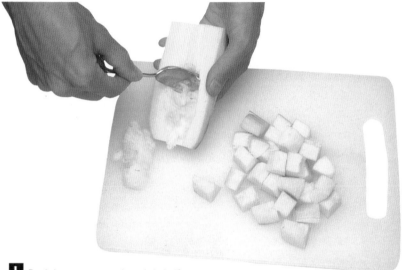

1 Peel the marrow and cut it in half. Scoop out the seeds. Cut the flesh into cubes.

2 Heat the oil in a large frying pan. Add the cumin seeds and the chopped chilli. Cook for 1 minute.

3 Add the marrow and water to the pan. Cover with foil or a lid and simmer for 8 minutes, stirring occasionally, until the marrow is just tender. Remove the cover and cook for 2 minutes more or until most of the water has evaporated.

4 Put the spinach leaves in a colander. Rinse well under cold water, drain and pat dry with kitchen paper. Tear into rough pieces.

5 Add the spinach to the marrow, replace the cover and cook gently for 1 minute. Serve hot.

COOK'S TIP

Be careful when handling chillies as the juice can burn sensitive skin. Wear rubber gloves or wash hands thoroughly after preparation.

6 Stir in the cream and cook over a high heat for 2 minutes. Add salt and pepper to taste, and serve. An Indian rice dish would be a good accompaniment. Alternatively, serve with naan bread.

Chilli Beans with Basmati Rice

Red kidney beans, tomatoes and chilli make a great combination. Serve with pasta or pitta bread instead of rice, if you prefer.

Serves 4

INGREDIENTS
350 g/12 oz/2 cups basmati rice
30 ml/2 tbsp olive oil
1 large onion, chopped
1 garlic clove, crushed
15 ml/1 tbsp hot chilli powder
15 ml/1 tbsp plain flour
15 ml/1 tbsp tomato purée
400 g/14 oz can chopped tomatoes
400 g/14 oz can red kidney
  beans, drained
150 ml/¼ pint/⅔ cup hot
  vegetable stock
chopped fresh parsley, to garnish
salt and freshly ground black pepper

basmati rice

chopped tomatoes

chilli powder

onion

tomato purée

garlic clove

stock cube

red kidney beans

plain flour

1 Wash the rice several times under cold running water. Drain well. Bring a large pan of water to the boil. Add the rice and cook for 10–12 minutes, until tender. Meanwhile, heat the oil in a frying pan. Add the onion and garlic and cook for 2 minutes.

2 Stir the chilli powder and flour into the onion and garlic mixture. Cook for 2 minutes, stirring frequently.

3 Stir in the tomato purée and chopped tomatoes. Rinse the kidney beans under cold water, drain well and add to the pan with the hot vegetable stock. Cover and cook for 12 minutes, stirring occasionally.

4 Season the chilli sauce with salt and pepper. Drain the rice and serve at once, with the chilli beans, sprinkled with a little chopped fresh parsley.

Spicy Cauliflower and Potato Salad

A delicious cold vegetable salad with a hot spicy dressing.

Serves 2–3

INGREDIENTS

1 medium cauliflower
2 medium potatoes
7.5 ml/1½ tsp caraway seeds
5 ml/1 tsp ground coriander
2.5 ml/½ tsp hot chilli powder
juice of 1 lemon
60 ml/4 tbsp olive oil
salt and freshly ground black pepper

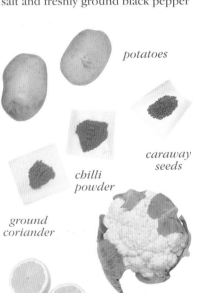

potatoes

caraway seeds

chilli powder

ground coriander

lemon

cauliflower

1 Break the cauliflower into small florets. Peel the potatoes and cut them into chunks.

2 Bring a large pan of water to the boil. Add the cauliflower florets and potato chunks and cook for 8 minutes until just tender.

3 Meanwhile, heat a non-stick frying pan. Add the caraway seeds and fry, shaking the pan constantly, for 1 minute. Tip the roasted seeds into a bowl and add the ground coriander and chilli powder, with salt and pepper to taste. Stir in the lemon juice and olive oil and mix to a paste.

4 Drain the vegetables well. Add them to the bowl and toss to coat in the chilli dressing. Serve at once, with hot pitta bread or brown rice.

Bengali-style Vegetables

A hot dry curry using spices that do not require long slow cooking.

Serves 4

INGREDIENTS

½ medium cauliflower, broken into
   small florets
1 large potato, peeled and cut into
   2.5 cm/1 in dice
115 g/4 oz French beans, trimmed
2 courgettes, halved lengthways
   and sliced
2 green chillies
2.5 cm/1 in piece of fresh root
   ginger, peeled
120 ml/4 fl oz/½ cup natural yogurt
10 ml/2 tsp ground coriander
2.5 ml/½ tsp ground turmeric
25 g/1 oz/2 tbsp ghee
2.5 ml/½ tsp garam masala
5 ml/1 tsp cumin seeds
10 ml/2 tsp sugar
pinch each of ground cloves,
   ground cinnamon and
      ground cardamom
salt and freshly ground black pepper

1 Bring a large pan of water to the boil. Add the cauliflower and potato and cook for 5 minutes. Add the beans and courgettes and cook for 2–3 minutes.

2 Meanwhile, cut the chillies in half, remove the seeds and roughly chop the flesh. Finely chop the ginger. Mix the chillies and ginger in a small bowl.

green chilli

cumin seeds

French beans

root ginger

cauliflower florets

potato

natural yogurt

ground turmeric

sugar

ghee

ground coriander

courgettes

ground cinnamon

ground cloves

garam masala

3 Drain the vegetables and tip them into a bowl. Add the chilli and ginger mixture, with the yogurt, ground coriander and turmeric. Season with plenty of salt and pepper and mix well.

4 Heat the ghee in a large frying pan. Add the vegetable mixture and cook over a high heat for 2 minutes, stirring from time to time.

5 Stir in the garam masala and cumin seeds and cook for 2 minutes.

6 Stir in the sugar and remaining spices and cook for 1 minute or until all the liquid has evaporated.

COOK'S TIP
If ghee is not available you can clarify your own butter. Melt 50 g/2 oz/¼ cup butter slowly in a small pan. Remove from the heat and leave for about 5 minutes. Pour off the clear yellow clarified butter, leaving the sediment in the pan.

Mushroom and Okra Curry with Fresh Mango Relish

This simple but delicious curry with its fresh gingery mango relish is best served with plain basmati rice.

Serves 4

INGREDIENTS
4 garlic cloves, roughly chopped
2.5 cm/1 in piece of fresh ginger root, peeled and roughly chopped
1–2 red chillies, seeded and chopped
175 ml/6 fl oz/¾ cup cold water
15 ml/1 tbsp sunflower oil
5 ml/1 tsp coriander seeds
5 ml/1 tsp cumin seeds
5 ml/1 tsp ground cumin
2 green cardamom pods, seeds removed and ground
pinch of ground turmeric
1 × 400 g/14 oz can chopped tomatoes
450 g/1 lb mushrooms, quartered if large
225 g/8 oz okra, trimmed and cut into 1 cm/½ in slices
30 ml/2 tbsp chopped fresh coriander
basmati rice, to serve

FOR THE MANGO RELISH
1 large ripe mango, about 500 g/1¼ lb in weight
1 small garlic clove, crushed
1 onion, finely chopped
10 ml/2 tsp grated fresh ginger root
1 fresh red chilli, seeded and finely chopped
pinch of salt and sugar

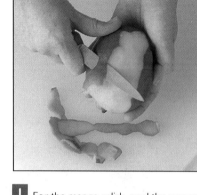

1 For the mango relish, peel the mango and cut off the flesh from the stone.

2 In a bowl mash the mango flesh with a fork or pulse in a food processor, and mix in the rest of the relish ingredients. Set to one side.

3 Place the garlic, ginger, chilli and 45 ml/3 tbsp of the water into a blender and blend until smooth.

4 Heat the sunflower oil in a large pan. Add the whole coriander and cumin seeds and allow them to sizzle for a few seconds. Add the ground cumin, ground cardamom and turmeric and cook for 1 minute more.

mango

okra

cardamom pods

chopped tomatoes

onion

garlic

ginger

cumin seeds

mushrooms

red chillies

coriander seeds

turmeric

5 Add the paste from the blender, the tomatoes, remaining water, mushrooms and okra. Stir to mix well and bring to the boil. Reduce the heat, cover, and simmer for 5 minutes.

6 Remove the cover, turn up the heat slightly and cook for another 5–10 minutes until the okra is tender. Stir in the fresh coriander and serve with rice and the mango relish.

Aloo Gobi

Cauliflower and potatoes are encrusted with Indian spices in this delicious recipe.

Serves 4

INGREDIENTS
450 g/1 lb potatoes, cut into
  2.5 cm/1 in chunks
30 ml/2 tbsp oil
5 ml/1 tsp cumin seeds
1 green chilli, finely chopped
450 g/1 lb cauliflower, broken
  into florets
5 ml/1 tsp ground coriander
5 ml/1 tsp ground cumin
1.5 ml/¼ tsp chilli powder
2.5 ml/½ tsp ground turmeric
2.5 ml/½ tsp salt
chopped fresh coriander, to garnish
tomato and onion salad and pickle,
  to serve

oil

ground coriander

chilli powder

ground cumin

cumin seeds

ground turmeric

cauliflower

salt

green chilli

potatoes

VARIATION
Try using sweet potatoes instead of ordinary potatoes for an alternative curry with a sweeter flavour.

1 Par-boil the potatoes in a large saucepan of boiling water for 10 minutes. Drain well and set aside.

2 Heat the oil in a large frying pan and fry the cumin seeds for 2 minutes until they begin to splutter. Add the chilli and fry for a further 1 minute.

3 Add the cauliflower florets and fry, stirring, for 5 minutes.

4 Add the potatoes and the ground spices and salt and cook for a further 7–10 minutes, or until both the vegetables are tender. Garnish with fresh coriander and serve with tomato and onion salad and pickle.

Masala Okra

Okra, or "ladies' fingers" are a popular Indian vegetable. In this recipe they are stir-fried with a dry, spicy masala to make a delicious side dish.

Serves 4

INGREDIENTS
450 g/1 lb okra
2.5 ml/½ tsp ground turmeric
5 ml/1 tsp chilli powder
15 ml/1 tbsp ground cumin
15 ml/1 tbsp ground coriander
1.5 ml/¼ tsp salt
1.5 ml/¼ tsp sugar
15 ml/1 tbsp lemon juice
15 ml/1 tbsp desiccated coconut
30 ml/2 tbsp chopped
   fresh coriander
45 ml/3 tbsp oil
2.5 ml/½ tsp cumin seeds
2.5 ml/½ tsp black mustard seeds
chopped fresh tomatoes, to garnish
poppadums, to serve

black mustard seeds · lemon juice · ground coriander · cumin seeds

ground cumin

sugar · chilli powder · okra

desiccated coconut · ground turmeric

salt · fresh coriander

1 Wash, dry and trim the okra. In a bowl, mix together the turmeric, chilli powder, cumin, ground coriander, salt, sugar, lemon juice, desiccated coconut and the fresh coriander.

2 Heat the oil in a large frying pan. Add the cumin seeds and mustard seeds and fry for about 2 minutes, or until they begin to splutter.

COOK'S TIP

When buying okra, choose firm, brightly coloured pods that are less than 10 cm/4 in long.

3 Add the spice mixture and continue to fry for 2 minutes.

4 Add the okra, cover, and cook over a low heat for 10 minutes, or until tender. Garnish with chopped fresh tomatoes and serve with poppadums.

Mixed Vegetable Curry

A good all-round vegetable curry that goes well with most Indian dishes. You can use any combination of vegetables that are in season for this basic recipe.

Serves 4

INGREDIENTS

30 ml/2 tbsp oil
2.5 ml/½ tsp black mustard seeds
2.5 ml/½ tsp cumin seeds
1 onion, thinly sliced
2 curry leaves
1 green chilli, finely chopped
2.5 cm/1 in piece root ginger, finely chopped
30 ml/2 tbsp curry paste
1 small cauliflower, broken into florets
1 large carrot, thickly sliced
115 g/4 oz French beans, cut into 2.5 cm/1 in lengths
1.5 ml/¼ tsp ground turmeric
1.5 ml/¼ tsp chilli powder
2.5 ml/½ tsp salt
2 tomatoes, finely chopped
50 g/2 oz frozen peas, thawed
150 ml/¼ pint/⅔ cup vegetable stock
fresh curry leaves, to garnish

vegetable stock   curry paste   peas   black mustard seeds   chilli powder   cauliflower   ground turmeric   cumin seeds   tomatoes   root ginger   French beans   carrot   curry leaves   onion   green chilli

1 Heat the oil in a large saucepan and fry the mustard seeds and cumin seeds for 2 minutes until they begin to splutter.

2 Add the onion and the curry leaves and fry for 5 minutes.

3 Add the chilli and ginger and fry for 2 minutes. Stir in the curry paste and fry for 3–4 minutes.

4 Add the cauliflower, carrot and French beans and cook for 4–5 minutes. Add the turmeric, chilli powder, salt and tomatoes and cook for 2–3 minutes.

5 Add the thawed peas and cook for a further 2–3 minutes.

6 Add the stock. Cover and simmer over a low heat for 10–13 minutes until all the vegetables are tender. Serve, garnished with curry leaves.

Spicy Potato Chips with Sesame Seeds

This recipe is a variation of the well-known dish Bombay Potatoes, in which the potatoes are fried to give them a crispy texture, and then tossed in spices and sesame seeds.

Serves 4

INGREDIENTS
900 g/2 lb potatoes
oil, for deep-frying
1.5 ml/¼ tsp ground turmeric
1.5 ml/¼ tsp chilli powder
1.5 ml/¼ tsp salt
30 ml/2 tbsp oil
1.5 ml/¼ tsp black mustard seeds
1 green chilli, finely chopped
1 garlic clove, crushed
30 ml/2 tbsp sesame seeds

oil
black mustard seeds
sesame seeds
ground turmeric
chilli powder
green chilli
potatoes
garlic
salt

1 Cut the potatoes into thick chips.

2 Heat the oil for deep-frying to 160°C/325°F. Fry the chips in batches for 5 minutes, until golden. Drain well on plenty of kitchen paper.

3 Put the chips in a bowl and sprinkle over the turmeric, chilli powder and salt. Cool, then toss the chips in the spices until they are evenly coated.

4 Heat the 30 ml/2 tbsp oil in a large saucepan and fry the mustard seeds for 2 minutes until they splutter. Add the chilli and garlic and fry for 2 minutes.

5 Add the sesame seeds and fry for 3–4 minutes until the seeds begin to brown. Remove from the heat.

6 Add the sesame seed mixture to the potatoes and toss together to coat evenly. Serve cold, or reheat for about 5 minutes in an oven preheated to 200°C/400°F/Gas 6.

COOK'S TIP
Make sure the chips are as uniform in size as possible to ensure that they cook evenly.

Courgette Curry

Thickly sliced courgettes are combined with authentic Indian spices for a delicious, colourful vegetable curry.

Serves 4

INGREDIENTS
675 g/1½ lb courgettes
45 ml/3 tbsp oil
2.5 ml/½ tsp cumin seeds
2.5 ml/½ tsp mustard seeds
1 onion, thinly sliced
2 garlic cloves, crushed
1.5 ml/¼ tsp ground turmeric
1.5 ml/¼ tsp chilli powder
5 ml/1 tsp ground coriander
5 ml/1 tsp ground cumin
2.5 ml/½ tsp salt
15 ml/1 tbsp tomato purée
400 g/14 oz can chopped tomatoes
150 ml/¼ pint/⅔ cup water
15 ml/1 tbsp chopped
    fresh coriander
5 ml/1 tsp garam masala

oil *mustard seeds* *chopped tomatoes*

ground cumin *cumin seeds* *chilli powder*

garam masala *tomato purée* *onion*

ground turmeric *ground coriander*

salt *garlic*

courgettes

fresh coriander

1 Trim the ends from the courgettes then cut into 1 cm/½ in thick slices.

2 Heat the oil in a large saucepan and fry the cumin and mustard seeds for 2 minutes until they begin to splutter.

3 Add the onion and garlic and fry for about 5–6 minutes.

4 Add the turmeric, chilli powder, coriander, cumin and salt and fry for about 2–3 minutes.

5 Add the sliced courgettes all at once, and cook for 5 minutes

6 Mix together the tomato purée and chopped tomatoes and add to the saucepan with the water. Cover and simmer for 10 minutes until the sauce thickens. Stir in the fresh coriander and garam masala, then cook for 5 minutes or until the courgettes are tender.

Vegetable Kashmiri

This is a delicious vegetable curry, in which fresh mixed vegetables are cooked in a spicy, aromatic yogurt sauce.

Serves 4

INGREDIENTS

10 ml/2 tsp cumin seeds
8 black peppercorns
2 green cardamom pods, seeds only
5 cm/2 in cinnamon stick
2.5 ml/¹/₂ tsp grated nutmeg
45 ml/3 tbsp oil
1 green chilli, chopped
2.5 cm/1 in piece root ginger, grated
5 ml/1 tsp chilli powder
2.5 ml/¹/₂ tsp salt
2 large potatoes, cut into
    2.5 cm/1 in chunks
225 g/8 oz cauliflower, broken
    into florets
225 g/8 oz okra, thickly sliced
150 ml/¹/₄ pint/²/₃ cup natural yogurt
150 ml/¹/₄ pint/²/₃ cup
    vegetable stock
toasted flaked almonds and fresh
    coriander sprigs, to garnish

vegetable stock | oil | chilli powder | black peppercorns

cauliflower | potatoes | cumin seeds

natural yogurt | salt | nutmeg | cinnamon stick | cardamom pods

root ginger | okra | green chilli

1 Grind the cumin seeds, peppercorns, cardamom seeds, cinnamon stick and nutmeg to a fine powder using a blender or a pestle and mortar.

2 Heat the oil in a large saucepan and fry the chilli and ginger for 2 minutes, stirring all the time.

3 Add the chilli powder, salt and ground spice mixture and fry for about 2–3 minutes, stirring all the time to prevent the spices from sticking.

4 Stir in the potatoes, cover, and cook for 10 minutes over a low heat, stirring from time to time.

5 Add the cauliflower and okra and cook for 5 minutes.

6 Add the yogurt and stock. Bring to the boil, then reduce the heat. Cover and simmer for 20 minutes, or until all the vegetables are tender. Garnish with toasted almonds and coriander sprigs.

Red Cabbage in Port and Red Wine

A sweet and sour, spicy red cabbage dish, with the added crunch of pears and walnuts.

Serves 6

INGREDIENTS
15 ml/1 tbsp walnut oil
1 onion, sliced
2 whole star anise
5 ml/1 tsp ground cinnamon
pinch of ground cloves
450 g/1 lb red cabbage, finely
    shredded
25 g/1 oz/2 tbsp dark brown sugar
45 ml/3 tbsp red wine vinegar
300 ml/½ pint/1¼ cups red wine
150 ml/¼ pint/⅔ cup port
2 pears, cut into 1 cm/½ in cubes
115 g/4 oz/½ cup raisins
salt and freshly ground black pepper
115 g/4 oz/½ cup walnut halves

brown sugar

red cabbage

pears

onion   *raisins*

walnut halves

star anise

port

red wine vinegar

red wine

1 Heat the oil in a large pan. Add the onion and cook gently for about 5 minutes until softened.

2 Add the star anise, cinnamon, cloves and cabbage and cook for about 3 minutes more.

3 Stir in the sugar, vinegar, red wine and port. Cover the pan and simmer gently for 10 minutes, stirring occasionally.

4 Stir in the cubed pears and raisins and cook for a further 10 minutes or until the cabbage is tender. Season to taste. Mix in the walnut halves and serve.

Beetroot and Celeriac Gratin

Beautiful ruby-red slices of beetroot and celeriac make a stunning light accompaniment to any main course dish.

Serves 6

INGREDIENTS
350 g/12 oz raw beetroot
350 g/12 oz celeriac
4 thyme sprigs
6 juniper berries, crushed
salt and freshly ground black pepper
100 ml/4 fl oz/½ cup fresh orange juice
100 ml/4 fl oz/½ cup vegetable stock

celeriac

orange juice

juniper berries

beetroot

thyme

1 Preheat the oven to 190°C/375°F/Gas 5. Peel and slice the beetroot very finely. Quarter and peel the celeriac and slice very finely.

2 Fill a 25 cm/10 in diameter, cast iron, ovenproof or flameproof frying pan with alternate layers of beetroot and celeriac slices, sprinkling with the thyme, juniper and seasoning between each layer.

3 Mix the orange juice and stock together and pour over the gratin. Place over a medium heat and bring to the boil. Boil for 2 minutes.

4 Cover with foil and place in the oven for 15–20 minutes. Remove the foil and raise the oven temperature to 200°C/400°F/Gas 6. Cook for a further 10 minutes.

Roasted Plum Tomatoes with Garlic

These are so simple to prepare, yet taste absolutely wonderful. Use a large, shallow earthenware dish that will allow the tomatoes to sear and char in a hot oven.

Serves 4

INGREDIENTS
8 plum tomatoes
12 garlic cloves
60 ml/4 tbsp extra virgin olive oil
3 bay leaves
salt and ground black pepper
45 ml/3 tbsp fresh oregano leaves,
   to garnish

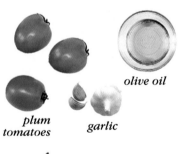

olive oil

plum tomatoes   *garlic*

oregano   *bay leaves*

1 Preheat the oven to 230°C/450°F/Gas 8. Halve the plum tomatoes, leaving a small part of the green stem intact for decoration.

2 Select an ovenproof dish that will hold all the tomatoes snugly in a single layer. Place the tomatoes in the dish with the cut side facing upwards, and push the whole, unpeeled garlic cloves between them.

4 Bake for about 45 minutes until the tomatoes have softened and are sizzling in the dish. They should be charred around the edges. Season with salt and a little more black pepper, if needed. Garnish with the fresh oregano leaves and serve immediately.

3 Brush the tomatoes with the oil, add the bay leaves and sprinkle black pepper over the top.

VARIATION
For a sweet alternative, use red or yellow peppers instead of the tomatoes. Cut each pepper in half and remove all the seeds before placing, cut side up, in an ovenproof dish.

COOK'S TIP
Select ripe, juicy tomatoes without any blemishes to get the best flavour out of this dish.

Courgettes with Onion and Garlic

Use a good-quality olive oil and sunflower oil. The olive oil gives the dish a delicious fragrance without overpowering the courgettes.

Serves 4

INGREDIENTS
15 ml/1 tbsp olive oil
15 ml/1 tbsp sunflower oil
1 large onion, chopped
1 garlic clove, crushed
4–5 medium courgettes, cut into
    1 cm/½ in slices
150 ml/¼ pint/⅔ cup
    vegetable stock
2.5 ml/½ tsp chopped fresh oregano
salt and ground black pepper
chopped fresh parsley, to garnish

courgettes   *garlic*

olive oil   *stock*

sunflower oil

oregano   *onion*   *parsley*

1 Heat the olive and sunflower oils in a large frying pan and fry the onion and garlic over a moderate heat for 5–6 minutes until the onion has softened and is beginning to brown.

2 Add the sliced courgettes and fry for about 4 minutes until they just begin to be flecked with brown, stirring frequently.

3 Stir in the stock, oregano and seasoning and simmer gently for 8–10 minutes or until the liquid has almost evaporated.

4 Spoon the courgettes into a warmed serving dish, sprinkle with chopped parsley and serve.

COOK'S TIP

Courgettes are very popular in Italy, grown in many kitchen gardens. They make a lovely summer dish, taking very little time to prepare. If you can find them, choose small courgettes, which tend to be much sweeter than the larger ones.

Herby Baked Tomatoes

Dress up sliced, sweet tomatoes with fresh herbs and a crisp breadcrumb topping.

Serves 4–6

INGREDIENTS

675 g/1½ lb (about 8) large red and
    yellow tomatoes
10 ml/2 tsp red wine vinegar
2.5 ml/½ tsp wholegrain mustard
1 garlic clove, crushed
10 ml/2 tsp chopped fresh parsley
10 ml/2 tsp snipped fresh chives
25 g/1 oz/½ cup fresh fine white
    breadcrumbs
salt and freshly ground black pepper
sprigs of flat-leaf parsley, to garnish

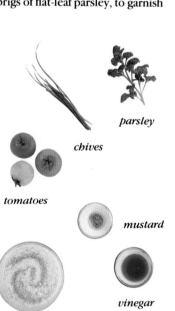

parsley

chives

tomatoes

mustard

vinegar

breadcrumbs

1 Pre-heat the oven to 200°C/400°F/Gas 6. Thickly slice the tomatoes and arrange half of them in a 900 ml/1½ pint/3¾ cup ovenproof dish.

2 Mix the vinegar, mustard, garlic clove and seasoning together. Stir in 10 ml/2 tsp of cold water. Sprinkle the tomatoes with half the parsley and chives, then drizzle over half the dressing.

3 Lay the remaining tomato slices on top, overlapping them slightly. Drizzle with the remaining dressing.

4 Sprinkle over the breadcrumbs. Bake in the pre-heated oven for 25 minutes or until the topping is golden. Sprinkle with the remaining parsley and chives. Serve immediately garnished with sprigs of flat-leaf parsley.

Courgettes in Citrus Sauce

If baby courgettes are unavailable, you can use larger ones, but they should be cooked whole so that they don't absorb too much water. Halve them lengthways and cut into 10 cm/4 in lengths.

Serves 4

INGREDIENTS
350 g/12 oz baby courgettes
4 spring onions, finely sliced
2.5 cm/1 in fresh root ginger, grated
30 ml/2 tbsp cider vinegar
15 ml/1 tbsp light soy sauce
5 ml/1 tsp soft light brown sugar
45 ml/3 tbsp vegetable stock
finely grated rind and juice of ½
    lemon and ½ orange
5 ml/1 tsp cornflour

orange

lemon

courgettes

ginger

spring onions

1 Cook the courgettes in lightly salted boiling water for 3-4 minutes, or until just tender. Drain well.

2 Meanwhile put all the remaining ingredients, except the cornflour, into a small saucepan and bring to the boil. Simmer for 3 minutes.

3 Blend the cornflour with 10 ml/2 tsp of cold water and add to the sauce. Bring to the boil, stirring continuously, until the sauce has thickened.

4 Pour the sauce over the courgettes and gently heat, shaking the pan to coat evenly. Transfer to a warmed serving dish and serve.

Mixed Mushroom Ragout

These mushrooms are delicious served hot or cold and can be made up to two days in advance.

Serves 4

INGREDIENTS
1 small onion, finely chopped
1 garlic clove, crushed
5 ml/1 tsp coriander seeds, crushed
30 ml/2 tbsp red wine vinegar
15 ml/1 tbsp soy sauce
15 ml/1 tbsp dry sherry
10 ml/2 tsp tomato purée
10 ml/2 tsp soft light brown sugar
150 ml/¼ pint/⅔ cup vegetable stock
115 g/4 oz baby button mushrooms
115 g/4 oz chestnut mushrooms, quartered
115 g/4 oz oyster mushrooms, sliced
salt and freshly ground black pepper
sprig of fresh coriander, to garnish

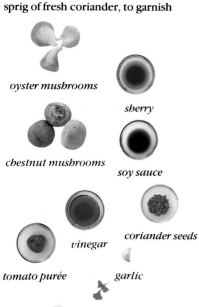

oyster mushrooms

sherry

chestnut mushrooms

soy sauce

vinegar

coriander seeds

tomato purée

garlic

coriander

button mushrooms

onion

1 Put the first nine ingredients into a large saucepan. Bring to the boil and reduce the heat. Cover and simmer for 5 minutes.

2 Uncover the saucepan and simmer for 5 more minutes, or until the liquid has reduced by half.

3 Add the baby button and chestnut mushrooms and simmer for 3 minutes. Stir in the oyster mushrooms and cook for a further 2 minutes.

4 Remove the mushrooms with a slotted spoon and transfer them to a serving dish.

5 Boil the juices for about 5 minutes, or until reduced to about 75 ml/5 tbsp. Season to taste.

6 Allow to cool for 2-3 minutes, then pour over the mushrooms. Serve hot or well chilled, garnished with a sprig of fresh coriander.

Baked Onions with Sun-dried Tomatoes

This wonderfully simple vegetable dish of baked onions brings together the flavours of a hot Italian summer – tomatoes, fresh herbs and olive oil.

Serves 4

INGREDIENTS
450 g/1 lb small onions, peeled
10 ml/2 tsp chopped fresh rosemary
    or 5 ml/1 tsp dried rosemary
2 garlic cloves, chopped
15 ml/1 tbsp chopped fresh parsley
120 ml/4 fl oz/½ cup sun-dried
    tomatoes in oil, drained and
    chopped
90 ml/6 tbsp olive oil
15 ml/1 tbsp white wine vinegar
salt and ground black pepper

olive oil

garlic

rosemary

small onions

sun-dried tomatoes

white wine vinegar

parsley

1 Preheat the oven to 150°C/300°F/Gas 2. Grease a shallow baking dish. Drop the onions into a saucepan of boiling water and cook for 5 minutes. Drain in a colander.

2 Spread the onions in the bottom of the prepared baking dish.

VARIATIONS
Other herbs can be used instead of the rosemary and parsley in this dish. Try using shredded fresh basil which will enhance the flavour of the sun-dried tomatoes, or fresh thyme, which complements the flavour of baked onions perfectly. If you can find small red onions, these would make a nice change, or even mix the two colours.

3 Combine the rosemary, garlic, parsley, salt and pepper in a small mixing bowl and sprinkle the mixture evenly over the onions in the dish.

4 Scatter the sun-dried tomatoes over the onions. Drizzle the olive oil and vinegar on top.

5 Cover the dish with a sheet of foil and bake for 45 minutes, basting occasionally. Remove the foil and bake for about 15 minutes more until the onions are golden brown all over. Serve immediately from the dish.

Grilled Aubergine Parcels

These are delicious little Italian bundles of tomatoes, Mozzarella cheese and basil, wrapped in slices of aubergine.

Serves 4

INGREDIENTS
2 large, long aubergines
225 g/8 oz mozzarella cheese
2 plum tomatoes
16 large basil leaves
30 ml/2 tbsp olive oil
salt and ground black pepper

FOR THE DRESSING
60 ml/4 tbsp olive oil
5 ml/1 tsp balsamic vinegar
15 ml/1 tbsp sun-dried tomato paste
15 ml/1 tbsp lemon juice

FOR THE GARNISH
30 ml/2 tbsp pine nuts, toasted
torn basil leaves

aubergine

mozzarella cheese

basil

lemon

balsamic vinegar

sun-dried tomato paste

plum tomatoes

olive oil

pine nuts

1 To make the dressing, whisk together the olive oil, vinegar, sun-dried tomato paste and lemon juice. Season to taste and set aside.

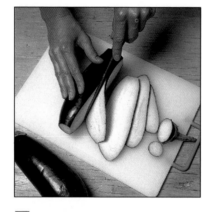

2 Remove the stalks from the aubergines and cut the aubergines lengthways into thin slices – the aim is to get 16 slices in total (each about 5 mm/¼ in thick), disregarding the first and last slices. (If you have a mandolin, it will cut perfect, even slices for you; otherwise use a sharp long-bladed knife.)

3 Bring a large pan of salted water to the boil and cook the aubergine slices for about 2 minutes or until just softened. Drain the sliced aubergines, then dry on kitchen paper. Set aside.

4 Cut the cheese into slices. Cut each tomato into eight slices, not counting the first and last slices.

5 Take two aubergine slices and place on a baking sheet or in a large flameproof dish, forming a cross. Place a slice of tomato in the centre of each cross, season with salt and pepper, then add a basil leaf, followed by a slice of cheese, another basil leaf, a slice of tomato and more seasoning.

6 Fold the ends of the aubergine slices around the cheese and tomato filling to make a neat parcel. Repeat with the rest of the assembled ingredients to make eight parcels. Chill the parcels for about 20 minutes.

7 Preheat the grill. Brush the parcels with olive oil and cook for about 5 minutes on each side or until golden. Serve hot, with the dressing, and sprinkled with pine nuts and basil.

Radicchio and Chicory Gratin

Radicchio and chicory take on a different flavour when cooked in this way. The creamy béchamel combines wonderfully with the bitter leaves.

Serves 4

INGREDIENTS
2 heads radicchio
2 heads chicory
120 ml/4 fl oz/½ cup sun-dried
    tomatoes in oil, drained
    and roughly chopped,
    oil reserved
salt and ground black pepper

FOR THE SAUCE
25 g/1 oz/2 tbsp butter
15 g/½ oz/2 tbsp plain flour
250 ml/8 fl oz/1 cup milk
pinch of grated nutmeg
50 g/2 oz/½ cup grated
    Emmenthal cheese
chopped fresh parsley,
    to garnish

radicchio

Emmenthal cheese

butter

chicory

sun-dried tomatoes

plain flour

milk

nutmeg

parsley

1 Preheat the oven to 180°C/350°F/ Gas 4. Grease a 1.2 litre/2 pint/5 cup baking dish. Trim the radicchio and chicory and discard any damaged or wilted leaves. Quarter them lengthways and arrange in the baking dish. Scatter over the sun-dried tomatoes and brush the leaves liberally with oil from the sun-dried tomato jar. Sprinkle with salt and pepper and cover with foil. Bake for 15 minutes, then remove the foil and bake for a further 10 minutes until the vegetables are softened.

COOK'S TIP
In Italy radicchio and chicory are often grilled on an outdoor barbecue. To do this, simply prepare the vegetables as above and brush with olive oil. Place cut-side down on the grill for 7–10 minutes until browned. Turn and grill for about 5 more minutes or until the other side is browned.

2 Make the béchamel sauce. Place the butter in a small saucepan and melt over a medium heat. When the butter is foaming, add the flour and cook for 1 minute, stirring. Remove from the heat and gradually add the milk, whisking all the time. Return to the heat, bring to the boil and simmer for 2–3 minutes until it thickens.

3 Season the sauce to taste and add the grated nutmeg.

4 Pour the sauce over the vegetables and sprinkle with the grated cheese. Bake for 20 minutes or until golden brown. Serve immediately, garnished with the chopped parsley.

Gorgonzola, Cauliflower and Walnut Gratin

This cauliflower dish is covered with a bubbly blue cheese sauce topped with chopped walnuts and cooked under the grill.

Serves 4

INGREDIENTS
1 large cauliflower, broken into florets
25 g/1 oz/2 tbsp butter
1 medium onion, finely chopped
45 ml/3 tbsp plain flour
450 ml/¾ pint/scant 2 cups milk
150 g/5 oz Gorgonzola or other blue
    cheese, cut into pieces
2.5 ml/½ tsp celery salt
pinch of cayenne papper
75 g/3 oz/¾ cup chopped walnuts
pinch of salt
fresh parsley, to garnish
115 g/4 oz green salad, to serve

onion

butter

Gorgonzola

walnuts

cauliflower

1 Bring a large saucepan of salted water to the boil and cook the cauliflower for 6 minutes. Drain and place in a flameproof gratin dish.

2 Heat the butter in a heavy saucepan. Add the onion and cook over a gentle heat to soften without colouring. Stir in the flour, then draw from the heat. Stir in the milk a little at a time until absorbed by the flour, stirring continuously. Add the cheese, celery salt and cayenne pepper. Simmer and stir to thicken.

3 Preheat a moderate grill. Spoon the sauce over the cauliflower, scatter with chopped walnuts and grill until golden. Garnish with the parsley and serve with a crisp green salad.

VARIATION

For a delicious alternative, substitute cauliflower with 1.1 kg/2½ lb fresh broccoli or combine both together.

236

Leek and Caraway Gratin with a Carrot Crust

Tender leeks are mixed with a creamy caraway sauce and a crunchy carrot topping.

Serves 4–6

INGREDIENTS

675 g/1½ lb leeks, cut into 5 cm/2 in
   pieces
150 ml/¼ pint/⅔ cup vegetable stock
   or water
45 ml/3 tbsp dry white wine
5 ml/1 tsp caraway seeds
pinch of salt
275 ml/10 fl oz skimmed milk as
   required
25 g/1 oz/2 tbsp butter
25 g/1 oz/¼ cup plain flour

FOR THE TOPPING

115 g/4 oz/2 cups fresh wholemeal
   breadcrumbs
115 g/4 oz/2 cups grated carrot
30 ml/2 tbsp chopped fresh parsley
75 g/3 oz Jarlsberg cheese, coarsely
   grated
25 g/1 oz/2 tbsp slivered almonds

parsley

vegetable stock

Jarlsberg

breadcrumbs

leek

butter

1 Place the leeks in a large pan. Add the stock or water, wine, caraway seeds and salt. Bring to a simmer, cover and cook for 5–7 minutes until the leeks are just tender.

2 With a slotted spoon, transfer the leeks to an ovenproof dish. Reduce the remaining liquid to half then make the amount up to 350 ml/12 fl oz/1½ cups with skimmed milk.

3 Preheat the oven to 180°C/350°F/ Gas 4. Melt the butter in a saucepan, stir in the flour and cook without allowing it to colour for 1–2 minutes. Gradually add the stock and milk, stirring well after each addition, until you have a smooth sauce. Simmer for 5–6 minutes then pour over the leeks in the dish.

4 Mix all the topping ingredients together in a bowl and sprinkle over the leeks. Bake for 20–25 minutes until golden.

Carrot Mousse with Mushroom Sauce

The combination of fresh vegetables in this impressive yet easy-to-make mousse makes healthy eating a pleasure.

Serves 4

INGREDIENTS
350 g/12 oz carrots, roughly chopped
1 small red pepper, seeded and
    roughly chopped
45 ml/3 tbsp vegetable stock or water
2 eggs
1 egg white
115 g/4 oz/½ cup quark or low fat soft
    cheese
15 ml/1 tbsp chopped fresh tarragon
salt and freshly ground black pepper
sprig of fresh tarragon, to garnish
boiled rice and leeks, to serve

FOR THE MUSHROOM SAUCE
25 g/1 oz/2 tbsp low fat spread
175 g/6 oz mushrooms, sliced
30 ml/2 tbsp plain flour
250 ml/8 fl oz/1 cup skimmed milk

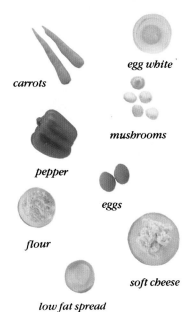

carrots

egg white

mushrooms

pepper

eggs

flour

soft cheese

low fat spread

1 Pre-heat the oven to 190°C/375°F/ Gas 5. Line the bases of four 150 ml/ ¼ pint/⅔ cup dariole moulds or ramekin dishes with non-stick baking paper. Put the carrots and red pepper in a small saucepan with the vegetable stock or water. Cover and cook for 5 minutes, or until tender. Drain well.

2 Lightly beat the eggs and egg white together. Mix with the quark or low fat soft cheese. Season to taste. Purée the cooked vegetables in a food processor or blender. Add the cheese mixture and process for a few seconds more until smooth. Stir in the chopped tarragon.

3 Divide the carrot mixture between the prepared dariole moulds or ramekin dishes and cover with foil. Place the dishes in a roasting tin half-filled with hot water. Bake in the pre-heated oven for 35 minutes, or until set.

4 For the mushroom sauce, melt 15 g/½ oz/1 tbsp of the low fat spread in a frying pan. Add the mushrooms and gently sauté for 5 minutes, until soft.

5 Put the remaining low fat spread in a small saucepan together with the flour and milk. Cook over a medium heat, stirring all the time, until the sauce thickens. Stir in the mushrooms and season to taste.

6 Turn out each mousse onto a serving plate. Spoon over a little sauce and serve the remainder separately. Garnish with a sprig of fresh tarragon and serve with boiled rice and leeks.

Spring Vegetable Stir-fry

A colourful, dazzling medley of fresh and sweet young vegetables.

Serves 4

INGREDIENTS
15 ml/1 tbsp peanut oil
1 garlic clove, sliced
2.5 cm/1 in piece of fresh ginger root, finely chopped
115 g/4 oz baby carrots
115 g/4 oz patty pan squash
115 g/4 oz baby sweetcorn
115 g/4 oz French beans, topped and tailed
115 g/4 oz sugar-snap peas, topped and tailed
115 g/4 oz young asparagus, cut into 7.5 cm/3 in pieces
8 spring onions, trimmed and cut into 5 cm/2 in pieces
115 g/4 oz cherry tomatoes

FOR THE DRESSING
juice of 2 limes
15 ml/1 tbsp runny honey
15 ml/1 tbsp soy sauce
5 ml/1 tsp sesame oil

1 Heat the peanut oil in a wok or large frying pan.

2 Add the garlic and ginger and stir-fry over a high heat for 1 minute.

3 Add the carrots, patty pan squash, sweetcorn and beans and stir-fry for another 3–4 minutes.

4 Add the sugar-snap peas, asparagus, spring onions and cherry tomatoes and stir-fry for a further 1–2 minutes.

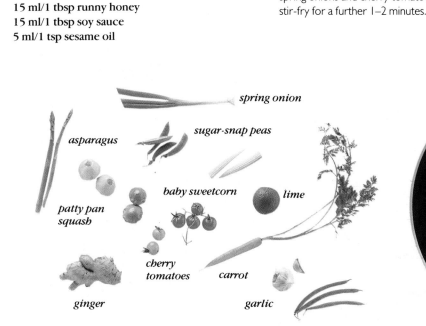

spring onion

asparagus

sugar-snap peas

patty pan squash

baby sweetcorn

lime

ginger

cherry tomatoes

carrot

garlic

French beans

5 Mix the dressing ingredients together and add to the pan.

6 Stir well then cover the pan. Cook for 2–3 minutes more until the vegetables are just tender but still crisp.

COOK'S TIP
Stir-fries take only moments to cook so prepare this dish at the last minute.

Black Bean and Vegetable Stir-fry

The secret of a quick stir-fry is to prepare all the ingredients first. This colourful vegetable mixture is coated in a classic Chinese sauce.

Serves 4

INGREDIENTS
8 spring onions
225 g/8 oz/2 cups button
  mushrooms
1 red pepper
1 green pepper
2 large carrots
60 ml/4 tbsp sesame oil
2 garlic cloves, crushed
60 ml/4 tbsp black bean sauce
90 ml/6 tbsp warm water
225 g/8 oz beansprouts
salt and freshly ground black pepper

1 Thinly slice the spring onions and button mushrooms.

spring onions

black bean sauce

sesame oil

button mushrooms

red pepper

beansprouts

carrots

garlic cloves

onion

green pepper

2 Cut both the peppers in half, remove the seeds and slice the flesh into thin strips.

3 Cut the carrots in half. Cut each half into thin strips lengthways. Stack the slices and cut through them to make very fine strips.

4 Heat the oil in a large wok or frying pan until very hot. Add the spring onions and garlic and stir-fry for 30 seconds.

5 Add the mushrooms, peppers and carrots. Stir-fry for 5–6 minutes over a high heat until the vegetables are just beginning to soften.

6 Mix the black bean sauce with the water. Add to the wok or pan and cook for 3–4 minutes. Stir in the beansprouts and stir-fry for 1 minute more, until all the vegetables are coated in the sauce. Season to taste. Serve at once.

COOK'S TIP
For best results the oil in the wok must be very hot before adding the vegetables.

Courgettes and Asparagus en Papillote

An impressive dinner party accompaniment, these puffed paper parcels should be broken open at the table by each guest, so that the wonderful aroma can be fully appreciated.

Serves 4

INGREDIENTS
2 medium courgettes
1 medium leek
225 g/8 oz young asparagus, trimmed
4 tarragon sprigs
4 whole garlic cloves, unpeeled
salt and freshly ground black pepper
1 egg, beaten

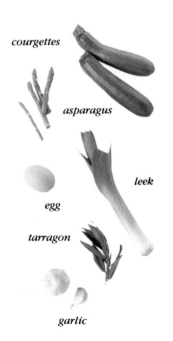

courgettes

asparagus

leek

egg

tarragon

garlic

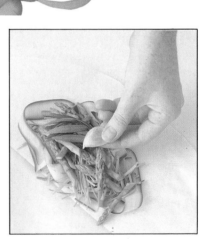

1 Preheat the oven to 200°C/400°F/ Gas 6. Using a potato peeler slice the courgettes lengthwise into thin strips.

2 Cut the leek into very fine julienne strips and cut the asparagus evenly into 5 cm/2 in lengths.

3 Cut out 4 sheets of greaseproof paper measuring 30 × 38 cm/12 × 15 in and fold in half. Draw a large curve to make a heart shape when unfolded. Cut along the inside of the line and open out.

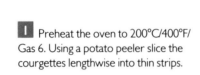

4 Divide the courgettes, asparagus and leek evenly between each paper heart, positioning the filling on one side of the fold line, and topping each with a sprig of tarragon and an unpeeled garlic clove. Season to taste.

COOK'S TIP

Experiment with other vegetables and herbs such as sugar-snap peas and mint or baby carrots and rosemary. The possibilities are endless.

5 Brush the edges lightly with the beaten egg and fold over.

6 Pleat the edges together so that each parcel is completely sealed. Lay the parcels on a baking tray and cook for 10 minutes. Serve immediately.

Broccoli and Chestnut Terrine

Served hot or cold, this versatile terrine is equally suitable for a dinner party as for a picnic.

Serves 4–6

INGREDIENTS

450 g/1 lb broccoli, cut into small florets

225 g/8 oz cooked chestnuts, roughly chopped

50 g/2 oz/1 cup fresh wholemeal breadcrumbs

60 ml/4 tbsp low-fat natural yogurt

30 ml/2 tbsp Parmesan cheese, finely grated

salt, grated nutmeg and freshly ground black pepper

2 eggs, beaten

yogurt

breadcrumbs

broccoli

chestnuts

egg

Parmesan

1 Preheat the oven to 180°C/350°F/Gas 4. Line a 900 g/2 lb loaf tin with non-stick baking paper.

2 Blanch or steam the broccoli for 3–4 minutes until just tender. Drain well. Reserve ¼ of the smallest florets and chop the rest finely.

3 Mix together the chestnuts, breadcrumbs, yogurt and Parmesan, and season to taste.

4 Fold in the chopped broccoli, reserved florets and the beaten eggs.

5 Spoon the broccoli mixture into the prepared tin.

6 Place in a roasting tin and pour in boiling water to come halfway up the sides of the loaf tin. Bake for 20–25 minutes. Remove from the oven and tip out onto a plate or tray. Serve cut into even slices.

Baked Squash

A creamy, sweet and nutty filling makes the perfect topping for tender buttery squash.

Serves 4

INGREDIENTS

2 butternut or acorn squash, 500 g/
  1¼ lb each
15 ml/1 tbsp olive oil
175 g/6 oz/¾ cup canned sweetcorn
  kernels, drained
115 g/4 oz/½ cup unsweetened
  chestnut purée
75 ml/5 tbsp low-fat yogurt
salt and freshly ground black pepper
50 g/2 oz/¼ cup fresh goat's cheese
snipped chives, to garnish

yogurt

chestnut purée

sweetcorn

butternut squash

goat's cheese

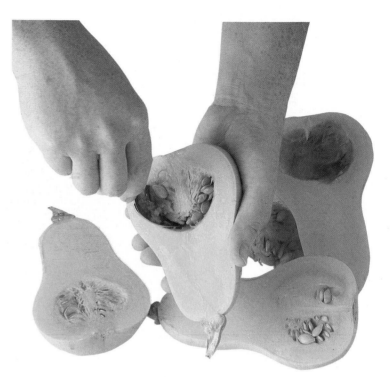

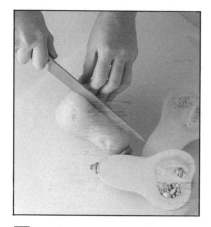

1 Preheat the oven to 180°C/350°F/ Gas 4. Cut the squash in half lengthwise.

2 Scoop out the seeds with a spoon and discard.

3 Place the squash halves on a baking sheet and brush the flesh lightly with the oil. Bake in the oven for 30 minutes.

4 Mix together the sweetcorn, chestnut purée and yogurt in a bowl. Season to taste.

5 Remove the squash from the oven and divide the chestnut mixture between them, spooning it into the hollows.

COOK'S TIP
Use mozzarella or other mild, soft cheeses in place of goat's cheese. The cheese can be omitted entirely for a lower-fat alternative.

6 Top each half with ¼ of the goat's cheese and return to the oven for a further 10–15 minutes. Garnish with snipped chives.

Mushrooms with Leeks and Stilton

Upturned mushrooms make perfect containers for this leek and Stilton filling.

Serves 2–3

INGREDIENTS
1 leek, thinly sliced
6 flat mushrooms
2 garlic cloves, crushed
30 ml/2 tbsp chopped fresh parsley
115 g/4 oz/¹/₂ cup butter, softened
115 g/4 oz Stilton cheese
freshly ground black pepper
frisée and tomato halves, to garnish

leek

butter

flat mushrooms

parsley

Stilton cheese

garlic cloves

1 Put the leek slices in a small pan with a little water. Cover and cook for about 5 minutes until tender. Drain, refresh under cold water and drain again.

2 Remove the stalks from the mushrooms and set them aside. Put the mushroom caps, hollows uppermost, on an oiled baking sheet.

3 Put the mushroom stalks, garlic and parsley in a food processor or blender. Process for 1 minute. Tip into a bowl, add the leek and butter and season with freshly ground black pepper to taste. Preheat the grill.

4 Crumble the Stilton into the mushroom mixture and mix well. Divide the Stilton mixture between the mushroom caps and grill for 6–7 minutes until bubbling. Serve garnished with frisée and halved tomatoes.

Tomato and Okra Stew

Okra is an unusual and delicious vegetable. It releases a sticky sap when cooked, which helps to thicken the stew.

Serves 4

INGREDIENTS
15 ml/1 tbsp olive oil
1 onion, chopped
400 g/14 oz can pimientos, drained
2 x 400 g/14 oz cans chopped
  tomatoes
275 g/10 oz okra
30 ml/2 tbsp chopped fresh parsley
salt and freshly ground black pepper

parsley

chopped
tomatoes

pimientos

onion

okra

1 Heat the oil in a pan. Add the onion and cook for 2–3 minutes.

2 Roughly chop the pimientos and add to the onion. Add the chopped tomatoes and mix well.

3 Cut the tops off the okra and cut into halves or quarters if large. Add to the tomato sauce in the pan. Season with plenty of salt and pepper.

4 Bring the vegetable stew to the boil, then lower the heat, cover the pan and simmer for 12 minutes until the vegetables are tender and the sauce has thickened. Stir in the chopped parsley and serve at once.

Vegetable Kebabs with Mustard and Honey

A colourful mixture of vegetables and tofu, skewered, glazed and grilled until tender.

Serves 4

INGREDIENTS
1 yellow pepper
2 small courgettes
225 g/8 oz piece of firm tofu
8 cherry tomatoes
8 button mushrooms
15 ml/1 tbsp wholegrain mustard
15 ml/1 tbsp clear honey
30 ml/2 tbsp olive oil
salt and freshly ground black pepper

TO SERVE
4 portions cooked mixed rice
  and wild rice
lime segments
flat leaf parsley

1 Cut the pepper in half and remove the seeds. Cut each half into quarters and cut each quarter in half.

2 Top and tail the courgettes and peel them decoratively, if you like. Cut each courgette into 8 chunks.

3 Cut the tofu into pieces of a similar size to the vegetables.

courgettes

cherry tomatoes

yellow pepper

clear honey

wholegrain mustard

button mushrooms

tofu

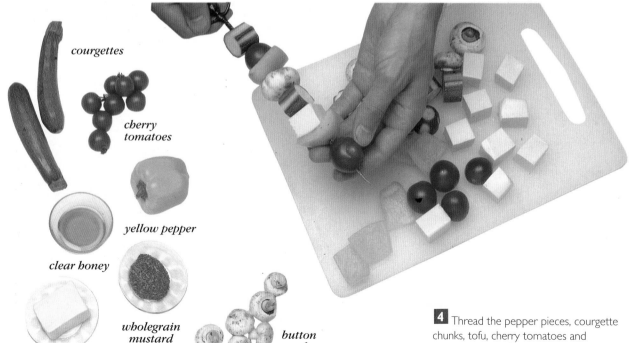

5 Whisk the mustard, honey and olive oil in a small bowl. Add salt and pepper to taste.

4 Thread the pepper pieces, courgette chunks, tofu, cherry tomatoes and mushrooms alternately on to four metal or bamboo skewers. Preheat the grill.

6 Put the kebabs on to a baking sheet. Brush with the mustard and honey glaze. Cook under the grill for 8 minutes, turning once or twice during cooking. Serve with a mixture of long grain and wild rice, and garnish with lime segments and parsley.

COOK'S TIP
If using bamboo skewers, soak them in a bowl of cold water before threading, to prevent them burning when placed under the grill.

Potato, Broccoli and Red Pepper Stir-fry

A hot and hearty stir-fry of vegetables with just a hint of fresh ginger.

Serves 2

INGREDIENTS

450 g/1 lb potatoes
45 ml/3 tbsp groundnut oil
50 g/2 oz/¼ cup butter
·1 small onion, chopped
1 red pepper, seeded and chopped
225 g/8 oz broccoli, broken
  into florets
2.5 cm/1 in piece of fresh root
  ginger, peeled and grated
salt and freshly ground black pepper

red pepper   butter

broccoli

onion

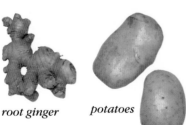

root ginger   potatoes

1 Peel the potatoes and cut them into 1 cm/½ in dice.

2 Heat the oil in a large frying pan and add the potatoes. Cook for 8 minutes over a high heat, stirring and tossing occasionally, until the potatoes are browned and just tender.

3 Drain off the oil. Add the butter to the potatoes in the pan. As soon as it melts, add the onion and red pepper. Stir-fry for 2 minutes.

4 Add the broccoli florets and ginger to the pan. Stir-fry for 2–3 minutes more, taking care not to break up the potatoes. Add salt and pepper to taste and serve at once.

COOK'S TIP

Although a wok is the preferred pan for stir-frying, for this recipe a flat frying pan is best to cook the potatoes quickly.

Bubble and Squeak with Fried Eggs

Next time you are serving mashed potato, make double the amount and chill half so that you can make this tasty dish the next day.

Serves 2

INGREDIENTS

½ Savoy cabbage
50 g/2 oz/¼ cup butter
1 small onion, finely chopped
450 g/1 lb mashed potato
15 ml/1 tbsp chopped fresh parsley
15 ml/1 tbsp vegetable oil
2 eggs
salt and freshly ground black pepper
2 tomatoes, halved, to serve

eggs

mashed potato

butter

onion

Savoy cabbage

parsley

1 Cut out and discard the hard core of the cabbage. Strip off and discard the outer layer of leaves. Finely slice the remaining cabbage and set aside.

2 Melt the butter in a large frying pan. Add the onion and fry for 2–3 minutes until just tender. Reduce the heat slightly, add the cabbage and cook, stirring constantly, for 2–3 minutes.

3 Add the mashed potato to the pan. Stir to combine. Cook for 5–6 minutes until the mixture starts to brown. Stir in the chopped parsley and add salt and pepper to taste. Transfer the mixture to a serving dish and keep hot.

4 Wipe the pan clean. Heat the oil and fry the eggs until just set. Serve the bubble and squeak on individual plates, adding a fried egg and two tomato halves to each portion. Sprinkle with black pepper.

Potato, Spinach and Pine Nut Gratin

Pine nuts add a satisfying crunch to this gratin of wafer-thin potato slices and spinach in a creamy cheese sauce.

Serves 2

INGREDIENTS
450 g/1 lb potatoes
1 garlic clove, crushed
3 spring onions, thinly sliced
150 ml/¼ pint/⅔ cup single cream
250 ml/8 fl oz/1 cup milk
225 g/8 oz frozen chopped
  spinach, thawed
115 g/4 oz Cheddar cheese, grated
25 g/1 oz/¼ cup pine nuts
salt and freshly ground black pepper

spinach

potatoes

garlic clove

pine nuts

spring onions

Cheddar cheese

single cream

1 Peel the potoates and cut them carefully into wafer-thin slices. Spread them out in a large, heavy-based, non-stick frying pan.

2 Scatter the crushed garlic and sliced spring onions evenly over the potatoes.

3 Pour the cream and milk over the potatoes. Place the pan over a gentle heat, cover and cook for 8 minutes or until the potatoes are tender.

4 Using both hands, squeeze the spinach dry. Add the spinach to the potatoes, mixing lightly. Cover the pan and cook for 2 minutes more.

5 Add salt and pepper to taste, then spoon the mixture into a gratin dish. Preheat the grill.

6 Sprinkle the grated cheese and pine nuts over the spinach mixture. Heat under the grill for 2–3 minutes until the topping is golden. A simple lettuce and tomato salad makes an excellent accompaniment to this dish.

Spinach and Potato Galette

Creamy layers of potato, spinach and herbs make a warming supper dish.

Serves 6

INGREDIENTS

900 g/2 lb large potatoes
450 g/1 lb fresh spinach
2 eggs
400 g/14 oz/1¾ cup low-fat cream cheese
15 ml/1 tbsp grainy mustard
50 g/2 oz chopped fresh herbs (e.g. chives, parsley, chervil or sorrel)
salt and freshly ground black pepper

mustard

parsley

cream cheese

spinach

egg

potatoes

chives

cherry tomatoes

chervil

sorrel

COOK'S TIP

Choose firm potatoes for this dish such as Cara, Desirée or Estima.

1 Preheat the oven to 180°C/350°F/Gas 4. Line a deep 23 cm/9 in cake tin with non-stick baking paper. Place the potatoes in a large pan and cover with cold water. Bring to the boil and cook for 10 minutes. Drain well and allow to cool slightly before slicing thinly.

4 Place a layer of the sliced potatoes in the lined tin, arranging them in concentric circles. Top with a spoonful of the cream cheese mixture and spread out. Continue layering, seasoning with salt and pepper as you go, until all the potatoes and the cream cheese mixture are used up.

2 Wash the spinach and place in a large pan with only the water that is clinging to the leaves. Cover and cook, stirring once, until the spinach has just wilted. Drain well in a sieve and squeeze out the excess moisture. Chop finely.

5 Cover the tin with a piece of foil and place in a roasting tin.

3 Beat the eggs with the cream cheese and mustard then stir in the chopped spinach and fresh herbs.

6 Fill the roasting tin with enough boiling water to come halfway up the sides, and cook in the oven for 45–50 minutes. Turn out onto a plate and serve hot or cold.

Potato Gratin

Don't rinse the potato slices before layering because the starch makes a thick sauce during cooking.

Serves 4

INGREDIENTS
1 garlic clove
5 large baking potatoes, peeled
45 ml/3 tbsp freshly grated
    Parmesan cheese
600 ml/1 pint/2½ cups vegetable
    stock
pinch of freshly grated nutmeg
salt and ground black pepper

potatoes

Parmesan cheese

stock

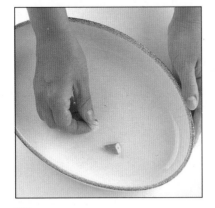

1 Pre-heat the oven to 200°C/400°F/Gas 6. Halve the garlic clove and rub over the base and sides of a gratin dish measuring about 20 × 30 cm/8 × 12 in.

2 Slice the potatoes very thinly and arrange a third of them in the dish. Sprinkle with a little grated cheese, salt and freshly ground black pepper. Pour over some of the stock to prevent the potatoes from discolouring.

3 Continue layering the potatoes and cheese as before, then pour over the rest of the stock. Sprinkle with the grated nutmeg.

4 Bake in the oven for 1¼-1½ hours or until the potatoes are tender and the tops well browned.

VARIATION

For a potato and onion gratin, thinly slice one medium onion and layer with the potato.

Cheese and Onion Slice

This inexpensive supper dish is made substantial with the addition of porridge oats.

Serves 4

INGREDIENTS
2 large onions, thinly sliced
1 garlic clove, crushed
150 ml/¼ pint/⅔ cup vegetable stock
5 ml/1 tsp vegetable extract
250 g/9 oz/3 cups porridge oats
115 g/4 oz/1 cup grated Edam cheese
30 ml/2 tbsp chopped fresh parsley
2 eggs, lightly beaten
1 medium potato, peeled
salt and freshly ground black pepper
coleslaw and tomatoes, halved,
   to serve

porridge oats

Edam cheese

eggs

parsley

onion

potato

1 Pre-heat the oven to 180°C/350°F/ Gas 4. Line the base of a 20 cm/8 in sandwich tin with non-stick baking paper. Put the onions, garlic clove and stock into a heavy-based saucepan and simmer until the stock has reduced entirely. Stir in the vegetable extract.

2 Spread the oats on a baking sheet and toast in the oven for 10 minutes. Mix with the onions, cheese, parsley, eggs, salt and freshly ground black pepper.

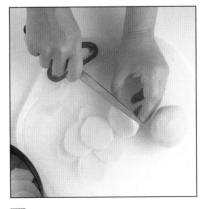

3 Thinly slice the potato and use it to line the base of the tin. Spoon in the oat mixture. Cover with a piece of foil.

4 Bake in the pre-heated oven for 35 minutes. Turn out onto a baking sheet and remove the lining paper. Put under a pre-heated hot grill to brown the potatoes. Cut into wedges and serve hot with coleslaw and halved tomatoes.

Potato Gnocchi with Hazelnut Sauce

These delicate potato dumplings are dressed with a creamy hazelnut sauce.

Serves 4

INGREDIENTS
675 g/1½ lb large potatoes
115 g/4 oz/1 cup plain flour

FOR THE HAZELNUT SAUCE
115 g/4 oz/½ cup hazelnuts, roasted
1 garlic clove, roughly chopped
½ tsp grated lemon rind
½ tsp lemon juice
30 ml/2 tbsp sunflower oil
150 g/5 oz/scant ¾ cup low-fat
   fromage blanc
salt and freshly ground black pepper

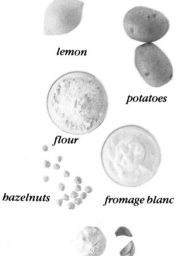

lemon

potatoes

flour

hazelnuts

fromage blanc

garlic

1 Place 65 g/2½ oz of the hazelnuts in a blender with the garlic, grated lemon rind and juice. Blend until coarsely chopped. Gradually add the oil and blend until smooth. Spoon into a bowl and mix in the fromage blanc. Season to taste.

2 Place the potatoes in a pan of cold water. Bring to the boil and cook for 20–25 minutes. Drain well in a colander.

When cool, peel and purée the potatoes whilst still warm by passing them through a food mill into a bowl.

3 Add the flour a little at a time (you may not need all the flour as potatoes vary in texture). Stop adding flour when the mixture is smooth and slightly sticky. Add salt to taste.

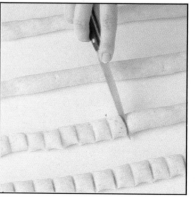

4 Roll out the mixture onto a floured board, into a long sausage about 1 cm/½ in in diameter. Cut into 2 cm/¾ in lengths.

5 Take 1 piece at a time and press it on to a floured fork. Roll each piece slightly while pressing it along the prongs and off the fork. Flip onto a floured plate or tray. Continue with the rest of the mixture.

COOK'S TIP

A light touch is the key to making soft gnocchi, so handle the dough as little as possible to prevent the mixture from becoming tough.

6 Bring a large pan of water to the boil and drop in 20–25 pieces at a time. They will rise to the surface very quickly. Let them cook for 10–15 seconds more, then lift them out with a slotted spoon. Drop into a dish and keep warm. Continue with the rest of the gnocchi. To heat the sauce, place in a heatproof bowl over a pan of simmering water and heat gently, being careful not to let the sauce curdle. Pour the sauce over the gnocchi. Roughly chop the remaining hazelnuts and scatter over the sauce.

SALADS

Parmesan and Poached Egg Salad with Croûtons

Soft poached eggs, hot garlic croûtons and cool, crisp salad leaves make an unforgettable combination.

Serves 2

INGREDIENTS
½ small loaf white bread
75 ml/5 tbsp extra virgin olive oil
2 eggs
115 g/4 oz mixed salad leaves
2 garlic cloves, crushed
7.5 ml/½ tbsp white wine vinegar
25 g/1 oz Parmesan cheese

Parmesan cheese

mixed salad leaves

white bread

garlic cloves

eggs

1 Remove the crust from the bread. Cut the bread into 2.5 cm/1 in cubes.

2 Heat 30 ml/2 tbsp of the oil in a frying pan. Cook the bread for about 5 minutes, tossing the cubes occasionally, until they are golden brown.

3 Meanwhile, bring a pan of water to the boil. Carefully slide in the eggs, one at a time. Gently poach the eggs for 4 minutes until lightly cooked.

4 Divide the salad leaves between two plates. Remove the croûtons from the pan and arrange them over the leaves. Wipe the pan clean with kitchen paper.

5 Heat the remaining oil in the pan, add the garlic and vinegar and cook over high heat for 1 minute. Pour the warm dressing over each salad.

COOK'S TIP
Add a dash of vinegar to the water before poaching the eggs. This helps to keep the whites together. To ensure that a poached egg has a good shape, swirl the water with a spoon, whirlpool-fashion, before sliding in the egg.

6 Place a poached egg on each salad. Scatter with shavings of Parmesan and a little freshly ground black pepper, if liked.

Classic Greek Salad

If you have ever visited Greece you'll know that a Greek salad with a chunk of bread makes a delicious, filling meal.

Serves 4

INGREDIENTS
1 cos lettuce
¹/₂ cucumber, halved lengthways
4 tomatoes
8 spring onions
75 g/3 oz/2¹/₂ cups Greek
  black olives
115 g/4 oz feta cheese
90 ml/6 tbsp white wine vinegar
150 ml/¹/₄ pint/²/₃ cup extra virgin
  olive oil
salt and freshly ground black pepper

tomatoes

cos lettuce

feta
cheese

black
olives

white wine
vinegar

cucumber

spring
onions

COOK'S TIP
The salad can be assembled in advance and chilled, but should only be dressed just before serving. Keep the dressing at room temperature as chilling deadens its flavour.

1 Tear the lettuce leaves into pieces and place them in a large mixing bowl. Slice the cucumber and add to the bowl.

2 Cut the tomatoes into wedges and put them into the bowl.

3 Slice the spring onions. Add them to the bowl with the olives and toss well.

4 Cut the feta cheese into cubes and add to the salad.

5 Put the vinegar, olive oil and seasoning into a small bowl and whisk well. Pour the dressing over the salad and toss to combine. Serve at once, with extra olives and chunks of bread, if liked.

Chicory, Fruit and Nut Salad

Mildly bitter chicory is wonderful with sweet fruit, and is especially delicious when complemented by a creamy curry sauce.

Serves 4

INGREDIENTS
45 ml/3 tbsp mayonnaise
15 ml/1 tbsp Greek yogurt
15 ml/1 tbsp mild curry paste
90 ml/6 tbsp single cream
1/2 iceberg lettuce
2 heads of chicory
50 g/2 oz/1/2 cup cashew nuts
50 g/2 oz/1 1/4 cups flaked coconut
2 red apples
75 g/3 oz/1/2 cup currants

currants

iceberg lettuce

curry paste

mayonnaise

cashew nuts

red apples

single cream

flaked coconut

chicory

1 Mix the mayonnaise, Greek yogurt, curry paste and single cream in a small bowl. Cover and chill until required.

2 Tear the iceberg lettuce into pieces and put into a mixing bowl.

3 Cut the root end off each head of chicory, separate the leaves and add them to the lettuce. Preheat the grill.

4 Toast the cashew nuts for 2 minutes until golden. Tip into a bowl and set aside. Spread out the coconut flakes on a baking sheet. Grill for 1 minute until golden.

5 Quarter the apples and cut out the cores. Slice the apples and add to the lettuce with the coconut, cashew nuts and currants.

COOK'S TIP
Watch the coconut and cashew
nuts very carefully when grilling,
as they brown very fast.

6 Spoon the dressing over the salad,
toss lightly and serve.

Grilled Pepper Salad

Grilled peppers are delicious served hot with a sharp dressing. You can also serve them cold.

Serves 2

INGREDIENTS
1 red pepper
1 green pepper
1 yellow or orange pepper
$^1/_2$ radicchio, separated into leaves
$^1/_2$ frisée, separated into leaves
7.5 ml/1$^1/_2$ tsp white wine vinegar
30 ml/2 tbsp extra virgin olive oil
175 g/6 oz goat's cheese
salt and freshly ground black pepper

frisée

green pepper *red pepper*

yellow pepper *goat's cheese*

radicchio *white wine vinegar*

1 Preheat the grill. Cut all the peppers in half. Cut each half into pieces.

2 Put the pepper pieces on a rack set over a grill pan. Grill for 10 minutes.

3 Meanwhile, divide the radicchio and frisée leaves between two plates. Chill until required.

4 Mix the vinegar and olive oil in a jar. Add salt and pepper to taste, close the jar tightly and shake well.

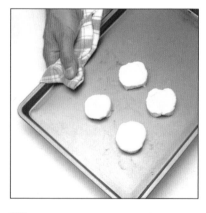

5 Slice the goat's cheese, place on a baking sheet and grill for 1 minute.

6 Arrange the peppers and grilled goat's cheese on the salads. Pour over the dressing and grind a little extra black pepper over each.

COOK'S TIP
Grill the peppers until they just start to blacken around the edges – don't let them burn.

Sesame Noodle Salad with Hot Peanuts

An orient-inspired salad with crunchy vegetables and a light soy dressing. The hot peanuts make a surprisingly successful union with the cold noodles.

Serves 4

INGREDIENTS
350 g/12 oz egg noodles
2 carrots, peeled and cut into fine
    julienne strips
½ cucumber, peeled and cut into
    1 cm/½ in cubes
115 g/4 oz celeriac, peeled and cut
    into fine julienne strips
6 spring onions, finely sliced
8 canned water chestnuts, drained
    and finely sliced
175 g/6 oz beansprouts
1 small fresh green chilli, seeded and
    finely chopped
30 ml/2 tbsp sesame seeds, to serve
115 g/4 oz/1 cup peanuts, to serve

FOR THE DRESSING
15 ml/1 tbsp dark soy sauce
15 ml/1 tbsp light soy sauce
15 ml/1 tbsp runny honey
15 ml/1 tbsp rice wine or dry sherry
15 ml/1 tbsp sesame oil

2 Drain the noodles, refresh in cold water, then drain again.

3 Mix the noodles with all of the prepared vegetables.

1 Preheat the oven to 200°C/400°F/Gas 6. Cook the egg noodles in boiling water, following the instructions on the side of the packet.

celeriac

beansprouts

green chilli

sesame seeds

spring onion

carrot

cucumber

water chestnuts

peanuts

noodles

4 Combine the dressing ingredients in a small bowl, then toss into the noodle and vegetable mixture. Divide the salad between 4 plates.

5 Place the sesame seeds and peanuts on separate baking trays and place in the oven. Take the sesame seeds out after 5 minutes and continue to cook the peanuts for a further 5 minutes until evenly browned.

6 Sprinkle the sesame seeds and peanuts evenly over each portion and serve at once.

Green Lentil and Cabbage Salad

This warm crunchy salad makes a satisfying meal if served with crusty French bread or wholemeal rolls.

Serves 4–6

INGREDIENTS
225 g/8 oz/1 cup puy lentils
1.3 litres/2¼ pints/6 cups cold water
1 garlic clove
1 bay leaf
1 small onion, peeled and studded
  with 2 cloves
15 ml/1 tbsp olive oil
1 red onion, finely sliced
2 garlic cloves, crushed
15 ml/1 tbsp thyme leaves
350 g/12 oz cabbage, finely shredded
finely grated rind and juice of 1 lemon
15 ml/1 tbsp raspberry vinegar
salt and freshly ground black pepper

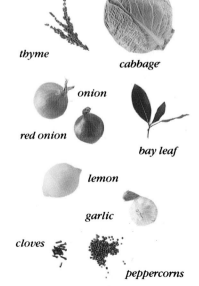

thyme

cabbage

onion

red onion

bay leaf

lemon

garlic

cloves

peppercorns

1 Rinse the lentils in cold water and place in a large pan with the water, peeled garlic clove, bay leaf and clove-studded onion. Bring to the boil and cook for 10 minutes. Reduce the heat, cover the pan and simmer gently for 15–20 minutes. Drain and remove the onion, garlic and bay leaf.

2 Heat the oil in a large pan. Add the red onion, garlic and thyme and cook for 5 minutes until softened.

3 Add the cabbage and cook for 3–5 minutes until just cooked but still crunchy.

4 Stir in the cooked lentils, lemon rind and juice and the raspberry vinegar. Season to taste and serve.

Tabbouleh with Fennel and Pomegranate

A fresh salad originating in the Middle East, with the added crunchiness of fennel and sweet pomegranate seeds. It is perfect for a summer lunch.

Serves 6

INGREDIENTS

225 g/8 oz/1 cup bulgur wheat
2 fennel bulbs
1 small fresh red chilli, seeded and finely chopped
1 celery stick, finely sliced
30 ml/2 tbsp olive oil
finely grated rind and juice of 2 lemons
6–8 spring onions, chopped
90 ml/6 tbsp chopped fresh mint
90 ml/6 tbsp chopped fresh parsley
1 pomegranate, seeds removed
salt and freshly ground black pepper

lemon

red chilli

celery

bulgur wheat

spring onion

fennel

pomegranate

parsley

mint

1 Place the bulgur wheat in a bowl and pour over enough cold water to cover. Leave to stand for 30 minutes.

2 Drain the wheat through a sieve, pressing out any excess water using a spoon.

3 Halve the fennel bulbs and cut into very fine slices.

4 Mix all the remaining ingredients together, including the soaked bulgur wheat and fennel. Season well, cover, and set aside for 30 minutes before serving.

Courgette Puffs with Salad and Balsamic Dressing

This unusual salad consists of deep-fried courgettes, flavoured with mint and served warm on a bed of salad leaves with a balsamic dressing.

Serves 2

INGREDIENTS
450 g/1 lb courgettes
75 g/3 oz/1½ cups fresh white
  breadcrumbs
1 egg
pinch of cayenne pepper
15 ml/1 tbsp chopped fresh mint
oil for deep-frying
15 ml/1 tbsp/3 tbsp balsamic vinegar
45 ml/3 tbsp extra virgin olive oil
200 g/7 oz mixed salad leaves
salt and freshly ground black pepper

courgettes

white breadcrumbs

balsamic vinegar

mixed salad leaves

egg *mint*

1 Top and tail the courgettes. Coarsely grate them and put into a colander. Squeeze out the excess water, then put the courgettes into a bowl.

2 Add the breadcrumbs, egg, cayenne, mint and seasoning. Mix well.

3 Shape the courgette mixture into balls, about the size of walnuts.

4 Heat the oil for deep-frying to 180°C/350°F or until a cube of bread, when added to the oil, browns in 30–40 seconds. Deep-fry the courgette balls in batches for 2–3 minutes. Drain on kitchen paper.

5 Whisk the vinegar and oil together and season well.

6 Put the salad leaves in a bowl and pour over the dressing. Add the courgette puffs and toss lightly together. Serve at once, while the courgette puffs are still crisp.

Vegetable and Satay Salad

Baby new potatoes, tender vegetables and crunchy chick-peas are smothered in a creamy peanut dressing.

Serves 4

INGREDIENTS
450 g/1 lb baby new potatoes
1 small head cauliflower, broken into small florets
225 g/8 oz French beans, trimmed
400 g/14 oz can chick-peas, drained
115 g/4 oz watercress sprigs
115 g/4 oz beansprouts
8 spring onions, sliced
60 ml/4 tbsp crunchy peanut butter
150 ml/¼ pint/⅔ cup hot water
5 ml/1 tsp chilli sauce
10 ml/2 tsp soft brown sugar
5 ml/1 tsp soy sauce
5 ml/1 tsp lime juice

cauliflower

soy sauce

watercress

spring onions

crunchy peanut butter

soft brown sugar

chick-peas

beansprouts

chilli sauce

French beans

lime

baby new potatoes

1 Put the potatoes into a pan and add water to just cover. Bring to the boil and cook for 10–12 minutes or until the potatoes are just tender when pierced with the point of a sharp knife. Drain and refresh under cold running water. Drain once again.

2 Meanwhile, bring another pan of salted water to the boil. Add the cauliflower and cook for 5 minutes, then add the beans and cook for 5 minutes more. Drain both vegetables, refresh under cold water and drain again.

3 Put the cauliflower and beans into a large bowl and add the chick-peas. Halve the potatoes and add. Toss lightly. Mix the watercress, beansprouts and spring onions together. Divide between four plates and pile the vegetables on top.

4 Put the peanut butter into a bowl and stir in the water. Add the chilli sauce, brown sugar, soy sauce and lime juice. Whisk well then drizzle the dressing over the vegetables.

Vegetables à la Greque

This simple side salad is made with winter vegetables, but you can vary it according to the season.

Serves 4

INGREDIENTS

175 ml/6 fl oz/¾ cup white wine
5 ml/1 tsp olive oil
30 ml/2 tbsp lemon juice
2 bay leaves
sprig of fresh thyme
4 juniper berries
450 g/1 lb leeks, trimmed and cut into
 2.5 cm/1 in lengths
1 small cauliflower, broken into
 florets
4 celery sticks, sliced on the diagonal
30 ml/2 tbsp chopped fresh parsley
salt and freshly ground black pepper

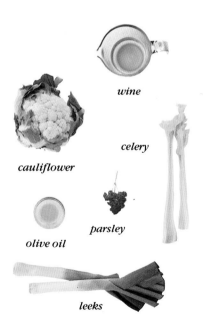

wine

celery

cauliflower

parsley

olive oil

leeks

1 Put the wine, oil, lemon juice, bay leaves, thyme and juniper berries into a large, heavy-based saucepan and bring to the boil. Cover and leave to simmer for 20 minutes.

2 Add the leeks, cauliflower and celery. Simmer very gently for 5–6 minutes or until just tender.

COOK'S TIP
Choose a dry or medium-dry white wine for this dish.

3 Remove the vegetables with a slotted spoon and transfer them to a serving dish. Briskly boil the cooking liquid for 15-20 minutes, or until reduced by half. Strain.

4 Stir the parsley into the liquid and season to taste. Pour over the vegetables and leave to cool. Chill in the refrigerator for at least 1 hour before serving.

Fruit and Fibre Salad

Fresh, fast and filling, this salad makes a great starter, supper or snack.

Serves 4–6

INGREDIENTS
225 g/8 oz red or white cabbage or a
    mixture of both
3 medium carrots
1 pear
1 red-skinned eating apple
200 g/7 oz can green flageolet beans,
    drained
50 g/2 oz/¼ cup chopped dates

FOR THE DRESSING
2.5 ml/½ tsp dry English mustard
10 ml/2 tsp clear honey
30 ml/2 tbsp orange juice
5 ml/1 tsp white wine vinegar
2.5 ml/½ tsp paprika
salt and freshly ground black pepper

carrot

dates

orange

flageolet beans

cabbage

pear

apple

1 Shred the cabbage very finely, discarding any tough stalks.

2 Cut the carrots into very thin strips, about 5 cm/2 in long.

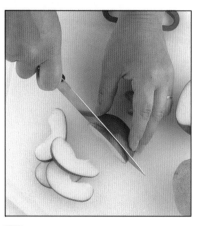

3 Quarter, core and slice the pear and apple, leaving the skin on.

4 Put the fruit and vegetables in a bowl with the beans and dates. Mix well.

5 For the dressing, blend the mustard with the honey until smooth. Add the orange juice, vinegar, paprika and seasoning and mix well.

6 Pour the dressing over the salad and toss to coat. Chill in the refrigerator for 30 minutes before serving.

Cracked Wheat and Mint Salad

Also known as bulgar wheat, burghul or pourgouri, cracked wheat has been partially cooked, so it requires only a short soaking before serving.

Serves 4

INGREDIENTS

250 g/9 oz/1⅔ cups cracked wheat
4 tomatoes
4 small courgettes, thinly sliced
  lengthways
4 spring onions, sliced on the diagonal
8 ready-to-eat dried apricots, chopped
40 g/1½ oz/¼ cup raisins
juice of 1 lemon
30 ml/2 tbsp tomato juice
45 ml/3 tbsp chopped fresh mint
1 garlic clove, crushed
salt and freshly ground black pepper
sprig of fresh mint, to garnish

1 Put the cracked wheat into a large bowl. Add enough cold water to come 2.5 cm/1 in above the level of the wheat. Leave to soak for 30 minutes, then drain well and squeeze out any excess water in a clean dish towel.

courgettes

cracked wheat

tomatoes

lemon

spring onions

2 Meanwhile plunge the tomatoes into boiling water for 1 minute and then into cold water. Slip off the skins. Halve, remove the seeds and cores and roughly chop the flesh.

3 Stir the chopped tomatoes, courgettes, spring onions, apricots, and raisins into the cracked wheat.

4 Put the lemon and tomato juice, mint, garlic clove and seasoning into a small bowl and whisk together with a fork. Pour over the salad and mix well. Chill in the refrigerator for at least 1 hour. Serve garnished with a sprig of mint.

Fresh Spinach and Avocado Salad

Young tender spinach leaves make a change from lettuce and are delicious served with avocado, cherry tomatoes and radishes in a tofu sauce.

Serves 2-3

INGREDIENTS
1 large avocado
juice of 1 lime
225 g/8 oz fresh baby spinach leaves
115 g/4 oz cherry tomatoes
4 spring onions, sliced
¹/₂ cucumber
50 g/2 oz radishes, sliced

FOR THE DRESSING
115 g/4 oz soft silken tofu
45 ml/3 tbsp milk
10 ml/2 tsp mustard
2.5 ml/¹/₂ tsp white wine vinegar
pinch of cayenne
salt and freshly ground black pepper

tofu   spring onions   spinach leaves

cherry tomatoes

avocado

white wine vinegar
mustard

cayenne   lime

cucumber

radishes   milk

1 Cut the avocado in half, remove the stone and strip off the skin. Cut the flesh into slices. Transfer to a plate, drizzle over the lime juice and set aside.

2 Wash and dry the spinach leaves. Put them in a mixing bowl.

COOK'S TIP
Use soft silken tofu rather than the firm block variety. It can be found in most supermarkets in long-life cartons.

3 Cut the larger cherry tomatoes in half and add all the tomatoes to the mixing bowl, with the spring onions. Cut the cucumber into chunks and add to the bowl with the sliced radishes.

4 Make the dressing. Put the tofu, milk, mustard, wine vinegar and cayenne in a food processor or blender. Add salt and pepper to taste. Process for 30 seconds until smooth. Scrape the dressing into a bowl and add a little extra milk if you like a thinner dressing. Sprinkle with a little extra cayenne and garnish with radish roses and herb sprigs, if liked.

New Spring Salad

This chunky salad makes a satisfying meal, use other spring vegetables, if you like.

Serves 4

INGREDIENTS

675 g/1½ lb small new
  potatoes, halved
400 g/14 oz can broad
  beans, drained
115 g/4 oz cherry tomatoes
50 g/2 oz/2½ cups walnut halves
30 ml/2 tbsp white wine vinegar
15 ml/1 tbsp wholegrain mustard
60 ml/4 tbsp olive oil
pinch of sugar
225 g/8 oz young asparagus
  spears, trimmed
6 spring onions, trimmed
salt and freshly ground black pepper
baby spinach leaves, to serve

*asparagus
spears*

*new
potatoes*

*wholegrain
mustard*

broad beans

*cherry
tomatoes*

*spring
onions*

walnut halves

1 Put the potatoes in a pan. Cover with cold water and bring to the boil. Cook for 10 –12 minutes, until tender. Meanwhile, tip the broad beans into a bowl. Cut the tomatoes in half and add them to the bowl with the walnuts.

2 Put the white wine vinegar, mustard, olive oil and sugar into a jar. Add salt and pepper to taste. Close the jar tightly and shake well.

3 Add the asparagus to the potatoes and cook for 3 minutes more. Drain the cooked vegetables well, cool under cold running water and drain again. Thickly slice the potatoes. Cut the spring onions into halves.

4 Add the asparagus, potatoes and spring onions to the bowl containing the broad bean mixture. Pour the dressing over the salad and toss well. Serve on a bed of baby spinach leaves.

Carrot, Raisin and Apricot Coleslaw

A tasty high fibre coleslaw, combining cabbage, carrots and dried fruit in a light yogurt dressing.

Serves 6

INGREDIENTS
350 g/12 oz/3 cups white cabbage, finely shredded
225 g/8 oz/1½ cups carrots, coarsely grated
1 red onion, sliced
3 celery sticks, sliced
175 g/6 oz/1 cup raisins
75 g/3 oz ready-to-eat dried apricots, chopped
120 ml/8 tbsp reduced-calorie mayonnaise
90 ml/6 tbsp low-fat plain yogurt
30 ml/2 tbsp chopped fresh mixed herbs
salt and ground black pepper

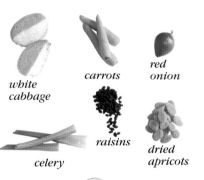

white cabbage
carrots
red onion
celery
raisins
dried apricots

low-fat plain yogurt
reduced-calorie mayonnaise
fresh mixed herbs
salt
black pepper

1 Put the cabbage and carrot in a large bowl.

2 Add the onion, celery, raisins and apricots and mix well.

3 In a small bowl, mix together the mayonnaise, yogurt, herbs and seasoning.

COOK'S TIP
Use other dried fruit such as sultanas and ready-to-eat dried pears or peaches in place of the raisins and apricots.

4 Add the mayonnaise dressing to the bowl and toss the ingredients together to mix. Cover and chill for several hours before serving.

Curried New Potato and Green Bean Salad

Tender new potatoes and green beans tossed together in a subtly flavoured light dressing make this salad ideal for serving with chargrilled vegetables and fresh wholemeal bread.

Serves 6

INGREDIENTS

225 g/8 oz/1½ cups green beans, trimmed and halved
675 g/1½ lb cooked baby new potatoes
2 bunches spring onions, chopped
115 g/4 oz/⅔ cup sultanas
75 g/3 oz ready-to-eat dried pears, finely chopped
90 ml/6 tbsp reduced-calorie mayonnaise
60 ml/4 tbsp low fat plain yogurt
30 ml/2 tbsp Greek yogurt
15 ml/1 tbsp tomato purée
15 ml/1 tbsp curry paste
30 ml/2 tbsp snipped fresh chives
salt and ground black pepper

green beans

baby new potatoes

spring onions

sultanas

dried pears

reduced-calorie mayonnaise

low fat plain yogurt

Greek yogurt

tomato purée

curry paste

chives

black pepper

salt

1 Cook the beans in boiling water for about 5 minutes, until tender. Rinse under cold running water to cool them quickly, drain and set aside.

2 Put the potatoes, beans, spring onions, sultanas and pears in a bowl and mix together.

3 In a small bowl, mix together the mayonnaise, yogurts, tomato purée, curry paste, chives and seasoning.

4 Add the dressing to the bowl and toss the ingredients together to mix. Cover and leave to stand for at least 1 hour before serving.

Cannellini Bean Pureé with Grilled Radicchio

The slightly bitter flavours of the radicchio and chicory make a wonderful marriage with the creamy citrus bean purée.

Serves 4

INGREDIENTS
1 × 400 g/14 oz can cannellini beans
45 ml/3 tbsp low-fat fromage blanc
finely grated zest, rind and juice of 1
    large orange
15 ml/1 tbsp finely chopped fresh
    rosemary
4 heads of chicory
2 medium radicchio
15 ml/1 tbsp walnut oil

chicory

fromage blanc

cannellini beans

rosemary

raddichio

orange

1 Drain the beans, rinse, and drain again. Purée the beans in a blender or food processor with the fromage blanc, orange zest, orange juice and rosemary. Set aside.

2 Cut the chicory in half lengthwise.

3 Cut each radicchio into 8 wedges

4 Lay out the chicory and radicchio on a baking tray and brush with walnut oil. Grill for 2–3 minutes. Serve with the puree and scatter over the orange rind.

COOK'S TIP
Other suitable beans to use are haricot, mung or broad beans.

Fruity Rice Salad

An appetizing and colourful rice salad combining many different flavours, ideal for a packed lunch.

Serves 4–6

INGREDIENTS

225 g/8 oz/1 cup mixed brown and
  wild rice
1 yellow pepper, seeded and diced
1 bunch spring onions, chopped
3 sticks celery, chopped
1 large beefsteak tomato, chopped
2 green-skinned eating
  apples, chopped
175 g/6 oz/¾ cup ready-to-eat dried
  apricots, chopped
115 g/4 oz/⅔ cup raisins
30 ml/2 tbsp unsweetened
  apple juice
30 ml/2 tbsp dry sherry
30 ml/2 tbsp light soy sauce
dash of Tabasco sauce
30 ml/2 tbsp chopped fresh parsley
15 ml/1 tbsp chopped fresh rosemary
salt and ground black pepper

mixed brown and wild rice *yellow pepper* *spring onions*
celery *beefsteak tomato* *eating apples*
dried apricots *raisins* *light soy sauce*
unsweetened apple juice *dry sherry*
Tabasco sauce *fresh parsley* *fresh rosemary*

1 Cook the rice in a large saucepan of lightly salted, boiling water for about 30 minutes (or according to the instructions on the packet) until tender. Rinse the rice under cold running water to cool quickly and drain thoroughly.

2 Place the pepper, spring onions, celery, tomato, apples, apricots, raisins and the cooked rice in a serving bowl and mix well.

3 In a small bowl, mix together the apple juice, sherry, soy sauce, Tabasco sauce, herbs and seasoning.

4 Pour the dressing over the rice mixture and toss the ingredients together to mix. Serve immediately or cover and chill in the fridge before serving.

Bulgur Wheat and Broad Bean Salad

This appetizing salad is ideal served with fresh crusty wholemeal bread and home-made chutney or pickle, and for non-vegetarians it can be served as an accompaniment to grilled lean meat or fish.

Serves 6

INGREDIENTS
350 g/12 oz/2 cups bulgur wheat
225 g/8 oz frozen broad beans
115 g/4 oz/1 cup frozen petit pois
225 g/8 oz cherry tomatoes, halved
1 sweet onion, chopped
1 red pepper, seeded and diced
50 g/2 oz mangetouts, chopped
50 g/2 oz watercress
15 ml/1 tbsp chopped fresh parsley
15 ml/1 tbsp chopped fresh basil
15 ml/1 tbsp chopped fresh thyme
fat-free French dressing
salt and ground black pepper

bulgur wheat *frozen broad beans* *frozen petit pois*

cherry tomatoes *sweet onion* *red pepper*

mangetouts *watercress* *fresh parsley*

fresh basil *fresh thyme* *fat-free French dressing*

salt *black pepper*

1 Soak and cook the bulgur wheat according to the packet instructions. Drain thoroughly and put into a serving bowl.

2 Meanwhile, cook the broad beans and petits pois in boiling water for about 3 minutes, until tender. Drain thoroughly and add to the prepared bulgur wheat.

3 Add the cherry tomatoes, onion, pepper, mangetouts and watercress to the bulgur wheat mixture and mix.

4 Add the herbs, seasoning and enough French dressing to taste, tossing the ingredients together. Serve immediately or cover and chill in the fridge before serving.

COOK'S TIP
Use cooked couscous, boiled brown rice or wholewheat pasta in place of the bulgur wheat.

PIZZAS

Basic Pizza Dough

This simple bread base is rolled out thinly for a traditional pizza recipe.

MAKES
1 × 25–30 cm/10–12 in round pizza base
4 × 13 cm/5 in round pizza bases
1 × 30 × 18 cm/12 × 7 in oblong pizza base

INGREDIENTS
175 g/6 oz/1 ½ cups strong white flour
1.25 ml/¼ tsp salt
5 ml/1 tsp easy-blend dried yeast
120–150 ml/4–5 fl oz/½–⅔ cups lukewarm water
15 ml/1 tbsp olive oil

1 Sift the flour and salt into a large mixing bowl.

2 Stir in the yeast.

3 Make a well in the centre of the dry ingredients. Pour in the water and oil and mix with a spoon to a soft dough.

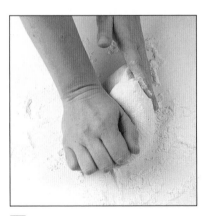
4 Knead the dough on a lightly floured surface for about 10 minutes until smooth and elastic.

5 Place the dough in a greased bowl and cover with clear film. Leave in a warm place to rise for about 1 hour or until the dough has doubled in size.

6 Knock back the dough. Turn on to a lightly floured surface and knead again for 2–3 minutes. Roll out as required and place on a greased baking sheet. Push up the dough to make a rim. The dough is now ready for topping.

Deep-pan Pizza Dough

This recipe produces a deep and spongy base.

MAKES
1 × 25 cm/10 in deep-pan pizza base

INGREDIENTS
225 g/8 oz/2 cups strong white flour
2.5 ml/½ tsp salt
5 ml/1 tsp easy-blend dried yeast
150 ml/¼ pint/⅔ cup lukewarm
   water
30 ml/2 tbsp olive oil

Follow the method for Basic Pizza Dough. When the dough has doubled in size, knock back and knead for 2–3 minutes. Roll out the dough to fit a greased 25 cm/10 in deep-pan pizza tin or sandwich tin. Let the dough prove for 10 minutes, then add the topping. Alternatively, shape and place on a greased baking sheet.

Wholemeal Pizza Dough

INGREDIENTS
75 g/3 oz/¾ cup strong wholemeal
   flour
75 g/3 oz/¾ cup strong white flour
1.25 ml/¼ tsp salt
5 ml/1 tsp easy-blend dried yeast
120–150 ml/4–5 fl oz/½–⅔ cup
   lukewarm water
15 ml/1 tbsp olive oil

Follow the method for Basic Pizza Dough. You may have to add a little extra water to form a soft dough, depending on the absorbency of the flour.

Cornmeal Pizza Dough

INGREDIENTS
175 g/6 oz/1½ cups strong white
   flour
25 g/1 oz/¼ cup cornmeal
1.25 ml/¼ tsp salt
5 ml/1 tsp easy-blend dried yeast
120–150 ml/4–5 fl oz/½–⅔ cup
   lukewarm water
15 ml/1 tbsp olive oil

Follow the method for Basic Pizza Dough.

Scone Pizza Dough

The joy of using a scone mixture is it's quick to make and uses storecupboard ingredients.

MAKES
1 × 25 cm/10 in round pizza base
1 × 30 × 18 cm/12 × 7 in oblong
    pizza base

INGREDIENTS
115 g/4 oz/1 cup self-raising flour
115 g/4 oz/1 cup self-raising
    wholemeal flour
pinch of salt
50 g/2 oz/4 tbsp butter, diced
about 150 ml/¼ pint/⅔ cup milk

1 Mix together the flours and salt in a mixing bowl. Rub in the butter until the mixture resembles fine breadcrumbs.

2 Add the milk and mix with a wooden spoon to a soft dough.

3 Knead lightly on a lightly floured surface until smooth. The dough is now ready to use.

Superquick Pizza Dough

If you're really pressed for time, try a packet pizza dough mix. For best results roll out the dough to a 25–30 cm/10–12 in circle; this is slightly larger than stated on the packet, but it does produce a perfect thin, crispy base. For a deep-pan version use two packets.

ALSO MAKES
4 × 13 cm/5 in round pizza bases
1 × 30 × 18 cm/12 × 7 in oblong
    pizza base

INGREDIENTS
1 × 150 g/5 oz packet pizza base mix
120 ml/4 fl oz/½ cup lukewarm water

1 Empty the contents of the packet into a mixing bowl.

2 Pour in the water and mix with a wooden spoon to a soft dough.

3 Turn the dough on to a lightly floured surface and knead for 5 minutes until smooth and elastic. The dough is now ready to use.

Tomato Sauce

Tomato sauce forms the basis of the topping in many of the recipes. Make sure it is well seasoned and thick before spreading it over the base. It will keep fresh in a covered container in the fridge for up to 3 days.

COVERS
1 × 25–30 cm/10–12 in round pizza base
1 × 30 × 18 cm/12 × 7 in oblong pizza base

INGREDIENTS
15 ml/1 tbsp olive oil
1 onion, finely chopped
1 garlic clove, crushed
1 × 400 g/14 oz can chopped tomatoes
15 ml/1 tbsp tomato purée
15 ml/1 tbsp chopped fresh mixed herbs, such as parsley, thyme, basil and oregano
pinch of sugar
salt and black pepper

1 Heat the oil in a pan, add the onion and garlic and gently fry for about 5 minutes until softened.

2 Add the tomatoes, tomato purée, herbs, sugar and seasoning.

3 Simmer, uncovered, stirring occasionally for 15–20 minutes or until the tomatoes have reduced to a thick pulp. Leave to cool.

Flavoured Oils

For extra flavour brush these over the pizza base before adding the topping. They also form a kind of protective seal that keeps the crust crisp and dry.

CHILLI
INGREDIENTS
150 ml/¼ pint/⅔ cup olive oil
10 ml/2 tsp tomato purée
15 ml/1 tbsp dried red chilli flakes

1 Heat the oil in a pan until very hot but not smoking. Stir in the tomato purée and red chilli flakes. Leave to cool.

2 Pour the chilli oil into a small jar or bottle. Cover and store in the fridge for up to 2 months (the longer you keep it the hotter it gets).

GARLIC
INGREDIENTS
3–4 whole garlic cloves
120 ml/4 fl oz/½ cup olive oil

1 Peel the garlic cloves and put them into a small jar or bottle.

2 Pour in the oil, cover and refrigerate for up to 1 month.

Margherita Pizza

(Tomato, Basil and Mozzarella)
This classic pizza is simple to prepare. The sweet flavour of sun-ripe tomatoes works wonderfully with the basil and mozzarella.

Serves 2–3

INGREDIENTS
1 pizza base, about 25–30 cm/10–12 in
   diameter
30 ml/2 tbsp olive oil
1 quantity Tomato Sauce
150 g/5 oz mozzarella
2 ripe tomatoes, thinly sliced
6–8 fresh basil leaves
30 ml/2 tbsp freshly grated Parmesan
black pepper

basil

mozzarella

Parmesan

olive oil

tomatoes

Tomato Sauce

1 Preheat the oven to 220°C/425°F/ Gas 7. Brush the pizza base with 15 ml/ 1 tbsp of the oil and then spread over the Tomato Sauce.

2 Cut the mozzarella into thin slices.

3 Arrange the sliced mozzarella and tomatoes on top of the pizza base.

4 Roughly tear the basil leaves, add and sprinkle with the Parmesan. Drizzle over the remaining oil and season with black pepper. Bake for 15–20 minutes until crisp and golden. Serve immediately.

Marinara Pizza

(Tomato and Garlic)

The combination of garlic, good quality olive oil and oregano give this pizza an unmistakably Italian flavour.

Serves 2–3

INGREDIENTS
60 ml/4 tbsp olive oil
675 g/1½ lb plum tomatoes, peeled, seeded and chopped
1 pizza base, about 25–30 cm/10–12 in diameter
4 garlic cloves, cut into slivers
15 ml/1 tbsp chopped fresh oregano
salt and black pepper

olive oil

oregano

plum tomatoes

garlic

1 Preheat the oven to 220°C/425°F/ Gas 7. Heat 30 ml/2 tbsp of the oil in a pan. Add the tomatoes and cook, stirring frequently for about 5 minutes until soft.

2 Place the tomatoes in a sieve and leave to drain for about 5 minutes.

3 Transfer the tomatoes to a food processor or blender and purée until smooth.

4 Brush the pizza base with half the remaining oil. Spoon over the tomatoes and sprinkle with garlic and oregano. Drizzle over the remaining oil and season. Bake for 15–20 minutes until crisp and golden. Serve immediately.

Fiorentina Pizza

Spinach is the star ingredient of this pizza. A grating of nutmeg to heighten its flavour gives this pizza its unique character.

Serves 2–3

INGREDIENTS
175 g/6 oz fresh spinach
45 ml/3 tbsp olive oil
1 small red onion, thinly sliced
1 pizza base, about 25–30 cm/10–12 in
   diameter
1 quantity Tomato Sauce
freshly grated nutmeg
150 g/5 oz mozzarella
1 size 3 egg
25 g/1 oz Gruyère, grated

mozzarella

Gruyère

Tomato Sauce

spinach

red onion

nutmeg

egg

1 Preheat the oven to 220°C/425°F/ Gas 7. Remove the stalks from the spinach and wash the leaves in plenty of cold water. Drain well and pat dry with kitchen paper.

2 Heat 15 ml/1 tbsp of the oil and fry the onion until soft. Add the spinach and continue to fry until just wilted. Drain off any excess liquid.

3 Brush the pizza base with half the remaining oil. Spread over the Tomato Sauce, then top with the spinach mixture. Grate over some nutmeg.

4 Thinly slice the mozzarella and arrange over the spinach. Drizzle over the remaining oil. Bake for 10 minutes, then remove from the oven.

5 Make a small well in the centre and drop the egg into the hole.

6 Sprinkle over the Gruyère and return to the oven for a further 5–10 minutes until crisp and golden. Serve immediately.

Chilli, Tomato and Spinach Pizza

This richly flavoured topping with a hint of spice makes a colourful and satisfying pizza.

Serves 3

INGREDIENTS
1–2 fresh red chillies
45 ml/3 tbsp tomato oil (from jar of sun-dried tomatoes)
1 onion, chopped
2 garlic cloves, chopped
50 g/2 oz (drained weight) sun-dried tomatoes in oil
400 g/14 oz can chopped tomatoes
15 ml/1 tbsp tomato purée
175 g/6 oz fresh spinach
1 pizza base, 25–30 cm/10–12 in diameter
75 g/3 oz smoked Bavarian cheese, grated
75 g/3 oz mature Cheddar, grated
salt and black pepper

smoked Bavarian cheese

chopped tomatoes

mature Cheddar

sun-dried tomatoes

onion

garlic

spinach

red chillies

tomato oil

1 Seed and finely chop the chillies.

2 Heat 30 ml/2 tbsp of the tomato oil in a pan, add the onion, garlic and chillies and gently fry for about 5 minutes until they are soft.

3 Roughly chop the sun-dried tomatoes. Add to the pan with the chopped tomatoes, tomato purée and seasoning. Simmer uncovered, stirring occasionally, for 15 minutes.

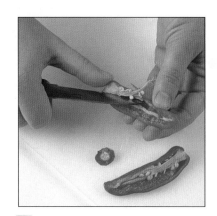

4 Remove the stalks from the spinach and wash the leaves in plenty of cold water. Drain well and pat dry with kitchen paper. Roughly chop the spinach.

5 Stir the spinach into the sauce. Cook, stirring, for a further 5–10 minutes until the spinach has wilted and no excess moisture remains. Leave to cool.

6 Meanwhile, preheat the oven to 220°C/425°F/Gas 7. Brush the pizza base with the remaining tomato oil, then spoon over the sauce. Sprinkle over the cheeses and bake for 15–20 minutes until crisp and golden. Serve immediately.

Three-cheese Pizza

You can use any combination of cheese you like. Edam and Cheddar both have good flavours and melting properties.

Serves 3–4

INGREDIENTS
45 ml/3 tbsp olive oil
3 medium onions, sliced
1 pizza base, 25–30 cm/10–12 in
    diameter
4 small tomatoes, peeled, seeded and
    cut into thin wedges
30 ml/2 tbsp chopped fresh basil
115 g/4 oz Dolcelatte
150 g/5 oz mozzarella
115 g/4 oz Red Leicester
black pepper
fresh basil leaves, to garnish

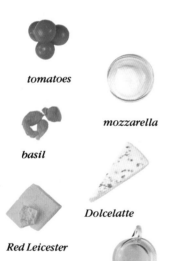

tomatoes

mozzarella

basil

Dolcelatte

Red Leicester

olive oil

onions

1 Preheat the oven to 220°C/425°F/ Gas 7. Heat 30 ml/2 tbsp of the oil in a frying pan, add the onions and gently fry for about 10 minutes, stirring occasionally. Leave to cool.

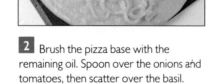

2 Brush the pizza base with the remaining oil. Spoon over the onions and tomatoes, then scatter over the basil.

3 Thinly slice the cheeses and arrange over the tomatoes and onions.

4 Grind over plenty of black pepper and bake for 15–20 minutes until crisp and golden. Garnish with basil leaves and serve immediately.

Tomato, Fennel and Parmesan Pizza

This pizza relies on the winning combination of tomatoes, fennel and Parmesan. The fennel adds both a crisp texture and a distinctive flavour.

Serves 2–3

INGREDIENTS
1 fennel bulb
45 ml/3 tbsp Garlic Oil
1 pizza base, 25–30 cm/10–12 in
  diameter
1 quantity Tomato Sauce
30 ml/2 tbsp chopped fresh flat-leaf
  parsley
50 g/2 oz mozzarella, grated
50 g/2 oz Parmesan, grated
salt and black pepper

flat-leaf parsley

mozzarella

Parmesan

Tomato Sauce

fennel bulb

Garlic Oil

1 Preheat the oven to 220°C/425°F/Gas 7. Trim and quarter the fennel lengthways. Remove the core and slice thinly.

2 Heat 30 ml/2 tbsp of the Garlic Oil in a frying pan and sauté the fennel for 4–5 minutes until just tender. Season.

3 Brush the pizza base with the remaining Garlic Oil and spread over the Tomato Sauce. Spoon the fennel on top and scatter over the flat-leaf parsley.

4 Mix together the mozzarella and Parmesan and sprinkle over. Bake for 15–20 minutes until crisp and golden. Serve immediately.

Spring Vegetable and Pine Nut Pizza

This colourful pizza is well worth the time it takes to prepare. You can vary the ingredients according to availability.

Serves 2–3

INGREDIENTS
1 pizza base, 25–30 cm/10–12 in diameter
45 ml/3 tbsp Garlic Oil
1 quantity Tomato Sauce
4 spring onions
2 courgettes
1 leek
115 g/4 oz asparagus tips
15 ml/1 tbsp chopped fresh oregano
30 ml/2 tbsp pine nuts
50 g/2 oz mozzarella, grated
30 ml/2 tbsp freshly grated Parmesan
black pepper

Parmesan

mozzarella

Tomato Sauce

spring onions

leek

courgette

asparagus

pine nuts

1 Preheat the oven to 220°C/425°F/Gas 7. Brush the pizza base with 15 ml/1 tbsp of the Garlic Oil, then spread over the Tomato Sauce.

2 Slice the spring onions, courgettes, leek and asparagus.

3 Heat half the remaining Garlic Oil in a frying pan and stir-fry the vegetables for 3–5 minutes.

4 Arrange the vegetables over the Tomato Sauce.

5 Sprinkle the oregano and pine nuts over the pizza.

6 Mix together the mozzarella and Parmesan and sprinkle over. Drizzle over the remaining Garlic Oil and season with black pepper. Bake for 15–20 minutes until crisp and golden. Serve immediately.

Roasted Vegetable and Goat's Cheese Pizza

Here is a pizza which incorporates the smoky flavours of oven-roasted vegetables with the distinctive taste of goat's cheese.

Serves 3

INGREDIENTS
1 aubergine, cut into thick chunks
2 small courgettes, sliced lengthways
1 red pepper, quartered and seeded
1 yellow pepper, quartered and seeded
1 small red onion, cut into wedges
90 ml/6 tbsp Garlic Oil
1 pizza base, 25–30 cm/10–12 in diameter
1 × 400 g/14 oz can chopped tomatoes, drained well
1 × 115 g/4 oz goat's cheese (with rind)
15 ml/1 tbsp chopped fresh thyme
black pepper
green olive tapenade, to serve

courgettes

aubergine

goat's cheese

Garlic Oil

tapenade

chopped tomatoes

peppers

1 Preheat the oven to 220°C/425°F/ Gas 7. Place the aubergine, courgettes, peppers and onion in a large roasting tin. Brush with 60 ml/4 tbsp of the Garlic Oil. Roast for about 30 minutes until lightly charred, turning the peppers half-way through cooking. Remove from the oven and set aside.

2 When the peppers are cool enough to handle, peel off the skins and cut the flesh into thick strips.

3 Brush the pizza base with half the remaining Garlic Oil and spread over the drained tomatoes.

4 Arrange the roasted vegetables on top of the pizza.

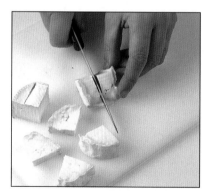

5 Cube the goat's cheese and arrange on top. Scatter over the thyme.

COOK'S TIP

If you place the roasted peppers in a plastic bag while they cool, peeling off the skins becomes easier.

6 Drizzle over the remaining Garlic Oil and season with black pepper. Bake for 15–20 minutes until crisp and golden. Spoon the tapenade over to serve.

New Potato, Rosemary and Garlic Pizza

New potatoes, smoked mozzarella, rosemary and garlic make the flavour of this pizza unique. For a delicious variation, use sage instead of rosemary.

Serves 2–3

INGREDIENTS
350 g/12 oz new potatoes
45 ml/3 tbsp olive oil
2 garlic cloves, crushed
1 pizza base, 25–30 cm/10–12 in
   diameter
1 red onion, thinly sliced
150 g/5 oz smoked mozzarella, grated
10 ml/2 tsp chopped fresh rosemary
salt and black pepper
30 ml/2 tbsp freshly grated Parmesan,
   to garnish

olive oil

Parmesan

smoked mozzarella

new potatoes

rosemary

red onion

garlic

1 Preheat the oven to 200°C/425°F/ Gas 7. Cook the potatoes in boiling salted water for 5 minutes. Drain well. When cool, peel and slice thinly.

2 Heat 30 ml/2 tbsp of the oil in a frying pan. Add the sliced potatoes and garlic and fry for 5–8 minutes until tender.

3 Brush the pizza base with the remaining oil. Scatter over the onion, then arrange the potatoes on top.

4 Sprinkle over the mozzarella and rosemary. Grind over plenty of black pepper and bake for 15–20 minutes until crisp and golden. Remove from the oven and sprinkle over the Parmesan to serve.

Fresh Herb Pizza

Cut this pizza into thin wedges and serve as part of a mixed antipasti.

Serves 8

INGREDIENTS
115 g/4 oz mixed fresh herbs, such as
    parsley, basil and oregano
3 garlic cloves, crushed
120 ml/4 fl oz/½ cup double cream
1 pizza base, 25–30 cm/10–12 in
    diameter
15 ml/1 tbsp Garlic Oil
115 g/4 oz Pecorino, grated
salt and black pepper

double cream

Garlic Oil

Pecorino

basil

parsley

garlic

2 In a bowl mix together the herbs, garlic, cream and seasoning.

3 Brush the pizza base with the Garlic Oil, then spread over the herb mixture.

4 Sprinkle over the Pecorino. Bake for 15–20 minutes until crisp and golden and the topping is still moist. Cut into thin wedges and serve immediately.

Tomato, Pesto and Black Olive Pizza

These individual pizzas take very little time to put together. Marinating the tomatoes gives them extra flavour.

Serves 4

INGREDIENTS
2 plum tomatoes
1 garlic clove, crushed
60 ml/4 tbsp olive oil
1 quantity Basic or Superquick Pizza
  Dough
30 ml/2 tbsp red pesto
150 g/5 oz mozzarella, thinly sliced
4 pitted black olives, chopped
15 ml/1 tbsp chopped fresh oregano
salt and black pepper
oregano leaves, to garnish

red pesto

mozzarella

oregano

plum tomatoes

black olives

1. Slice the tomatoes thinly crossways, then cut each slice in half. Place the tomatoes in a shallow dish with the garlic. Drizzle over 30 ml/2 tbsp of the oil and season. Leave to marinate for 15 minutes.

2. Meanwhile, preheat the oven to 220°C/425°F/Gas 7. Divide the dough into four pieces and roll out each one on a lightly floured surface to a 13 cm/5 in circle. Place well apart on two greased baking sheets, then push up the dough edges to make a rim. Brush the pizza bases with half the remaining oil and spread over the pesto.

3. Drain the tomatoes, then arrange a fan of alternate slices of tomatoes and mozzarella on each base.

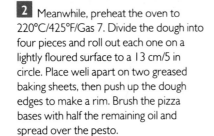

4. Sprinkle over the olives and oregano. Drizzle over the remaining oil on top and bake for 15–20 minutes until crisp and golden. Garnish with the oregano leaves and serve immediately.

Red Onion, Gorgonzola and Sage Pizza

This topping combines the richness of Gorgonzola with the earthy flavours of sage and sweet red onions.

Serves 4

INGREDIENTS
1 quantity Basic or Superquick Pizza
  Dough
30 ml/2 tbsp Garlic Oil
2 small red onions
150 g/5 oz Gorgonzola *piccante*
2 garlic cloves
10 ml/2 tsp chopped fresh sage
black pepper

sage

garlic

Gorgonzola

Garlic Oil

red onions

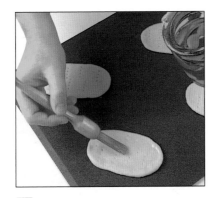

1 Preheat the oven to 220°C/425°F/ Gas 7. Divide the dough into eight pieces and roll out each one on a lightly floured surface to a small oval about 5 mm/¼ in thick. Place well apart on two greased baking sheets and prick with a fork. Brush the bases well with 15 ml/1 tbsp of the Garlic Oil.

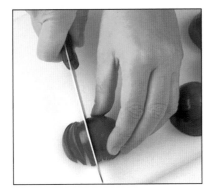

2 Halve, then slice the onions into thin wedges. Scatter over the pizza bases.

3 Remove the rind from the Gorgonzola. Cut the cheese into small cubes, then scatter it over the onions.

4 Cut the garlic lengthways into thin strips and sprinkle over, along with the sage. Drizzle the remaining oil on top and grind over plenty of black pepper. Bake for 10–15 minutes until crisp and golden. Serve immediately.

Mini Pizzas

For a quick supper dish try these delicious little pizzas made with fresh and sun-dried tomatoes.

Makes 4

INGREDIENTS
1 × 150 g/5 oz packet pizza mix
8 halves sun-dried tomatoes in olive
  oil, drained
50 g/2 oz/½ cup black olives, pitted
225 g/8 oz ripe tomatoes, sliced
50 g/2 oz/¼ cup goat's cheese
30 ml/2 tbsp fresh basil leaves

basil

tomatoes

*sun-dried
tomatoes*

black olives

goat's cheese

1 Preheat the oven to 200°C/400°F/ Gas 6. Make up the pizza base following the instructions on the side of the packet.

2 Divide the dough into 4 and roll each piece out to a 13 cm/5 in disc. Place on a lightly oiled baking sheet.

3 Place the sun-dried tomatoes and olives in a blender or food processor and blend until smooth. Spread the mixture evenly over the pizza bases.

4 Top with the tomato slices and crumble over the goat's cheese. Bake for 10–15 minutes. Sprinkle with the fresh basil and serve.

COOK'S TIP

You could use loose sun-dried tomatoes (preserved without oil) instead. Leave in a bowl of warm water for 10–15 minutes to soften, drain and blend with the olives.

Quattro Formaggi Pizzas

Rich and tasty, these individual pizzas are very quick to assemble and the aroma of melting cheese is irresistible.

Serves 4

INGREDIENTS
1 quantity Basic or Superquick Pizza
   Dough
15 ml/1 tbsp Garlic Oil
½ small red onion, very thinly sliced
50 g/2 oz Dolcelatte
50 g/2 oz mozzarella
50 g/2 oz Gruyère, grated
30 ml/2 tbsp freshly grated Parmesan
15 ml/1 tbsp chopped fresh thyme
black pepper

Garlic Oil

red onion

mozzarella

Parmesan

Gruyère

Dolcelatte

thyme

1 Preheat the oven to 220°C/425°F/ Gas 7. Divide the dough into four pieces and roll out each one on a lightly floured surface into a 13 cm/5 in circle. Place well apart on two greased baking sheets, then push up the dough edges to make a thin rim. Brush with Garlic Oil and top with the red onion.

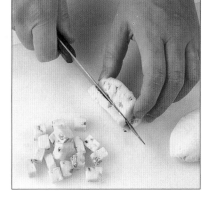

2 Cut the Dolcelatte and mozzarella into cubes and scatter over the bases.

3 Mix together the Gruyère, Parmesan and thyme and sprinkle over.

4 Grind over plenty of black pepper. Bake for 15–20 minutes until crisp and golden and the cheese is bubbling. Serve immediately.

Wild Mushroom Pizzettes

Serve these extravagant pizzas as a starter. Fresh wild mushrooms add a distinctive flavour to the topping but a mixture of cultivated mushrooms such as shiitake, oyster and chestnut mushrooms would do just as well.

Serves 4

INGREDIENTS
45 ml/3 tbsp olive oil
350 g/12 oz fresh wild mushrooms, washed and sliced
2 shallots, chopped
2 garlic cloves, finely chopped
30 ml/2 tbsp chopped fresh mixed thyme and flat-leaf parsley
1 quantity Basic or Superquick Pizza Dough
40 g/1½ oz Gruyère, grated
30 ml/2 tbsp freshly grated Parmesan
salt and black pepper

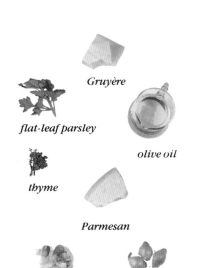

Gruyère

flat-leaf parsley

olive oil

thyme

Parmesan

garlic   *shallots*

wild mushrooms

1 Preheat the oven to 220°C/425°F/Gas 7. Heat 30 ml/2 tbsp of the oil in a frying pan. Add the mushrooms, shallots and garlic and fry over a moderate heat until all the juices have evaporated.

2 Stir in half the herbs and seasoning, then set aside to cool.

3 Divide the dough into four pieces and roll out each one on a lightly floured surface to a 13 cm/5 in circle. Place well apart on two greased baking sheets, then push up the dough edges to form a thin rim. Brush the pizza bases with the remaining oil and top with the wild mushroom mixture.

4 Mix together the Gruyère and Parmesan, then sprinkle over. Bake for 15–20 minutes until crisp and golden. Remove from the oven and scatter over the remaining herbs to serve.

Feta, Roasted Garlic and Oregano Pizzas

This is a pizza for garlic lovers! Mash down the cloves as you eat – they should be soft and will have lost their pungency.

Serves 4

INGREDIENTS
1 medium garlic bulb, unpeeled
45 ml/3 tbsp olive oil
1 medium red pepper, quartered and seeded
1 medium yellow pepper, quartered and seeded
2 plum tomatoes
1 quantity Basic or Superquick Pizza Dough
175 g/6 oz feta, crumbled
black pepper
15–30 ml/1–2 tbsp chopped fresh oregano, to garnish

oregano

feta

plum tomatoes

olive oil

peppers

garlic bulb

1 Preheat the oven to 220°C/425°F/Gas 7. Break the garlic into cloves, discarding the outer papery layers. Toss in 15 ml/1 tbsp of the oil.

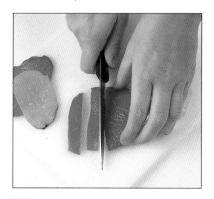

2 Place the peppers skin-side up on a baking sheet and grill until the skins are evenly charred. Place in a covered bowl for 10 minutes, then peel off the skins. Cut the flesh into strips.

3 Put the tomatoes in a bowl and pour over boiling water. Leave for 30 seconds, then plunge into cold water. Peel, seed and roughly chop the flesh. Divide the dough into four pieces and roll out each one on a lightly floured surface to a 13 cm/5 in circle.

4 Place the dough circles well apart on two greased baking sheets, then push up the dough edges to form a thin rim. Brush with half the remaining oil and scatter over the chopped tomatoes. Top with the peppers, crumbled feta and garlic cloves. Drizzle over the remaining oil and season with black pepper. Bake for 15–20 minutes until crisp and golden. Garnish with chopped oregano and serve immediately.

French Bread Pizzas with Artichokes

Crunchy French bread makes an ideal base for these quick pizzas.

Serves 4

INGREDIENTS
15 ml/1 tbsp sunflower oil
1 onion, chopped
1 green pepper, seeded and
  chopped
200 g/7 oz can chopped tomatoes
15 ml/1 tbsp tomato purée
$^1\!/_2$ French stick
400 g/14 oz can artichoke
  hearts, drained
115 g/4 oz mozzarella cheese, sliced
15 ml/1 tbsp poppy seeds
salt and freshly ground black pepper

mozzarella cheese

French stick

tomato purée

chopped tomatoes

green pepper

poppy seeds

onion

artichoke hearts

1 Heat the oil in a frying pan. Add the chopped onion and pepper and cook for 4 minutes until just softened.

2 Stir in the chopped tomatoes and tomato purée. Cook for 4 minutes. Remove from the heat and add salt and pepper to taste.

3 Cut the piece of French stick in half lengthways. Cut each half in four to give eight pieces in all.

4 Spoon a little of the pepper and tomato mixture over each piece of bread. Preheat the grill.

5 Slice the artichoke hearts. Arrange them on top of the pepper and tomato mixture. Cover with the mozzarella slices and sprinkle with the poppy seeds.

6 Arrange the French bread pizzas on a rack over a grill pan and grill for 6–8 minutes until the cheese melts and is beginning to brown. Serve at once.

Aubergine, Shallot and Sun-dried Tomato Calzone

Aubergines, shallots and sun-dried tomatoes make an unusual filling for calzone. Add more or less red chilli flakes, depending on personal taste.

Serves 2

INGREDIENTS
45 ml/3 tbsp olive oil
3 shallots, chopped
4 baby aubergines
1 garlic clove, chopped
50 g/2 oz (drained weight) sun-dried tomatoes in oil, chopped
1.25 ml/¼ tsp dried red chilli flakes
10 ml/2 tsp chopped fresh thyme
1 quantity Basic or Superquick Pizza Dough
75 g/3 oz mozzarella, cubed
salt and black pepper
15–30 ml/1–2 tbsp freshly grated Parmesan, to serve

Parmesan

mozzarella

thyme

olive oil

baby aubergines

shallots

red chilli flakes

1 Preheat the oven to 220°C/425°F/ Gas 7. Trim the aubergines, then cut into small cubes.

2 Cook the shallots until soft in a frying pan. Add the aubergines, garlic, sun-dried tomatoes, red chilli flakes, thyme and seasoning. Cook for 4–5 minutes, stirring frequently, until the aubergine is beginning to soften.

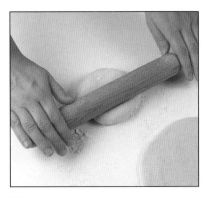

3 Divide the dough in half and roll out each piece on a lightly floured surface to an 18 cm/7 in circle.

4 Spread the aubergine mixture over half of each circle, leaving a 2.5 cm/1 in border, then scatter over the mozzarella.

5 Dampen the edges with water, then fold over the other half of dough to enclose the filling. Press the edges firmly together to seal. Place on two greased baking sheets.

6 Brush with half the remaining oil and make a small hole in the top of each to allow the steam to escape. Bake for 15–20 minutes until golden. Remove from the oven and brush with the remaining oil. Sprinkle over the Parmesan and serve immediately.

Spinach and Ricotta Panzerotti

These make great party food to serve with drinks or as tasty appetizers for a crowd.

Makes 20–24

INGREDIENTS
115 g/4 oz frozen chopped spinach, defrosted and squeezed dry
50 g/2 oz ricotta
50 g/2 oz freshly grated Parmesan
generous pinch freshly grated nutmeg
2 quantities Basic or Superquick Pizza Dough
1 egg white, lightly beaten
vegetable oil for deep-frying
salt and black pepper

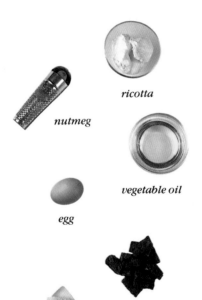

ricotta

nutmeg

vegetable oil

egg

frozen spinach

Parmesan

1 Place the spinach, ricotta, Parmesan, nutmeg and seasoning in a bowl and beat until smooth.

2 Roll out the dough on a lightly floured surface to about 3 mm/⅛ in thick. Using a 7.5 cm/3 in plain round cutter stamp out 20–24 circles.

3 Spread a teaspoon of spinach mixture over one half of each circle.

4 Brush the edges of the dough with a little egg white.

5 Fold the dough over the filling and press the edges firmly together to seal.

COOK'S TIP
Do serve these as soon as possible after frying, they will become much less appetizing if left to cool.

6 Heat the oil in a large heavy-based pan or deep-fat fryer to 180°C/350°F. Deep-fry the panzerotti a few at a time for 2–3 minutes until golden. Drain on kitchen paper and serve immediately.

DESSERTS

Fresh Fig, Apple and Date Salad

Sweet Mediterranean figs and dates combine especially well with crisp dessert apples. A hint of almond serves to unite the flavours.

Serves 4

INGREDIENTS
6 large apples
juice of ½ lemon
175 g/6 oz fresh dates
25 g/1 oz white marzipan
5 ml/1 tsp orange flower water
60 ml/4 tbsp natural yogurt
4 fresh figs
4 shelled almonds, toasted

apples

figs

almonds

dates

1 Core the apples. Slice thinly, then cut into fine matchsticks. Moisten with lemon juice to keep them white.

2 Remove the stones from the dates and cut the flesh into thin strips. Combine them with the apple slices.

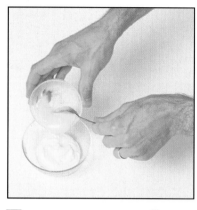

3 Soften the marzipan with orange flower water and combine with the yogurt. Mix well.

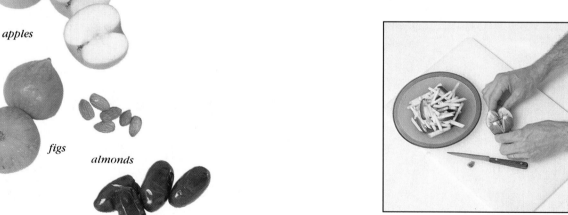

4 Pile the apples and dates in the centre of 4 plates. Remove the stem from each of the figs and divide the fruit into quarters without cutting right through the base. Squeeze the base with the thumb and forefinger of each hand to open up the fruit.

5 Place a fig in the centre of the salad, spoon in the yogurt filling and decorate with a toasted almond.

Strawberries with Raspberry and Passion Fruit Sauce

Fragrant strawberries release their finest flavour when moistened with a sauce of fresh raspberries and scented passion fruit.

Serves 4

INGREDIENTS
350 g/12 oz raspberries
45 ml/3 tbsp caster sugar
1 passion fruit
700 g/1½ lb small strawberries
8 plain finger biscuits, to serve

biscuits

passion fruit

raspberries

strawberries

1 Place the raspberries and sugar into a stain-resistant saucepan and soften over a gentle heat to release the juices. Simmer for 5 minutes. Allow to cool.

2 Halve the passion fruit and scoop out the seeds and juice.

3 Turn the raspberries into a food processor or blender, add the passion fruit and blend smoothly.

COOK'S TIP
Berry fruits offer their best flavour when served at room temperature.

4 Pass the fruit sauce through a fine nylon sieve to remove the seeds.

5 Fold the strawberries into the sauce, then spoon into four stemmed glasses. Serve with the biscuits.

Mixed Melon Salad with Wild Strawberries

Ice-cold melon is a delicious way to end a meal. Here several varieties are combined with strongly flavoured wild or woodland strawberries. If wild berries are not available, use ordinary strawberries or raspberries.

Serves 4

INGREDIENTS
1 cantaloupe or charentais melon
1 galia melon
900 g/2 lb water melon
175 g/6 oz wild strawberries
4 sprigs fresh mint

wild strawberries

galia melon

mint

cantaloupe melon

water melon

COOK'S TIP
Ripe melons should give slightly when pressed at the base, and should give off a fruity, melony scent. Buy carefully if you plan to use the fruit on the day.

1 Halve the cantaloupe, galia and water melons.

2 Remove the seeds from the cantaloupe and galia with a spoon.

3 With a melon scoop, take out as many balls as you can from all 3 melons. Combine in a large bowl and refrigerate.

4 Add the wild strawberries and turn out into 4 stemmed glass dishes.

5 Decorate with sprigs of mint.

324

Winter Fruit Salad

A colourful, refreshing and nutritious fruit salad, which is ideal served with reduced-fat Greek-style yogurt or cream.

Serves 6

INGREDIENTS

225 g/8 oz can pineapple cubes in fruit juice
200 ml/7 fl oz/scant 1 cup freshly squeezed orange juice
200 ml/7 fl oz/scant 1 cup unsweetened apple juice
30 ml/2 tbsp orange or apple liqueur
30 ml/2 tbsp clear honey (optional)
2 oranges, peeled
2 green-skinned eating apples, chopped
2 pears, chopped
4 plums, stoned and chopped
12 fresh dates, stoned and chopped
115 g/4 oz/½ cup ready-to-eat dried apricots
fresh mint sprigs, to decorate

pineapple cubes in fruit juice

freshly squeezed orange juice

unsweetened apple juice

orange or apple liqueur

clear honey

oranges

green-skinned eating apples

pears

plums

fresh dates

dried apricots

1 Drain the pineapple, reserving the juice. Put the pineapple juice, orange juice, apple juice, liqueur and honey, if using, in a large serving bowl and stir.

2 Segment the oranges, catching any juice in the bowl, and put the orange segments and pineapple in the fruit juice mixture.

3 Add the apples and pears to the bowl.

COOK'S TIP
Use other unsweetened fruit juices such as pink grapefruit and pineapple juice in place of the orange and apple juice.

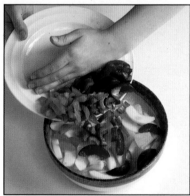

4 Stir in the plums, dates and apricots, cover and chill for several hours. Decorate with fresh mint sprigs to serve.

Apricot and Banana Compote

This compote is delicious served on its own or with low-fat custard or ice cream. Served for breakfast, it makes a tasty start to the day.

Serves 4

INGREDIENTS
225 g/8 oz/1 cup ready-to-eat
  dried apricots
300 ml/½ pint/1¼ cups
  unsweetened orange juice
150 ml/¼ pint/⅔ cup unsweetened
  apple juice
5 ml/1 tsp ground ginger
3 medium bananas, sliced
25 g/1 oz/¼ cup toasted
  flaked almonds

dried apricots

unsweetened orange juice

unsweetened apple juice

ground ginger

bananas

toasted flaked almonds

1 Put the apricots in a saucepan with the fruit juices and ginger and stir. Cover, bring to the boil and simmer gently for 10 minutes, stirring occasionally.

2 Set aside to cool, leaving the lid on. Once cool, stir in the sliced bananas.

3 Spoon the fruit and juices into a serving dish.

4 Serve immediately, or cover and chill for several hours before serving. Sprinkle with flaked almonds just before serving.

COOK'S TIP
Use other combinations of dried and fresh fruit such as prunes or figs and apples or peaches.

Apples and Raspberries in Rose Pouchong Syrup

Inspiration for this dessert stems from the fact that the apple and the raspberry belong to the rose family. The subtle flavours are shared here in an infusion of rose-scented tea.

Serves 4

INGREDIENTS
5 ml/1 tsp rose pouchong tea
5 ml/1 tsp rose water (optional)
50 g/2 oz/¼ cup sugar
5 ml/1 tsp lemon juice
5 dessert apples
175 g/6 oz/1½ cups fresh raspberries

tea

apples

sugar

raspberries

COOK'S TIP
If fresh raspberries are out of season, use the same weight of frozen fruit or a 400 g/14 oz can of well drained fruit.

1 Warm a large tea pot. Add the rose pouchong tea and 900 ml/1 ½ pints/3¾ cups of boiling water together with the rose water, if using. Allow to stand and infuse for 4 minutes.

2 Measure the sugar and lemon juice into a stainless steel saucepan. Strain in the tea and stir to dissolve the sugar.

3 Peel and core the apples, then cut into quarters.

4 Poach the apples in the syrup for about 5 minutes.

5 Transfer the apples and syrup to a large metal tray and leave to cool to room temperature.

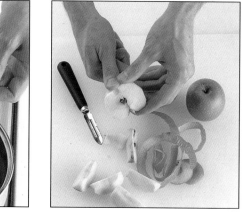

6 Pour the cooled apples and syrup into a bowl, add the raspberries and mix to combine. Spoon into individual dishes or bowls and serve warm.

Watermelon Sorbet

A slice of this refreshing sorbet is the perfect way to cool down on a hot sunny day.

Serves 4–6

INGREDIENTS
½ small watermelon, weighing about
    1 kg/2¼ lb
75 g/3 oz/½ cup caster sugar
60 ml/4 tbsp cranberry juice or water
30 ml/2 tbsp lemon juice
sprigs of fresh mint, to decorate

cranberry juice

sugar

watermelon   *lemon juice*

1 Cut the watermelon into 4–6 equal-sized wedges (depending on the number of servings you require). Scoop out the pink flesh, discarding the seeds but reserving the shell.

2 Line a freezer-proof bowl, about the same size as the melon, with clear film. Arrange the melon skins in the bowl to re-form the shell, fitting them together snugly so that there are no gaps. Put in the freezer.

3 Put the sugar and cranberry juice or water in a saucepan and stir over a low heat until the sugar dissolves. Bring to the boil and simmer for 5 minutes. Leave the sugar syrup to cool.

4 Put the melon flesh and lemon juice in a blender and process to a smooth purée. Stir in the sugar syrup and pour into a freezer-proof container. Freeze for 3–3½ hours, or until slushy.

5 Tip the sorbet into a chilled bowl and whisk to break up the ice crystals. Return to the freezer for another 30 minutes, whisk again, then tip into the melon shell and freeze until solid.

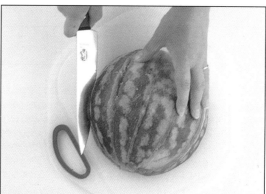

6 Remove from the freezer and leave to defrost at room temperature for 15 minutes. Take the melon out of the bowl and cut into wedges with a warmed sharp knife. Serve with sprigs of fresh mint.

COOK'S TIP
If preferred, this pretty pink sorbet can be served scooped into balls. Do this before the mixture is completely frozen and re-freeze the balls on a baking sheet, ready to serve.

Brown Bread Ice Cream

This dish sounds homely but tastes heavenly.
Toasted wholemeal breadcrumbs have a
wonderful nutty flavour, especially when
accentuated with hazelnuts.

Serves 6

INGREDIENTS
50 g/2 oz/½ cup roasted and
    chopped hazelnuts, ground
75 g/3 oz/1½ cups fresh
    wholemeal breadcrumbs
50 g/2 oz/4 tbsp demerara sugar
3 egg whites
115 g/4 oz/½ cup caster sugar
300 ml/½ pint/1¼ cups double cream
few drops of vanilla essence
fresh mint sprigs, to decorate

FOR THE SAUCE
225 g/8 oz blackcurrants
75 g/3 oz/6 tbsp caster sugar
15 ml/1 tbsp crème de cassis

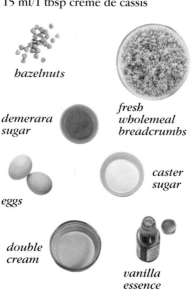

hazelnuts

demerara sugar

fresh wholemeal breadcrumbs

eggs

caster sugar

double cream

vanilla essence

blackcurrants

crème de cassis

1 Preheat the grill. Combine the hazelnuts and breadcrumbs on a baking sheet, then sprinkle over the demerara sugar. Grill, stirring frequently, until the mixture is crisp and evenly browned. Leave to cool.

2 Whisk the egg whites in a grease-free bowl until stiff, then gradually whisk in the caster sugar until thick and glossy. Whip the cream until it forms soft peaks and fold into the meringue with the breadcrumb mixture and vanilla essence.

3 Spoon the mixture into a 1.2 litre/ 2 pint/5 cup loaf tin. Smooth the top level, then cover and freeze for several hours, or until firm.

5 To serve, turn out the ice cream on to a plate and cut into slices. Arrange each slice on a serving plate, spoon over a little sauce and decorate with fresh mint sprigs.

4 Meanwhile, make the sauce. Put the blackcurrants in a small bowl with the sugar. Toss gently to mix and leave for 30 minutes. Purée the blackcurrants in a blender or food processor, then press through a nylon sieve into a bowl. Stir in the crème de cassis and chill well.

COOK'S TIP
To string blackcurrants, run a fork down the stalks so that the berries are pulled off by the tines.

Chocolate Chip Banana Pancakes

Serve these delicious pancakes as a dessert topped with cream and toasted almonds.

Makes 16

INGREDIENTS
2 ripe bananas
200 ml/7 fl oz/scant 1 cup milk
2 eggs
150 g/5 oz/1¼ cups self-raising flour
25 g/1 oz/⅓ cup ground almonds
15 ml/1 tbsp caster sugar
25 g/1 oz plain chocolate chips
butter, for frying
pinch of salt

FOR THE TOPPING
150 ml/¼ pint/⅔ cup double cream
15 ml/1 tbsp icing sugar
50 g/2 oz/½ cup toasted flaked
   almonds, to decorate

chocolate chips   bananas

flour

eggs

almonds

milk

1 In a bowl, mash the bananas with a fork, combine with half of the milk and beat in the eggs. Sieve in the flour, ground almonds, sugar and salt. Make a well in the centre and pour in the remaining milk. Add the chocolate chips and stir to produce a thick batter.

2 Heat a knob of butter in a non-stick frying pan. Spoon the pancake mixture into heaps, allowing room for them to spread. When bubbles emerge, turn the pancakes over and cook briefly on the other side.

3 Loosely whip the cream with the icing sugar to sweeten it slightly. Spoon the cream onto pancakes and decorate with flaked almonds.

COOK'S TIP

For banana and blueberry pancakes, replace the chocolate with 115 g/ 4 oz/1 cup fresh blueberries. Hot pancakes are also delicious when accompanied by ice cream.

Plum, Rum and Raisin Brulée

Crack through the crunchy caramel to find the juicy plums and smooth creamy centre of this dessert.

Serves 4

INGREDIENTS
25 g/1 oz/3 tbsp raisins
15 ml/1 tbsp dark rum
350 g/12 oz medium plums (about 6)
juice of 1 orange
15 ml/1 tbsp clear honey
225 g/8 oz/2 cups low fat soft cheese
90 g/3½ oz/½ cup granulated sugar

raisins

rum

orange

plums

honey

1 Put the raisins into a small bowl and sprinkle over the rum. Leave to soak for 5 minutes.

2 Quarter the plums and remove their stones. Put into a large, heavy-based saucepan together with the orange juice and honey. Simmer gently for 5 minutes or until soft. Stir in the soaked raisins. Reserve 15 ml/1 tbsp of the juice, then divide the rest between four 150 ml/¼ pint/⅔ cup ramekin dishes.

3 Blend the low fat soft cheese with the reserved 15 ml/1 tbsp of plum juice. Spoon over the plums and chill in the refrigerator for 1 hour.

4 Put the sugar into a large, heavy-based saucepan with 45 ml/3 tbsp cold water. Heat gently, stirring, until the sugar has dissolved. Boil for 15 minutes or until it turns golden brown. Cool for 2 minutes, then carefully pour over the ramekins. Cool and serve.

Raspberry and Passion Fruit Chinchillas

Few desserts are so strikingly easy to make as this one: beaten egg whites and sugar baked in a dish, turned out and served with a handful of soft fruit.

VARIATION

If raspberries are out of season, use either fresh, bottled or canned soft berry fruit such as strawberries, blueberries or redcurrants.

Serves 4

INGREDIENTS
25 g/1 oz/2 tbsp butter, softened
5 egg whites
150 g/5 oz/⅔ cup caster sugar
2 passion fruit
250 ml/8 fl oz/1 cup ready-made
   custard from a carton or can
milk, as required
675 g/1½ lb/6 cups fresh raspberries
icing sugar, for dusting

raspberries

egg whites

passion fruit

icing sugar

1 Preheat the oven to 180°C/350°F/ Gas 4. Brush four 300 ml/½ pint soufflé dishes with a visible layer of soft butter.

2 Whisk the egg whites in a mixing bowl until firm. (You can use an electric whisk.) Add the sugar a little at a time and whisk into a firm meringue.

3 Halve the passion fruit, take out the seeds with a spoon and fold them into the meringue.

4 Turn the meringue out into the prepared dishes, stand in a deep roasting pan which has been half-filled with boiling water and bake for 10 minutes. The meringue will rise above the tops of the soufflé dishes.

5 Turn the chinchillas out upside-down onto a serving plate. Thin the custard with a little milk and pour around the edge.

6 Top with raspberries, dredge with icing sugar and serve warm or cold.

Ice Cream Strawberry Shortcake

This pudding is an American classic, and couldn't be easier to make. Fresh juicy strawberries, store-bought flan cases and rich vanilla ice cream are all you need to create an irresistible feast of a dessert.

Serves 4

INGREDIENTS
3 × 15 cm/6 in sponge flan cases,
   or shortbreads
1.2 litres/2 pints/5 cups vanilla or
   strawberry ice cream
675 g/1½ lb hulled fresh strawberries
icing sugar, for dusting

strawberries

vanilla ice cream

flan case

1 If using flan cases, trim the raised edges with a serrated knife.

2 Sandwich the flan cases, or shortbreads with two-thirds of the ice cream and the strawberries.

3 Place the remaining ice cream on top, finish with strawberries, dust with icing sugar and serve.

COOK'S TIP

Don't worry if the shortbread falls apart when you cut into it. Messy cakes are best. Ice Cream Strawberry Shortbread can be assembled up to 1 hour in advance and kept in the freezer without spoiling the fruit.

Malted Chocolate and Banana Dip

Malted drinks and "smoothies" are all the fashion and this delectable dip is lovely served with chunks of fruit.

Serves 4

INGREDIENTS
50 g/2 oz plain chocolate
2 large ripe bananas
15 ml/1 tbsp malt extract

plain chocolate

bananas

malt extract

I Break the chocolate into pieces and place in a small heatproof bowl. Stand the bowl over a pan of gently simmering water and stir the chocolate occasionally until it melts. Allow to cool.

2 Cut the bananas into pieces and process them until finely chopped in a blender or food processor.

3 With the motor running, pour in the malt extract, and continue processing until the mixture is thick and frothy.

4 Drizzle in the chocolate in a steady stream and process until well blended. Serve immediately.

COOK'S TIP

This smooth dip can be prepared in advance and chilled. When ready to serve, stir in some lightly whipped cream to soften and enrich the mixture.

Papaya and Coconut Dip

Sweet and smooth papaya teams up well with
rich coconut cream to make a luscious sweet dip.

Serves 6

INGREDIENTS
2 ripe papayas
200 ml/7 fl oz/scant 1 cup
   crème fraîche
1 piece stem ginger
fresh coconut, to decorate

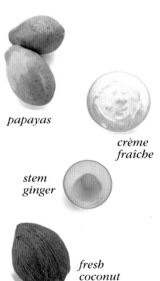

papayas

*crème
fraîche*

*stem
ginger*

*fresh
coconut*

1 Halve each papaya lengthways, then
scoop out and discard the seeds. Cut a
few slices and reserve for decoration.

2 Scoop out the flesh and process
it until smooth in a blender or a
food processor.

3 Stir in the crème fraîche and process
until well blended. Finely chop the stem
ginger and stir it into the mixture, then
chill until ready to serve.

4 Pierce a hole in the "eye" of the
coconut and drain off the liquid, then
break open the coconut. Hold it securely
in one hand and hit it sharply with a
hammer.

5 Remove the shell from a piece of
coconut, then snap the nut into pieces
no wider than 2 cm/¾ in.

6 Use a swivel-bladed vegetable peeler
to shave off 2 cm/¾ in lengths of
coconut. Scatter these over the dip with
the reserved papaya before serving.

COOK'S TIP

If fresh coconut is not available,
buy coconut strands and lightly
toast in a hot oven until golden.

Grilled Pineapple with Rum-custard Sauce

Freshly ground black pepper may seem an unusual ingredient to put with pineapple, until you realise that peppercorns are the fruit of a tropical vine. If the idea does not appeal, make the sauce without pepper.

Serves 4

INGREDIENTS
1 ripe pineapple
25 g/1 oz/2 tbsp butter
fresh strawberries, sliced, to serve

FOR THE SAUCE
1 egg
2 egg yolks
30 ml/2 tbsp caster sugar
30 ml/2 tbsp dark rum
2.5 ml/½ tsp freshly ground
   black pepper

butter

rum

eggs

pineapple

black pepper

caster sugar

1 Remove the top and bottom from the pineapple with a serrated knife. Pare away the outer skin from top to bottom, remove the core and cut into slices.

2 Preheat a moderate grill. Dot the pineapple slices with butter and grill for about 5 minutes.

3 To make the sauce, place all the ingredients in a bowl. Set over a saucepan of simmering water and whisk with a hand-held mixer for about 3–4 minutes or until foamy and cooked. Scatter the strawberries over the pineapple and serve with the sauce.

COOK'S TIP

The sweetest pineapples are picked and exported when ripe. Contrary to popular belief, pineapples do not ripen well after picking. Choose fruit that smells sweet and yields to firm pressure from your thumbs.

Oranges with Saffron Yogurt

This is a popular Indian dessert after a hot and spicy curry.

Serves 4

INGREDIENTS

4 large oranges
1.25 ml/¼ tsp ground cinnamon
150 ml/¼ pint/⅔ cup natural yogurt
10 ml/2 tsp caster sugar
3-4 saffron strands
1.5 ml/¼ tsp ground ginger
15 ml/1 tbsp chopped pistachio
    nuts, toasted
fresh lemon balm or mint leaves,
    to decorate

yogurt

saffron
strands

caster sugar

mint
leaves

pistachio
nuts

oranges

ground
cinnamon

ground ginger

1 Slice the bottom off each of the oranges. Working from the top of the orange, cut across the top of the orange and down one side. Follow the contours of the orange. Repeat until all the peel and pith has been removed, reserving any juice. Peel the remaining oranges in the same way.

2 Slice the oranges thinly and remove any pips. Lay in a single layer, overlapping the slices, on a shallow serving platter. Sprinkle the ground cinnamon over the oranges. Cover the platter with clear film and chill.

3 Mix the yogurt, sugar, saffron and ginger together in a bowl and leave to infuse for 5–10 minutes. Sprinkle with the chopped nuts. To serve, spoon the yogurt and nut mixture over the chilled orange slices.

COOK'S TIP

For a more unusual dessert use deliciously juicy blood oranges, which look dramatic and have a wonderful flavour.

Stuffed Peaches with Mascarpone Cream

Mascarpone is a thick, velvety Italian cream cheese, made from cow's milk. It is often used in desserts, or eaten with fresh fruit.

Serves 4

INGREDIENTS

4 large peaches, halved and stoned
40 g/1 ½ oz amaretti biscuits, crumbled
30 ml/2 tbsp ground almonds
45 ml/3 tbsp sugar
15 ml/1 tbsp cocoa powder
150 ml/¼ pint/⅔ cup sweet wine
25 g/1 oz/2 tbsp butter

FOR THE MASCARPONE CREAM

30 ml/2 tbsp caster sugar
3 egg yolks
15 ml/1 tbsp sweet wine
225 g/8 oz/1 cup mascarpone cheese
150 ml/¼ pint/⅔ cup double cream

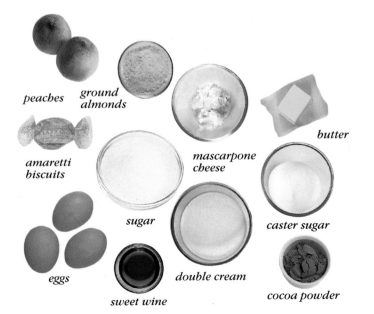

peaches   ground almonds

amaretti biscuits   mascarpone cheese   butter

sugar   caster sugar

eggs   double cream   cocoa powder

sweet wine

1 Preheat the oven to 200°C/400°F/ Gas 6. Using a teaspoon, scoop some of the flesh from the cavities in the peaches, to make a reasonable space for stuffing. Chop the scooped-out flesh.

2 Mix together the amaretti biscuits, ground almonds, sugar, cocoa and peach flesh. Add enough wine to make the mixture into a thick paste. Place the peaches in a buttered ovenproof dish and fill them with the amaretti and almond stuffing. Dot with butter, then pour the remaining wine into the dish. Bake for 35 minutes.

3 To make the mascarpone cream, beat the caster sugar and egg yolks until thick and pale. Stir in the wine, then fold in the mascarpone. Whip the double cream to soft peaks and fold into the mixture. Remove the peaches from the oven and leave to cool. Serve the peaches at room temperature, with the mascarpone cream.

Feather-light Peach Pudding

On chilly days, try this hot fruit pudding with its tantalizing sponge topping.

Serves 4

INGREDIENTS

400 g/14 oz can peach slices in
  natural juice
50 g/2 oz/4 tbsp low fat spread
40 g/1½ oz/¼ cup soft light
  brown sugar
1 egg, beaten
65 g/2½ oz/½ cup plain
  wholemeal flour
50 g/2 oz/½ cup plain flour
5 ml/1 tsp baking powder
2.5 ml/½ tsp ground cinnamon
60 ml/4 tbsp skimmed milk
2.5 ml/½ tsp vanilla essence
10 ml/2 tsp icing sugar, for dusting
low fat ready-to-serve custard,
  to serve

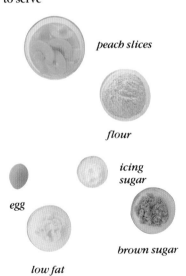

peach slices

flour

icing
sugar

egg

brown sugar

low fat
custard

1 Pre-heat the oven to 180°C/350°F/ Gas 4. Drain the peaches and put into a 1 litre/1¾ pint/4 cup pie dish with 30 ml/ 2 tbsp of the juice.

2 Put all the remaining ingredients, except the icing sugar into a mixing bowl. Beat for 3–4 minutes, until thoroughly combined.

COOK'S TIP

For a simple sauce, blend 5 ml/1 tsp arrowroot with 15 ml/1 tbsp peach juice in a small saucepan. Stir in the remaining peach juice from the can and bring to the boil. Simmer for 1 minute until thickened and clear.

3 Spoon the sponge mixture over the peaches and level the top evenly. Cook in the oven for 35-40 minutes, or until springy to the touch.

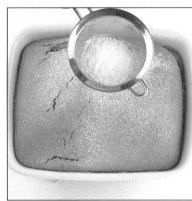

4 Lightly dust the top with icing sugar before serving hot with the custard.

Spiced Bread Pudding with Cranberry Sauce

Nutmeg is a warm, aromatic spice and is particularly suited to old-fashioned puddings.

Serves 6-8

INGREDIENTS

50 g/2 oz butter, melted
750 ml/1¼ pints/3 cups milk
3 eggs
90 g/3½ oz caster sugar
5 ml/1 tsp vanilla essence
10 ml/2 tsp ground cinnamon
2.5 ml/½ tsp grated nutmeg
400 g/14 oz cubed bread cut from a day-old French loaf
50 g/2 oz chopped walnut kernels
75 g/3 oz sultanas

FOR THE CRANBERRY SAUCE

350 g/12 oz cranberries, fresh or frozen
finely grated peel and juice of 1 large orange
25 g/1 oz caster sugar

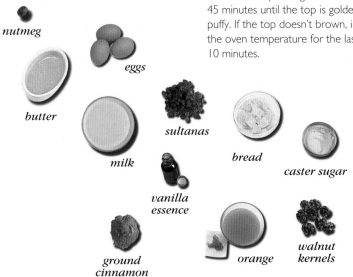

nutmeg

eggs

butter

sultanas

milk

bread

caster sugar

vanilla essence

orange

walnut kernels

ground cinnamon

1 Brush the butter generously into the bottom and sides of a medium-sized ovenproof dish. Pour any remaining butter into the milk. Beat the eggs until light and frothy, then beat in the sugar, vanilla essence, cinnamon and nutmeg. Stir in the milk and mix well.

2 Arrange the bread cubes in the prepared dish, scattering the walnuts and sultanas over the top.

3 Preheat the oven to 180°C/350°F/ Gas 4. Pour the custard over the bread, coating each piece thoroughly. Leave to stand for 45 minutes.

4 Bake the pudding in the oven for 45 minutes until the top is golden and puffy. If the top doesn't brown, increase the oven temperature for the last 10 minutes.

5 To make the cranberry sauce, put the berries into a saucepan with the orange peel and juice and the sugar.

6 Stir over a low heat until the sugar dissolves, then cook until the berries pop and the mixture thickens and becomes syrupy. Serve the sauce hot or cold.

Ginger and Lemon Puddings with Custard

The flavours of lemon and ginger complement each other perfectly in these light little puddings.

Serves 8

INGREDIENTS

3 lemons
75 g/3 oz drained stem ginger, plus
    30ml/2 tbsp syrup from the jar
60ml/4 tbsp golden syrup
175 g/6 oz self-raising flour
10 ml/2 tsp ground ginger
115 g/4 oz butter, softened
115 g/4 oz caster sugar
2 eggs, beaten
45-60ml/3-4 tbsp milk

FOR THE VANILLA CUSTARD

150 ml/¼ pint/⅔ cup milk
150 ml/¼ pint/⅔ cup double cream
1 vanilla pod, split
3 egg yolks
5ml/1 tsp cornflour
25 g/1 oz caster sugar

caster sugar *golden syrup*

eggs *lemons* *butter* *ground ginger* *double cream*

milk *vanilla pod*

COOK'S TIP

Use vanilla sugar for additional flavour. Place a vanilla pod in a jar of caster sugar and leave for at least a week before using.

1 Preheat the oven to 160°C/325°F/Gas 3. Grease 8 individual pudding basins. Set one lemon aside for the sauce. Grate the rind from the remaining lemons and reserve. Remove all the pith from one of the grated lemons and slice into 8 thin rounds. Squeeze the juice from the second grated lemon. Chop the stem ginger.

2 Mix 15ml/1 tbsp of the ginger syrup with 30ml/2 tbsp of the golden syrup and 5ml/1 tsp of the lemon juice. Divide among the greased pudding basins. Place a slice of lemon in the bottom of each basin.

3 Sift the flour and ground ginger into a bowl. In a separate bowl, beat the butter and sugar together until pale and fluffy. Beat in the eggs, then fold in the flour mixture. Add enough milk to give a soft consistency, then stir in the lemon rind. Spoon into the pudding basins.

4 Cover each basin with foil and stand in a roasting tin. Add boiling water to come halfway up the basins. Overwrap with foil, sealing well. Bake for 30-45 minutes, until cooked through.

5 To make the lemon and ginger sauce, grate the rind and squeeze the juice from the remaining lemon. Place in a pan with the remaining ginger syrup and golden syrup, bring to the boil, and simmer for 2 minutes. Keep warm.

6 To make the custard, mix the milk and cream in a pan. Add the vanilla pod and heat until almost boiling. Remove from the heat and leave for 10 minutes. Whisk together the egg yolks, cornflour and sugar, then strain into the milk and cream. Whisk until blended, then return to the clean pan and heat, stirring, until thick. Turn out the puddings, spoon over the sauce and serve with the custard.

Red Berry Sponge Tart

When soft berry fruits are in season, try making this delicious sponge tart. Serve warm from the oven with scoops of vanilla ice cream.

Serves 4

INGREDIENTS
softened butter, for greasing
450 g/1 lb/4 cups soft berry fruits
    such as raspberries, blackberries,
    blackcurrants, redcurrants,
    strawberries or blueberries
2 eggs, at room temperature
50 g/2 oz/¼ cup caster sugar, plus
    extra to taste (optional)
15 ml/1 tbsp plain flour
50 g/2 oz/¾ cup ground almonds
vanilla ice cream, to serve

eggs

ground almonds

flour   *caster sugar*

redcurrants

blackcurrants

raspberries   *strawberries*

1 Preheat the oven to 190°C/375°F/ Gas 5. Brush a 23 cm/9 in flan tin with softened butter and line the bottom with a circle of non-stick baking paper. Scatter the fruit in the bottom of the tin with a little sugar if the fruits are tart.

2 Whisk the eggs and sugar together for about 3–4 minutes or until they leave a thick trail across the surface. Combine the flour and almonds, then fold into the egg mixture with a spatula – retaining as much air as possible.

3 Spread the mixture on top of the fruit base and bake in the preheated oven for 15 minutes. Turn out onto a serving plate and serve with vanilla ice cream.

VARIATION
When berry fruits are out of season, use bottled fruits, but ensure that they are well drained before use.

Pear Tart Tatin with Cardamom

Cardamom is a versatile spice which is good with sweet or savoury dishes. It is delicious with pears.

Serves 2-4

INGREDIENTS

50 g/2 oz butter, melted
50 g/2 oz caster sugar
seeds from 10 cardamom pods
225 g/8 oz puff pastry, thawed if
    frozen
4-5 ripe pears
cream, to serve

caster sugar   butter

cardamom pods

puff pastry

pears

COOK'S TIP
You will need to use a heavy-based tin for this recipe. If you do not have a heavy cake tin, use an ovenproof omelette pan.

1 Preheat the oven to 220°C/425°F/Gas 7. Spread the butter over the base of an 18 cm/7 in flameproof round tin, sprinkle with the sugar and scatter over the cardamom seeds. Roll out the pastry to a circle slightly larger than the tin, prick the pastry lightly and chill.

2 Peel, core and halve the pears lengthways. Arrange the pears, rounded side down, on the butter and sugar. Set the pan over a medium heat until the sugar melts and begins to bubble. If any areas are browning more than others, move the pan, but do not stir.

3 As soon as the sugar has caramelized, quickly remove the pan from the heat, so that the sugar does not burn. Place the pastry on top, tucking the edges down the side of the pan. Bake in the oven for 25 minutes until the pastry is well risen and golden.

4 Leave the tart in the pan for 2-3 minutes until the juices have stopped bubbling. Invert over a plate and shake to release the tart. It may be necessary to slide a spatula underneath the pears to loosen them. Serve the tart warm with cream.

Crunchy Apple and Almond Flan

Generations of cooks have taken pride in making this traditional flan, with its attractive arrangement of tender apples topped with nut crumble.

Serves 8

INGREDIENTS
175 g/6 oz/1½ cups plain flour
75 g/3 oz/6 tbsp butter, cubed
25 g/1 oz/⅓ cup ground almonds
25 g/1 oz/2 tbsp caster sugar
1 egg yolk
15 ml/1 tbsp cold water
1.5 ml/¼ tsp almond essence
675 g/1½ lb cooking apples
25 g/1 oz/3 tbsp raisins (optional)
sifted icing sugar, to decorate

FOR THE CRUNCHY TOPPING
115 g/4 oz/1 cup plain flour
1.5 ml/¼ tsp mixed spice
50 g/2 oz/4 tbsp butter, diced
50 g/2 oz/⅓ cup demerara sugar
50 g/2 oz/½ cup flaked almonds

plain flour

butter

caster sugar

egg

ground almonds

demerara sugar

almond essence

cooking apples

raisins

flaked almonds

1 Process the flour and butter in a food processor until it resembles fine breadcrumbs. Stir in the ground almonds and sugar. Whisk the egg yolk, water and almond essence together and add to the dry ingredients to form a dough. Knead lightly, wrap and leave for 20 minutes.

2 Meanwhile, make the crunchy topping. Sift the flour and mixed spice into a bowl and rub in the butter. Stir in the sugar and almonds.

3 Roll out the pastry on a lightly floured surface and use it to line a 23cm/9 in loose-based flan tin, taking care to press it neatly into the edges and to make a lip around the top edge. Roll off the excess pastry to neaten the edge. Chill for 15 minutes.

6 Leave the flan to cool in the tin for 10 minutes. Serve warm or cold, dusted with sifted icing sugar.

4 Preheat the oven to 190°C/375°F/Gas 5. Place a baking sheet in the oven to preheat. Peel, core and slice the apples thinly. Arrange in the flan case in concentric circles, doming the centre.

5 Scatter over the raisins, if using. Cover the apples with the crunchy topping, pressing it on lightly. Bake on the hot baking sheet for 25–30 minutes, or until golden brown and the apples are tender when tested with a fine skewer.

COOK'S TIP

Do not be tempted to put any sugar with the apples, as this makes them produce too much liquid. All the sweetness necessary is in the pastry and topping.

Ricotta Cheesecake

Low-fat ricotta cheese is excellent for cheesecake fillings because it has a good, firm texture. Here it is enriched with eggs and cream and enlivened with tangy orange and lemon rind to make a Sicilian-style dessert.

Serves 8

INGREDIENTS
450 g/1 lb/2 cups low-fat
    ricotta cheese
120 ml/4 fl oz/½ cup double cream
2 eggs
1 egg yolk
75 g/3 oz/⅓ cup caster sugar
finely grated rind of 1 orange
finely grated rind of 1 lemon
blanched thin strips of orange and
    lemon rind, to decorate

FOR THE PASTRY
175 g/6 oz/1½ cups plain flour
45 ml/3 tbsp caster sugar
115 g/4 oz/½ cup chilled
    butter, diced
1 egg yolk
pinch of salt

double cream

ricotta cheese

caster sugar   plain flour

orange

eggs

butter   lemon

1 Make the pastry. Sift the flour, sugar and salt on to a cold work surface. Make a well in the centre and put in the diced butter and egg yolk. Gradually work the flour into the diced butter and egg yolk, using your fingertips.

2 Gather the dough together, reserve about a quarter for the lattice, then press the rest into a 23 cm/9 in fluted tart tin with a removable base. Chill the pastry case for 30 minutes.

3 Meanwhile, preheat the oven to 190°C/375°F/Gas 5 and make the filling. Put all the ricotta, cream, eggs, egg yolk, sugar and orange and lemon rinds in a large bowl and beat together until the ingredients are evenly mixed.

6 Bake the cheesecake for 30–35 minutes until golden and set. Transfer to a wire rack and leave to cool thoroughly, then carefully remove the side of the tin and slide the cheesecake on to a serving plate. Decorate with blanched thin strips of orange and lemon rind before serving.

4 Prick the bottom of the pastry case, then line with foil and fill with baking beans. Bake blind for 15 minutes, then transfer to a wire rack, remove the foil and beans and allow the tart shell to cool in the tin.

5 Spoon the cheese and cream filling into the pastry case and level the surface. Roll out the reserved dough and cut into strips. Arrange the strips on the top of the filling in a lattice pattern, sticking them in place with water.

VARIATIONS

Add 50–115 g/2–4 oz/⅓–⅔ cup finely chopped candied peel to the filling in step 3, or 50 g/ 2 oz/⅓ cup plain chocolate chips.

For a really rich dessert, you can add both candied peel and some grated plain chocolate.

Baked Blackberry Cheesecake

This light, low-fat cheesecake is best made with wild blackberries, if they are in season, but cultivated ones will do; or substitute other soft fruit, such as raspberries or blueberries.

Serves 4–6

INGREDIENTS
175 g/6 oz/¾ cup cottage cheese
150 g/5 oz/⅔ cup low-fat natural
    yogurt
15 ml/1 tbsp plain wholemeal flour
25 g/1 oz/2 tbsp golden caster sugar
1 egg, plus 1 egg white
finely grated rind and juice of
    ½ lemon
200 g/7 oz/2 cups fresh or frozen
    and thawed blackberries

cottage cheese

*low-fat
natural yogurt*

*plain
wholemeal flour*

*golden caster
sugar*

eggs

lemon

blackberries

COOK'S TIP
If you prefer to use canned blackberries, choose those canned in natural juice and drain the fruit well before adding it to the cheesecake mixture. The juice can be served with the cheesecake.

1 Preheat the oven to 180°C/350°F/Gas 4. Lightly grease and base-line an 18 cm/7 in sandwich cake tin.

2 Place the cottage cheese in a food processor and process until smooth. Alternatively, rub it through a sieve. Scrape the smooth mixture into a bowl.

3 Stir in the yogurt, flour, sugar, egg and egg white. Fold in the lemon rind and juice and the blackberries, reserving a few for decoration.

4 Tip the mixture into the prepared tin and level the surface. Bake for 30–35 minutes, or until the mixture is just set. Switch off the oven and leave for a further 30 minutes.

5 Run a knife around the edge of the cheesecake, and then turn it out. Remove the lining paper and place the cheesecake on a warm serving plate.

6 Decorate the cheesecake with the reserved blackberries. Serve warm.

Apple Brown Betty

Crisp, spicy breadcrumbs layered with lemony
apples make a simply delicious dessert.

Serves 6

INGREDIENTS
50 g/2 oz/1 cup fresh white
 breadcrumbs
50 g/2 oz/4 tbsp butter, plus extra
 for greasing
175 g/6 oz/1 cup soft light
 brown sugar
2.5 ml/½ tsp ground cinnamon
1.5 ml/¼ tsp ground cloves
1.5 ml/¼ tsp grated nutmeg
900 g/2 lb cooking apples
juice of 1 lemon
25 g/1 oz/¼ cup finely chopped
 walnuts

*fresh white
breadcrumbs*

butter

*soft light
brown
sugar*

*ground
cinnamon*

*grated
nutmeg*

cooking apples

lemon

*chopped
walnuts*

1 Preheat the grill. Spread out the
breadcrumbs on a baking sheet or in a
roasting tin and toast under the grill until
golden, stirring frequently to colour them
evenly. Set aside.

2 Preheat the oven to 190°C/375°F/
Gas 5. Grease a large, deep ovenproof
dish with a little butter. Mix the sugar
with the spices. Cut the butter into tiny
pieces, then set aside.

3 Peel, core, and slice the apples. Toss
immediately with the lemon juice to
prevent them from turning brown.

4 Sprinkle a thin layer of breadcrumbs
into the dish. Cover with one-third of
the apples and sprinkle with one-third of
the sugar and spice mixture. Add
another layer of breadcrumbs and dot
with one-third of the butter. Repeat the
layers twice more, sprinkling the nuts on
top of the final layer of breadcrumbs
before dotting the remaining butter over
the surface.

5 Bake for 35–40 minutes, until the
apples are tender and the top is golden
brown. Serve warm.

Pear and Cherry Crunch

A triumph of contrasting textures and flavours, this pudding pairs fresh and dried fruit with a nut and crumb topping.

Serves 6

INGREDIENTS
115 g/4 oz/½ cup butter, plus extra
    for greasing
1 kg/2¼ lb pears, about 8
45 ml/3 tbsp lemon juice
175 g/6 oz/3 cups fresh
    white breadcrumbs
75 g/3 oz/⅔ cup dried cherries or
    stoned prunes, chopped
65 g/2½ oz/⅔ cup coarsely
    chopped hazelnuts
115 g/4 oz/⅔ cup soft light
    brown sugar
fresh mint sprigs, to decorate
whipped cream, to serve

butter

pears

lemon

*fresh white
breadcrumbs*

prunes

hazelnuts

*soft light
brown
sugar*

1 Preheat the oven to 190°C/375°F/ Gas 5. Grease a 20 cm/8 in square cake tin. Peel, core and chop the pears. Place them in a bowl and sprinkle them with the lemon juice to prevent them from turning brown.

2 Melt 75 g/3 oz/6 tbsp of the butter. Stir in the breadcrumbs. Spread a scant one-third of the crumb mixture on the bottom of the prepared tin.

3 Top with half the pears. Sprinkle over half the dried cherries or prunes, half the hazelnuts and half the sugar. Repeat the layers, then sprinkle the remaining crumbs over the surface.

4 Dice the remaining butter and dot it over the surface. Bake for 30–35 minutes, until golden. Serve hot, with whipped cream. Decorate each portion with a sprig of fresh mint.

Spiced Apple Cake

Grated apple and chopped dates give this cake a natural sweetness – omit 25 g/1 oz of the sugar if the fruit is very sweet.

Serves 8

INGREDIENTS

225 g/8 oz/2 cups self-raising wholemeal flour
5 ml/1 tsp baking powder
10 ml/2 tsp ground cinnamon
175 g/6 oz/1 cup chopped dates
75 g/3 oz/½ cup light muscovado sugar
15 ml/1 tbsp pear and apple spread
120 ml/4 fl oz/½ cup apple juice
2 eggs
90 ml/6 tbsp sunflower oil
2 eating apples, cored and grated
15 ml/1 tbsp chopped walnuts

ground cinnamon

apple juice *sunflower oil*

self-raising wholemeal flour

chopped walnuts

chopped dates

baking powder

muscovado sugar

pear and apple spread *eating apples*

eggs

1 Preheat the oven to 180°C/350°F/ Gas 4. Grease and line a deep round 20 cm/8 in cake tin. Sift the flour, baking powder and cinnamon into a mixing bowl, then mix in the dates and make a well in the centre.

2 Mix the sugar with the pear and apple spread in a small bowl. Gradually stir in the apple juice. Add to the dry ingredients with the eggs, oil and apples. Mix thoroughly.

COOK'S TIP

It is not necessary to peel the apples – the skin adds extra fibre and softens on cooking.

3 Spoon the mixture into the prepared cake tin, sprinkle with the walnuts and bake for 60–65 minutes or until a skewer inserted into the centre of the cake comes out clean. Transfer to a wire rack, remove the lining paper and leave to cool.

Apple Crumble Cake

This is a wonderful way of using windfall apples, and it makes a satisfying and tasty sweet for a cool autumn evening.

Serves 8–10

INGREDIENTS
50 g/2 oz/4 tbsp butter, softened, plus extra for greasing
75 g/3 oz/6 tbsp caster sugar
1 egg, beaten
115 g/4 oz/1 cup self-raising flour, sifted
2 cooking apples
50 g/2 oz/⅓ cup sultanas

FOR THE TOPPING
75 g/3 oz/¾ cup self-raising flour
2.5 ml/½ tsp ground cinnamon
40 g/1½ oz/3 tbsp butter
25 g/1 oz/2 tbsp caster sugar

FOR THE DECORATION
1 red dessert apple, cored, thinly sliced and tossed in lemon juice
30 ml/2 tbsp caster sugar
ground cinnamon, for sprinkling

butter *caster sugar* *egg*

self-raising flour *cooking apples*

sultanas *ground cinnamon*

1 Preheat the oven to 180°C/350°F/ Gas 4. Grease and base-line a deep 18 cm/7 in springform tin. Make the topping. Sift the flour and cinnamon into a mixing bowl. Rub in the butter until the mixture resembles breadcrumbs, then stir in the sugar. Set aside.

2 Put the butter, sugar, egg and flour into a bowl and beat for 1–2 minutes until smooth. Spoon the mixture into the prepared tin.

3 Peel, core and slice the cooking apples into a bowl. Add the sultanas. Spread the mixture evenly over the cake mixture, then sprinkle with the crumble topping. Bake for about 1 hour.

4 Allow to cool in the tin for 10 minutes before turning out on to a wire rack and peeling off the lining paper. Serve warm or cool, decorated with slices of red dessert apple with a sprinkling of caster sugar and cinnamon.

COOK'S TIP
This cake can be kept for up to 2 days in an airtight container.

Farmhouse Apple and Sultana Cake

A slice of this tasty, moist and fruity cake makes an ideal teatime treat.

Serves 12

INGREDIENTS
175 g/6 oz/¾ cup half-fat spread
175 g/6 oz/¾ cup soft light
  brown sugar
3 eggs
225 g/8 oz/2 cups self-raising
  wholemeal flour, sifted
115 g/4 oz/1 cup self-raising white
  flour, sifted
5 ml/1 tsp baking powder, sifted
10 ml/2 tsp ground mixed spice
350 g/12 oz cooking apples, peeled,
  cored and diced
175 g/6 oz/1 cup sultanas
75 ml/5 tbsp skimmed milk
30ml/2 tbsp demerara sugar

half-fat spread

light soft brown sugar

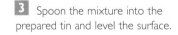
eggs

self-raising wholemeal flour

self-raising white flour

baking powder

ground mixed spice

cooking apples

sultanas

skimmed milk

demerara sugar

1 Preheat the oven to 160°C/325°F/ Gas 3. Lightly grease a deep, 20 cm/8 in round, loose-bottomed cake tin and line with non-stick baking paper. Put the half-fat spread, soft brown sugar, eggs, flours, baking powder and spice in a bowl and beat well together until thoroughly mixed.

2 Fold in the apples, sultanas and sufficient milk to make a soft dropping consistency.

3 Spoon the mixture into the prepared tin and level the surface.

4 Sprinkle the top with demerara sugar. Bake for about 1½ hours, until risen, golden brown and firm to the touch. Cool in the tin for a few minutes, then turn out on to a wire rack to cool completely. Serve in slices.

Carrot and Coconut Cake

A satisfying cake made with a delicious combination of flavours.

Serves 10

INGREDIENTS

115 g/4 oz/8 tbsp half-fat spread
115 g/4 oz/½ cup caster sugar
2 eggs
175 g/6 oz/1½ cups self-raising wholemeal flour, sifted
50 g/2 oz/3 cups bran
5 ml/1 tsp baking powder, sifted
90 ml/6 tbsp skimmed milk
225 g/8 oz/1⅔ cups carrots, coarsely grated
115 g/4 oz desiccated coconut
50 g/2 oz/⅓ cup sultanas
finely grated rind of 1 orange
15–30 ml/1–2 tbsp golden granulated sugar, to sprinkle

half-fat spread

caster sugar

eggs

self-raising wholemeal flour

bran

baking powder

skimmed milk

carrots

sultanas

orange

dessicated coconut

golden granulated sugar

1 Preheat the oven to 180°C/350°F/Gas 4. Lightly grease a deep 18 cm/7 in round cake tin and line with non-stick baking paper. Put the half-fat spread, caster sugar, eggs, flour, bran, baking powder and milk in a bowl and beat together until thoroughly mixed.

2 Fold in the carrots, coconut, sultanas, orange rind and extra milk, to make a soft dropping consistency.

3 Spoon the mixture into the prepared tin and level the surface.

4 Sprinkle the top with granulated sugar and bake for about 1 hour, until risen, golden brown and firm to the touch. Cool in the tin for a few minutes, then turn out on to a wire rack to cool completely. Serve in slices.

Nectarine Amaretto Cake

Try this delicious cake with low fat fromage frais for dessert, or serve it solo for afternoon tea. The syrup makes it moist but not soggy.

Serves 8

INGREDIENTS
3 eggs, separated
175 g/6 oz/³/₄ cup caster sugar
grated rind and juice of 1 lemon
50 g/2 oz/¹/₃ cup semolina
40 g/1¹/₂ oz/¹/₃ cup ground almonds
25 g/1 oz/¹/₄ cup plain flour
2 nectarines or peaches, halved
  and stoned
60 ml/4 tbsp Apricot Glaze

FOR THE SYRUP
75 g/3 oz/6 tbsp caster sugar
90 ml/6 tbsp water
30 ml/2 tbsp Amaretto liqueur

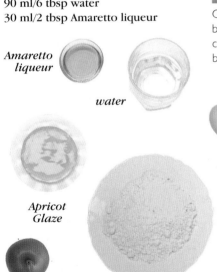

Amaretto liqueur

water

Apricot Glaze

eggs

semolina

caster sugar

ground almonds

plain flour

lemon

nectarines

1 Preheat the oven to 180°C/350°F/ Gas 4. Grease a 20 cm/8 in round loose-bottomed cake tin. Whisk the egg yolks, caster sugar, lemon rind and juice in a bowl until thick, pale and creamy.

2 Fold in the semolina, almonds and flour until smooth.

3 Whisk the egg whites in a grease-free bowl until fairly stiff. Using a metal spoon, stir a generous spoonful of the whites into the semolina mixture to lighten it, then fold in the remaining egg whites. Spoon the mixture into the prepared cake tin.

4 Bake for 30–35 minutes until the centre of the cake springs back when lightly pressed. Remove the cake from the oven and carefully loosen around the edge with a palette knife. Prick the top of the cake with a skewer and leave to cool slightly in the tin.

COOK'S TIP

To make Apricot Glaze, place a few spoonfuls of apricot jam in a small pan along with a squeeze of lemon juice. Heat the jam, stirring until it is melted. Push through a fine sieve.

5 Meanwhile, make the syrup. Heat the sugar and water in a small pan, stirring until dissolved, then boil without stirring for 2 minutes. Add the Amaretto liqueur and drizzle slowly over the cake.

6 Remove the cake from the tin and transfer it to a serving plate. Slice the nectarines or peaches, arrange them over the top and brush with the warm Apricot Glaze.

Spiced Chocolate Cake

This cake is flavoured with aromatic cinnamon, cloves, nutmeg and cardamom and makes a perfect end to a meal.

Makes 24

INGREDIENTS

3 eggs
200 g/7 oz caster sugar
115 g/4 oz plain flour
5 ml/1 tsp ground cinnamon
1.5 ml/¼ tsp ground cloves
1.5 ml/¼ tsp freshly grated nutmeg
1.5 ml/¼ tsp ground cardamom
275 g/10 oz unblanched almonds, coarsely ground
25 g/1 oz candied lemon peel, finely chopped
25 g/1 oz candied orange peel, finely chopped
40 g/1½ oz plain chocolate, grated
2.5 ml/½ tsp grated lemon rind
2.5 ml/½ tsp grated orange rind
10 ml/2 tsp rosewater

FOR THE ICING

1 egg white
10 ml/2 tsp cocoa powder, mixed with 15 ml/1 tbsp boiling water and cooled
115 g/4 oz icing sugar
15 ml/2 tbsp sugar crystals

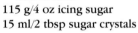
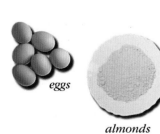

eggs

almonds

cinnamon

nutmeg

cloves

chocolate

rose water

candied peel

orange rind

lemon rind

COOK'S TIP
Do not worry when the top of the cake cracks when you cut it; it is meant to be like that!

1 Preheat the oven to 160°C/325°F/ Gas 3. Line a 30 x 23 cm/12 x 9 in Swiss roll tin with rice paper.

2 Whisk the eggs and caster sugar in a large bowl until thick and pale. Sift in the flour, cinnamon, ground cloves, nutmeg and cardamom and then stir in all the remaining dry ingredients.

3 Spoon evenly into the prepared tin and brush with the rosewater. Bake for 30-35 minutes until firm. Turn out of the tin.

4 To make the icing, stir the egg white into the cocoa mixture, sift in the icing sugar and mix. Spread over the cake while still warm. Sprinkle with sugar crystals and then return to the oven for 5 minutes. Cut into squares when cold.

Banana Gingerbread Slices

Bananas make this spicy bake delightfully moist.
The flavour develops on keeping, so store the
gingerbread for a few days before cutting into
slices, if possible.

Makes 20 slices

INGREDIENTS

275 g/10 oz/2½ cups plain flour
5 ml/1 tsp bicarbonate of soda
20 ml/4 tsp ground ginger
10 ml/2 tsp mixed spice
115 g/4 oz/⅔ cup soft light
   brown sugar
60 ml/4 tbsp sunflower oil
30 ml/2 tbsp molasses or
   black treacle
30 ml/2 tbsp malt extract
2 eggs
60 ml/4 tbsp orange juice
3 ripe bananas
115 g/4 oz/⅔ cup raisins or sultanas

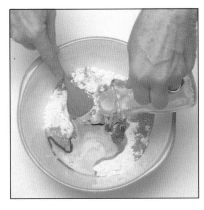

1 Preheat the oven to 180°C/350°F/
Gas 4. Lightly grease and line a 28 ×
18 cm/11 × 7 in shallow baking tin.

2 Sift the flour, bicarbonate of soda
and spices into a mixing bowl. Place the
sugar in the sieve over the bowl, add
some of the flour mixture and rub
through the sieve with a wooden spoon.

3 Make a well in the centre of the dry
ingredients and add the oil, molasses or
treacle, malt extract, eggs and orange
juice. Mix thoroughly.

orange juice

malt extract *raisins*

plain flour

mixed spice

soft light brown sugar

eggs

sunflower oil

bicarbonate of soda

ground ginger *bananas* *molasses*

5 Scrape the mixture into the
prepared baking tin. Bake for about
35–40 minutes or until the centre of
the gingerbread springs back when
lightly pressed.

4 Mash the bananas on a plate. Add
the raisins or sultanas to the gingerbread
mixture then mix in the mashed bananas.

6 Leave the gingerbread in the tin to cool for 5 minutes, then turn out on to a wire rack to cool completely. Transfer to a board and cut into 20 slices to serve.

COOK'S TIP
If your brown sugar is lumpy, mix it with a little flour and it will be easier to sift.

Chocolate and Banana Brownies

Nuts traditionally give brownies their chewy texture. Here oat bran is used instead, creating a moist, morish, yet healthy alternative.

Makes 9

INGREDIENTS
75 ml/5 tbsp fat reduced cocoa
    powder
15 ml/1 tbsp caster sugar
75 ml/5 tbsp skimmed milk
3 large bananas, mashed
215 g/7½ oz/1 cup soft light
    brown sugar
5 ml/1 tsp vanilla essence
5 egg whites
75 g/3 oz/¾ cup self-raising flour
75 g/3 oz/¾ cup oat bran
15 ml/1 tbsp icing sugar, for dusting

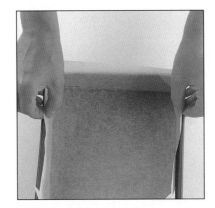

cocoa powder

vanilla essence

oat bran

egg

bananas

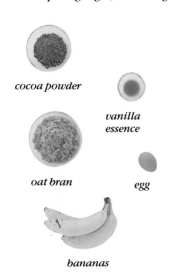

1 Pre-heat the oven to 180°C/350°F/ Gas 4. Line a 20 cm/8 in square tin with non-stick baking paper.

2 Blend the fat reduced cocoa powder and caster sugar with the skimmed milk. Add the bananas, soft brown sugar and vanilla essence.

COOK'S TIP

Store these brownies in an airtight tin for a day before eating – they improve with keeping.

3 Lightly beat the egg whites with a fork. Add the chocolate mixture and continue to beat well. Sift the flour over the mixture and fold in with the oat bran. Pour into the prepared tin.

4 Cook in the pre-heated oven for 40 minutes or until firm. Cool in the tin for 10 minutes, then turn out onto a wire rack. Cut into squares and lightly dust with icing sugar before serving.

Apricot and Almond Fingers

These apricot and almond fingers will stay moist for several days.

Makes 18

INGREDIENTS

225 g/8 oz/2 cups self-raising flour
115 g/4 oz/²⁄₃ cup light muscovado sugar
50 g/2 oz/¹⁄₃ cup semolina
175 g/6 oz/1 cup ready-to-use dried apricots, chopped
2 eggs
30 ml/2 tbsp malt extract
30 ml/2 tbsp clear honey
60 ml/4 tbsp skimmed milk
60 ml/4 tbsp sunflower oil
few drops of almond essence
30 ml/2 tbsp flaked almonds

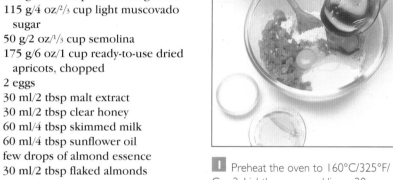

clear honey

sunflower oil

skimmed milk

eggs

ready-to-use dried apricots

light muscovado sugar

self-raising flour

semolina

malt extract

flaked almonds

1 Preheat the oven to 160°C/325°F/ Gas 3. Lightly grease and line a 28 × 18 cm/11 × 7 in shallow baking tin. Sift the flour into a bowl and add the muscovado sugar, semolina, dried apricots and eggs. Add the malt extract, clear honey, milk, sunflower oil and almond essence. Mix well until smooth.

2 Turn the mixture into the prepared tin, spread to the edges and sprinkle with the flaked almonds.

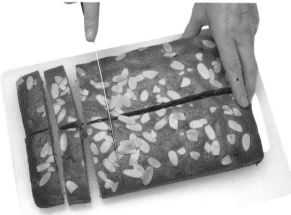

3 Bake for 30–35 minutes or until the centre of the cake springs back when lightly pressed. Transfer to a wire rack to cool. Remove the paper, place the cake on a board and cut it into 18 slices with a sharp knife.

Coffee Sponge Drops

These are delicious on their own, but taste even better with a filling made by mixing low fat soft cheese with drained and chopped stem ginger.

Makes 12

INGREDIENTS
50 g/2 oz/¹/₂ cup plain flour
15 ml/1 tbsp instant coffee powder
2 eggs
75 g/3 oz/6 tbsp caster sugar

FOR THE FILLING
115 g/4 oz/¹/₂ cup low fat soft cheese
40 g/1¹/₂ oz/¹/₄ cup chopped
   stem ginger

instant coffee powder

eggs

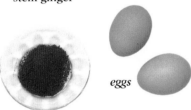

plain flour

caster sugar

low fat soft cheese

stem ginger

1 Preheat the oven to 190°C/375°F/ Gas 5. Line two baking sheets with non-stick baking paper. Make the filling by beating together the soft cheese and stem ginger. Chill until required. Sift the flour and instant coffee powder together.

2 Combine the eggs and caster sugar in a bowl. Beat with a hand-held electric whisk until thick and mousse-like (when the whisk is lifted a trail should remain on the surface of the mixture for at least 15 seconds).

3 Carefully add the sifted flour and coffee mixture and gently fold in with a metal spoon, being careful not to knock out any air.

4 Spoon the mixture into a piping bag fitted with a 1 cm/¹/₂ in plain nozzle. Pipe 4 cm/1¹/₂ in rounds on the baking sheets. Bake for 12 minutes. Cool on a wire rack. Sandwich together with the filling.

Oaty Crisps

These biscuits are very crisp and crunchy – ideal to serve with morning coffee.

Makes 18

INGREDIENTS
175 g/6 oz/1¾ cups rolled oats
75 g/3 oz/½ cup light muscovado
  sugar
1 egg
60 ml/4 tbsp sunflower oil
30 ml/2 tbsp malt extract

malt extract   sunflower oil

*rolled
oats*

*light muscovado
sugar*

egg

1 Preheat the oven to 190°C/375°F/ Gas 5. Lightly grease two baking sheets. Mix the rolled oats and brown sugar in a bowl, breaking up any lumps in the sugar. Add the egg, sunflower oil and malt extract, mix well, then leave to soak for 15 minutes.

2 Using a teaspoon, place small heaps of the mixture well apart on the prepared baking sheets. Press the heaps into 7.5 cm/3 in rounds with the back of a dampened fork.

VARIATION

To give these crisp biscuits a coarser texture, substitute jumbo oats for some or all of the rolled oats.

3 Bake the biscuits for 10–15 minutes until golden brown. Leave them to cool for 1 minute, then remove with a palette knife and cool on a wire rack.

Banana and Apricot Chelsea Buns

Old favourites are given a low fat twist with a delectable fruit filling.

Serves 9

INGREDIENTS
90 ml/6 tbsp warm skimmed milk
5 ml/1 tsp dried yeast
pinch of sugar
225 g/8 oz/2 cups strong plain flour
10 ml/2 tsp mixed spice
2.5 ml/½ tsp salt
25 g/1 oz/2 tbsp soft margarine
50 g/2 oz/¼ cup caster sugar
1 egg

FOR THE FILLING
1 large ripe banana
175 g/6 oz/1 cup ready-to-eat
   dried apricots
30 ml/2 tbsp light muscovado sugar

FOR THE GLAZE
30 ml/2 tbsp caster sugar
30 ml/2 tbsp water

dried yeast

egg

ready-to-eat dried apricots

soft margarine

muscovado sugar

mixed spice

banana

caster sugar

strong plain flour

salt

skimmed milk

1 Grease an 18 cm/7 in square cake tin. Put the warm milk in a jug. Sprinkle the yeast on top. Add a pinch of sugar to help activate the yeast, mix well and leave for 30 minutes.

2 Sift the flour, spice and salt into a mixing bowl. Rub in the margarine, then stir in the sugar. Make a central well, pour in the yeast mixture and the egg. Gradually mix in the flour to make a soft dough, adding extra milk if needed.

3 Turn the dough out on to a floured surface and knead for 5 minutes until smooth and elastic. Return to the clean bowl, cover with a damp dish towel and leave in a warm place to rise for about 2 hours until doubled in bulk.

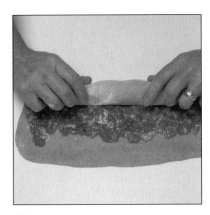

5 Knead the risen dough on a floured surface for 2 minutes, then roll out to a 30 x 23 cm/12 x 9 in rectangle. Spread the banana and apricot filling over the dough and roll up lengthways like a Swiss roll, with the join underneath.

4 Meanwhile prepare the filling. Mash the banana in a bowl. Using kitchen scissors, snip the apricots, then stir them into the mashed banana with the sugar.

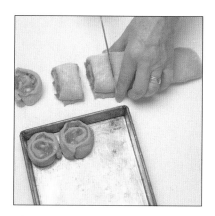

6 Cut the roll into 9 pieces and place, cut side down, in the prepared tin. Cover and leave to rise in a warm place for about 30 minutes. Preheat the oven to 200°C/400°F/Gas 6.

7 Bake the buns for 20–25 minutes until golden brown and cooked in the centre. Meanwhile make the glaze. Mix the caster sugar and water in a small saucepan. Heat, stirring, until dissolved, then boil for 2 minutes. Brush the glaze over the buns while still hot, then remove the buns from the tin and leave them to cool on a wire rack.

Raspberry Muffins

These American muffins are made using baking powder and low fat buttermilk, giving them a light and spongy texture. They are delicious to eat at any time of day.

Makes 10–12

INGREDIENTS
275 g/10 oz/2½ cups plain flour
15 ml/1 tbsp baking powder
115 g/4 oz/½ cup caster sugar
1 egg
250 ml/8 fl oz/1 cup buttermilk
60 ml/4 tbsp sunflower oil
150 g/5 oz/1 cup raspberries

egg

buttermilk

sunflower oil

caster sugar

plain flour

baking powder

raspberries

1 Preheat the oven to 200°C/400°F/ Gas 6. Arrange 12 paper cases in a deep muffin tin. Sift the flour and baking powder into a mixing bowl, stir in the sugar, then make a well in the centre.

2 Mix the egg, buttermilk and sunflower oil together in a bowl, pour into the flour mixture and mix quickly until just combined.

3 Add the raspberries and lightly fold in with a metal spoon. Spoon the mixture into the paper cases to within a third of the top.

4 Bake the muffins for 20–25 minutes until golden brown and firm in the middle. Transfer to a wire rack and serve warm or cold.

Date and Apple Muffins

You will only need one or two of these wholesome muffins per person as they are very filling.

Makes 12

INGREDIENTS

150 g/5 oz/1¼ cups self-raising wholemeal flour
150 g/5 oz/1¼ cups self-raising white flour
5 ml/1 tsp ground cinnamon
5 ml/1 tsp baking powder
25 g/1 oz/2 tbsp soft margarine
75 g/3 oz/½ cup light muscovado sugar
1 eating apple
250 ml/8 fl oz/1 cup apple juice
30 ml/2 tbsp pear and apple spread
1 egg, lightly beaten
75 g/3 oz/½ cup chopped dates
15 ml/1 tbsp chopped pecan nuts

chopped dates
egg
pecan nuts
self-raising wholemeal flour
ground cinnamon
muscovado sugar
self-raising white flour
apple juice
soft margarine
pear and apple spread
eating apple
baking powder

1 Preheat the oven to 200°C/400°F/Gas 6. Arrange 12 paper cases in a deep muffin tin. Put the wholemeal flour in a mixing bowl. Sift in the white flour with the cinnamon and baking powder. Rub in the margarine until the mixture resembles breadcrumbs, then stir in the muscovado sugar.

2 Quarter and core the apple, chop the flesh finely and set aside. Stir a little of the apple juice with the pear and apple spread until smooth. Mix in the remaining juice, then add to the rubbed-in mixture with the egg. Add the chopped apple to the bowl with the dates. Mix quickly until just combined.

3 Divide the mixture among the muffin cases.

4 Sprinkle with the chopped pecan nuts. Bake the muffins for 20–25 minutes until golden brown and firm in the middle. Remove to a wire rack and serve while still warm.

Chive and Potato Scones

These little scones should be fairly thin, soft and crisp on the outside. Serve them for breakfast.

Makes 20

INGREDIENTS
450 g/1 lb potatoes
115 g/4 oz/1 cup plain flour, sifted
30 ml/2 tbsp olive oil
30 ml/2 tbsp snipped chives
salt and freshly ground black pepper
low fat spread, for topping
  (optional)

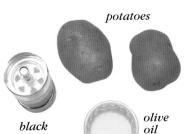

potatoes

black pepper

olive oil

chives

plain flour

salt

1 Cook the potatoes in a saucepan of boiling salted water for 20 minutes or until tender, then drain thoroughly. Return the potatoes to the clean pan and mash them. Preheat a griddle or heavy-based frying pan.

2 Add the flour, olive oil and snipped chives with a little salt and pepper to the hot mashed potato in the pan. Mix to a soft dough.

COOK'S TIP

Cook the scones over a low heat so that the outsides do not burn before the insides are cooked through.

3 Roll out the dough on a well-floured surface to a thickness of 5 mm/¼ in and stamp out rounds with a 5 cm/2 in plain pastry cutter. Lightly grease the griddle or frying pan.

4 Cook the scones, in batches, on the hot griddle or frying pan for about 10 minutes, turning once, until they are golden brown on both sides. Keep the heat low. Top with a little low fat spread, if you like, and serve immediately.

Cheese and Chive Scones

Feta cheese makes an excellent substitute for butter in these tangy savoury scones.

Makes 9

INGREDIENTS
115 g/4 oz/1 cup self-raising flour
150 g/5 oz/1 cup self-raising
  wholemeal flour
2.5 ml/½ tsp salt
75 g/3 oz feta cheese
15 ml/1 tbsp snipped fresh chives
150 ml/¼ pint/⅔ cup skimmed milk,
  plus extra for glazing
1.25 ml/¼ tsp cayenne pepper

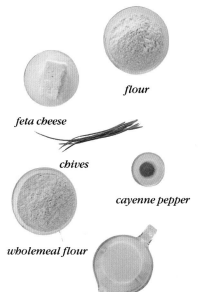

flour

feta cheese

chives

cayenne pepper

wholemeal flour

milk

1 Pre-heat the oven to 200°C/400°F/ Gas 6. Sift the flours and salt into a mixing bowl, adding any bran left over from the flour in the sieve.

2 Crumble the feta cheese and rub into the dry ingredients. Stir in the chives, then add the milk and mix to a soft dough.

3 Turn out onto a floured surface and lightly knead until smooth. Roll out to 2 cm/¾ in thick and stamp out nine scones with a 6 cm/2½ in biscuit cutter.

4 Transfer the scones to a non-stick baking sheet. Brush with skimmed milk, then sprinkle over the cayenne pepper. Bake in the oven for 15 minutes, or until golden brown. Serve warm or cold.

Curry Crackers

These spicy, crisp little biscuits are very low fat and are ideal for serving with drinks.

Makes 12

INGREDIENTS

50 g/2 oz/¹/₂ cup plain flour
1.5 ml/¹/₄ tsp salt
5 ml/1 tsp curry powder
1.5 ml/¹/₄ tsp chilli powder
15 ml/1 tbsp chopped fresh
  coriander
30 ml/2 tbsp water

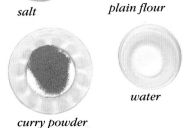

fresh coriander

chilli powder

salt

plain flour

water

curry powder

1 Preheat the oven to 180°C/350°F/ Gas 4. Sift the flour and salt into a mixing bowl, then add the curry powder and chilli powder. Make a well in the centre and add the chopped fresh coriander and water. Gradually incorporate the flour and mix to a firm dough.

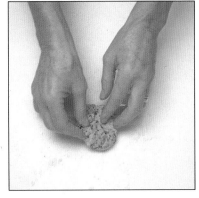

2 Turn on to a lightly floured surface, knead until smooth, then leave to rest for 5 minutes.

VARIATIONS
Omit the curry and chilli powders and add 15 ml/1 tbsp caraway, fennel or mustard seeds.

3 Cut the dough into 12 pieces and knead into small balls. Roll each ball out very thinly to a 10 cm/4 in round.

4 Arrange the rounds on two ungreased baking sheets, then bake for 15 minutes, turning over once during cooking. Cool on a wire rack.

Oatcakes

Try serving these oatcakes with reduced-fat hard cheeses. They are also delicious topped with thick honey for breakfast.

Makes 8

INGREDIENTS
175 g/6 oz/1 cup medium oatmeal,
    plus extra for sprinkling
2.5 ml/¹/₂ tsp salt
pinch of bicarbonate of soda
15 g/¹/₂ oz/1 tbsp butter
75 ml/5 tbsp water

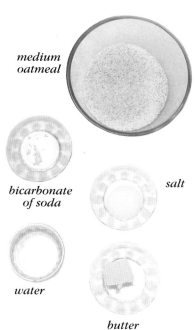

medium oatmeal

bicarbonate of soda

salt

water

butter

1 Preheat the oven to 150°C/300°F/ Gas 2. Mix the oatmeal with the salt and bicarbonate of soda in a mixing bowl.

2 Melt the butter with the water in a small saucepan. Bring to the boil, then add to the oatmeal mixture and mix to a moist dough.

COOK'S TIP

To achieve a neat round, place a 25 cm/10 in cake board or plate on top of the oatcake. Cut away any excess dough with a palette knife, then remove the board or plate.

3 Turn the dough on to a surface sprinkled with oatmeal and knead to a smooth ball. Turn a large baking sheet upside-down, grease it, sprinkle it lightly with oatmeal and place the ball of dough on top. Sprinkle the dough with oatmeal, then roll out to a 25 cm/10 in round.

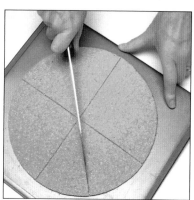

4 Cut the round into 8 sections, ease them apart slightly and bake for about 50–60 minutes until crisp. Leave to cool on the baking sheet, then remove the oatcakes with a palette knife.

Drop Scones

These little scones are delicious spread with jam.

Makes 18

INGREDIENTS

225 g/8 oz/2 cups self-raising flour
2.5 ml/½ tsp salt
15 ml/1 tbsp caster sugar
1 egg, beaten
300 ml/½ pint/1¼ cups skimmed
　milk

egg

self-raising flour

salt

skimmed milk

caster sugar

1 Preheat a griddle, heavy-based frying pan or an electric frying pan. Sift the flour and salt into a mixing bowl. Stir in the sugar and make a well in the centre.

2 Add the egg and half the milk, then gradually incorporate the surrounding flour to make a smooth batter. Beat in the remaining milk.

3 Lightly grease the griddle or pan. Drop tablespoons of the batter on to the surface, leaving them until they bubble and the bubbles begin to burst.

4 Turn the drop scones over with a palette knife and cook until the underside is golden brown. Keep the cooked drop scones warm and moist by wrapping them in a clean napkin while cooking successive batches.

VARIATION

For savoury scones, omit the sugar and add 2 chopped spring onions and 15 ml/1 tbsp freshly grated Parmesan cheese to the batter. Serve with cottage cheese.

Pineapple and Cinnamon Drop Scones

Making the batter with pineapple juice instead of milk cuts down on fat and adds to the taste.

Makes 24

INGREDIENTS

115 g/4 oz/1 cup self-raising wholemeal flour
115 g/4 oz/1 cup self-raising white flour
5 ml/1 tsp ground cinnamon
15 ml/1 tbsp caster sugar
1 egg
300 ml/½ pint/1¼ cups pineapple juice
75 g/3 oz/½ cup semi-dried pineapple, chopped

egg
semi-dried pineapple
pineapple juice
self-raising wholemeal flour
caster sugar
ground cinnamon
self-raising white flour

1 Preheat a griddle, heavy-based frying pan or an electric frying pan. Put the wholemeal flour in a mixing bowl. Sift in the white flour, add the cinnamon and sugar and make a well in the centre.

2 Add the egg with half the pineapple juice and gradually incorporate the surrounding flour to make a smooth batter. Beat in the remaining juice with the chopped pineapple.

COOK'S TIP

Drop scones do not keep well and are best eaten freshly cooked.

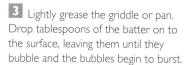

3 Lightly grease the griddle or pan. Drop tablespoons of the batter on to the surface, leaving them until they bubble and the bubbles begin to burst.

4 Turn the drop scones with a palette knife and cook until the underside is golden brown. Keep the cooked scones warm and moist by wrapping them in a clean napkin while continuing to cook successive batches.

Malt Loaf

This is a rich and sticky loaf. If it lasts long enough to go stale, try toasting it for a delicious tea-time treat.

Serves 8

INGREDIENTS

150 ml/¼ pint/⅔ cup warm
   skimmed milk
5 ml/1 tsp dried yeast
pinch of caster sugar
350 g/12 oz/3 cups plain flour
1.5 ml/¼ tsp salt
30 ml/2 tbsp light muscovado sugar
175 g/6 oz/generous 1 cup sultanas
15 ml/1 tbsp sunflower oil
45 ml/3 tbsp malt extract

FOR THE GLAZE

30 ml/2 tbsp caster sugar
30 ml/2 tbsp water

malt extract

sultanas

salt

plain flour

skimmed milk

light muscovado sugar

dried yeast

sunflower oil

VARIATION

To make buns, divide the dough into 10 pieces, shape into rounds, leave to rise, then bake for about 15–20 minutes. Brush with the glaze while still hot.

1 Place the warm milk in a bowl. Sprinkle the yeast on top and add the sugar. Leave for 30 minutes until frothy. Sift the flour and salt into a mixing bowl, stir in the muscovado sugar and sultanas, and make a well in the centre.

2 Add the yeast mixture with the oil and malt extract. Gradually incorporate the flour and mix to a soft dough, adding a little extra milk if necessary.

3 Turn on to a floured surface and knead for about 5 minutes until smooth and elastic. Grease a 450 g/1 lb loaf tin.

4 Shape the dough and place it in the prepared tin. Cover with a damp dish towel and leave in a warm place for 1–2 hours until well risen. Preheat the oven to 190°C/375°F/Gas 5.

5 Bake the loaf for 30–35 minutes, or until it sounds hollow when it is tapped underneath.

6 Meanwhile, prepare the glaze by dissolving the sugar in the water in a small pan. Bring to the boil, stirring, then lower the heat and simmer for 1 minute. Place the loaf on a wire rack and brush with the glaze while still hot. Leave the loaf to cool before serving.

Banana and Ginger Teabread

Serve this teabread in slices with low fat spread. The stem ginger adds an interesting flavour.

Serves 6–8

INGREDIENTS

175 g/6 oz/1½ cups self-raising flour
5 ml/1 tsp baking powder
40 g/1½ oz/3 tbsp soft margarine
50 g/2 oz/⅓ cup dark muscovado sugar
50 g/2 oz/⅓ cup drained stem ginger, chopped
60 ml/4 tbsp skimmed milk
2 ripe bananas, mashed

baking powder

stem ginger

muscovado sugar

bananas

self-raising flour

skimmed milk

soft margarine

1 Preheat the oven to 180°C/350°F/ Gas 4. Grease and line a 450 g/1 lb loaf tin. Sift the flour and baking powder into a mixing bowl.

2 Rub in the margarine until the mixture resembles breadcrumbs.

VARIATION

To make Banana and Sultana Teabread, add 5 ml/1 tsp mixed spice and omit the stem ginger. Stir in 115 g/4 oz/⅔ cup sultanas.

3 Stir in the sugar. Add the ginger, milk and bananas and mix to a soft dough.

4 Spoon into the prepared tin and bake for 40–45 minutes. Run a palette knife around the edges to loosen them, turn the teabread on to a wire rack and leave to cool.

Pear and Sultana Teabread

This is an ideal teabread to make when pears are plentiful – an excellent use for windfalls.

Serves 6–8

INGREDIENTS

25 g/1 oz/scant ⅓ cup rolled oats
50 g/2 oz/⅓ cup light muscovado
  sugar
30 ml/2 tbsp pear or apple juice
30 ml/2 tbsp sunflower oil
1 large or 2 small pears
115 g/4 oz/1 cup self-raising flour
115 g/4 oz/⅔ cup sultanas
2.5 ml/½ tsp baking powder
10 ml/2 tsp mixed spice
1 egg

small pears
egg
baking powder
sunflower oil
self-raising flour
rolled oats
sultanas
mixed spice
light muscovado sugar
pear juice

1 Preheat the oven to 180°C/350°F/ Gas 4. Grease and line a 450 g/1 lb loaf tin with non-stick baking paper. Put the oats in a bowl with the sugar, pour over the pear or apple juice and oil, mix well and leave to stand for 15 minutes.

2 Quarter, core and grate the pear(s). Add to the oat mixture with the flour, sultanas, baking powder, mixed spice and egg, then mix together thoroughly.

3 Spoon the mixture into the prepared loaf tin and level the top. Bake for 50–60 minutes or until a skewer inserted into the centre comes out clean.

4 Transfer the teabread on to a wire rack and peel off the lining paper. Leave to cool completely.

COOK'S TIP

Health food shops sell concentrated pear and apple juice, ready for diluting as required.

Courgette and Walnut Loaf

Cardamom seeds impart their distinctive aroma to this loaf. Serve spread with ricotta and honey for a delicious snack.

Makes 1 loaf

INGREDIENTS
3 × size 3 eggs
75 g/3 oz/⅓ cup light muscovado
    sugar
100 ml/4 fl oz/½ cup sunflower oil
225 g/8 oz/2 cups wholemeal flour
5 ml/1 tsp baking powder
5 ml/1 tsp bicarbonate of soda
5 ml/1 tsp ground cinnamon
3 ml/¾ tsp ground allspice
7.5 ml/½ tbsp green cardamoms,
    seeds removed and crushed
150 g/5 oz courgette, coarsely grated
115 g/4 oz/½ cup walnuts, chopped
50 g/2 oz/¼ cup sunflower seeds

courgettes

egg

walnuts

sunflower oil

muscovado sugar

wholemeal flour

sunflower seeds

cardamom pods

1 Preheat the oven to 180°C/350°F/ Gas 4. Line the base and sides of a 900 g/ 2 lb loaf tin with non-stick baking paper.

2 Beat the eggs and sugar together and gradually add the oil.

3 Sift the flour into a bowl together with the baking powder, bicarbonate of soda, cinnamon and allspice.

4 Mix into the egg mixture with the rest of the ingredients, reserving 15 g/1 tbsp of the sunflower seeds for the top.

5 Spoon into the loaf tin, level off the top, and sprinkle with the reserved sunflower seeds.

6 Bake for 1 hour or until a skewer inserted in the centre comes out clean. Leave to cool slightly before turning out onto a wire rack to cool completely.

Banana and Cardamom Bread

The combination of banana and cardamom is delicious in this soft-textured moist loaf. It is perfect for tea time, served with low fat spread and jam.

Serves 6

INGREDIENTS

150 ml/¼ pint/⅔ cup warm water
5 ml/1 tsp dried yeast
pinch of sugar
10 cardamom pods
400 g/14 oz/3½ cups strong
  white flour
5 ml/1 tsp salt
30 ml/2 tbsp malt extract
2 ripe bananas, mashed
5 ml/1 tsp sesame seeds

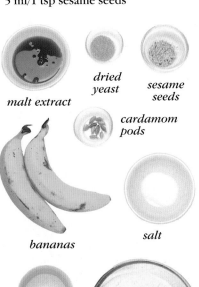

malt extract   *dried yeast*   *sesame seeds*

cardamom pods

bananas   *salt*

water

strong white flour

COOK'S TIP

Make sure the bananas are really ripe, so that they impart maximum flavour to the bread.

If you prefer, place the dough in one piece in a 450 g/1 lb loaf tin and bake for an extra 5 minutes.

1 Put the water in a small bowl. Sprinkle the yeast on top, add the sugar and mix well. Leave for 10 minutes.

2 Split the cardamom pods. Remove the seeds and chop them finely.

3 Sift the flour and salt into a mixing bowl and make a well in the centre. Add the yeast mixture with the malt extract, chopped cardamom seeds and bananas.

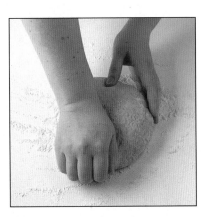

4 Gradually incorporate the flour and mix to a soft dough, adding a little extra water if necessary. Turn the dough on to a floured surface and knead for about 5 minutes until smooth and elastic. Return to the clean bowl, cover with a damp dish towel and leave to rise for about 2 hours until doubled in bulk.

5 Grease a baking sheet. Turn the dough on to a floured surface, knead briefly, then shape into a plait. Place the plait on the baking sheet and cover loosely with a plastic bag (ballooning it to trap the air). Leave until well risen. Preheat the oven to 220°C/425°F/Gas 7.

6 Brush the plait lightly with water and sprinkle with the sesame seeds. Bake for 10 minutes, then lower the oven temperature to 200°C/400°F/Gas 6. Cook for 15 minutes more, or until the loaf sounds hollow when it is tapped underneath. Cool on a wire rack.

Coriander Brioches

The warm flavour of coriander combines particularly well with orange in this recipe.

Makes 12

INGREDIENTS

225 g/8 oz strong white bread flour
10 ml/2 tsp easy-blend dried yeast
2.5 ml/½ tsp salt
15 ml/1 tbsp caster sugar
10 ml/2 tsp coriander seeds, coarsely ground
grated rind of 1 orange, plus extra to decorate
30ml/2 tbsp hand-hot water
2 eggs, beaten
50 g/2 oz unsalted butter, melted
1 small egg, beaten, to glaze

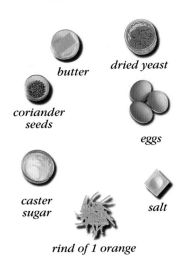

butter

dried yeast

coriander seeds

eggs

caster sugar

salt

rind of 1 orange

COOK'S TIP
These individual brioches look particularly attractive if they are made in special brioche tins. However, they can also be made in bun tins or muffin tins.

1 Sift the flour into a bowl and stir in the yeast, salt, sugar, coriander seeds and orange rind. Add the water, eggs and butter. Beat to make a soft dough. Turn on to a lightly floured surface and knead for 5 minutes, then place in a lightly oiled bowl, cover and leave in a warm place for 1 hour until doubled in bulk.

2 Turn on to a floured surface, knead again briefly and roll into a sausage. Cut into 12 pieces. Break off a quarter of each piece and set aside. Shape the larger pieces of dough into balls and place in 12 greased individual brioche tins.

3 Lightly flour your hands and roll each of the small pieces of dough into small sausages. Then lightly flour the handle of a wooden spoon and press in to the centre of each of the large dough balls to make a small hole. Place the dough sausages into the holes made by the spoon handle.

4 Place the brioche tins on a baking sheet. Cover with lightly oiled clear film and leave in a warm place until the dough rises almost to the top of the tins. Preheat the oven to 220°C/425°F/Gas 7. Brush the brioches with beaten egg and bake for 15 minutes until golden brown. Scatter over extra orange rind to decorate, and serve the brioches warm.

Sage Soda Bread

This wonderful loaf, quite unlike bread made with
yeast, has a velvety texture and a powerful sage aroma.

Makes 1 loaf

INGREDIENTS
225 g/8 oz/2 cups wholemeal flour
115 g/4 oz/1 cup strong white flour
2.5 ml/½ tsp salt
5 ml/1 tsp bicarbonate of soda
30 ml/2 tbsp shredded fresh sage
300–450 ml/½–¾ pint/1¼–1¾
   cups buttermilk

white flour

wholemeal flour

sage

buttermilk

1 Preheat the oven to 220°C/425°F/
Gas 7. Sift the dry ingredients into a bowl.

2 Stir in the sage and add enough
buttermilk to make a soft dough.

COOK'S TIP

As an alternative to the sage, try using
finely chopped rosemary or thyme.

3 Shape the dough into a round loaf
and place on a lightly oiled baking sheet.

4 Cut a deep cross in the top. Bake in
the oven for 40 minutes until the loaf is
well risen and sounds hollow when
tapped on the bottom. Leave to cool on a
wire rack.

Austrian Three-Grain Bread

A mixture of grains gives this close-textured bread a delightful nutty flavour. Make two smaller twists if preferred.

Serves 8–10

INGREDIENTS
475 ml/16 fl oz/2 cups warm water
10 ml/2 tsp dried yeast
pinch of sugar
225 g/8 oz/2 cups strong white flour
7.5 ml/1½ tsp salt
225 g/8 oz/2 cups malted
    brown flour
225 g/8 oz/2 cups rye flour
30 ml/2 tbsp linseed
75 g/3 oz/½ cup medium oatmeal
45 ml/3 tbsp sunflower seeds
30 ml/2 tbsp malt extract

sunflower seeds

medium oatmeal

strong white flour

dried yeast

linseed

malt extract

water

rye flour

malted brown flour

salt

1 Put half the water in a jug. Sprinkle the yeast on top. Add the sugar, mix well and leave for 10 minutes.

2 Sift the white flour and salt into a mixing bowl and add the other flours. Set aside 5 ml/1 tsp of the linseed and add the rest to the flour mixture with the oatmeal and sunflower seeds. Make a well in the centre.

3 Add the yeast mixture to the bowl with the malt extract and the remaining water. Gradually incorporate the flour.

4 Mix to a soft dough, adding extra water if necessary. Turn out on to a floured surface and knead for about 5 minutes until smooth and elastic. Return to the clean bowl, cover with a damp dish towel and leave to rise for about 2 hours until doubled in bulk.

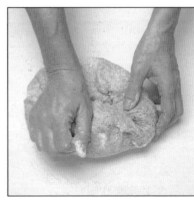

5 Flour a baking sheet. Turn the dough on to a floured surface, knead for 2 minutes then divide in half. Roll each half into a 30 cm/12 in long sausage.

6 Twist the two cylinders together, dampen the ends, and press to seal. Lift the twist onto the prepared baking sheet. Brush it with water, sprinkle with the remaining linseed, and cover loosely with a large plastic bag (ballooning it to trap the air inside). Let stand in a warm place until well risen. Preheat the oven to 425°F.

7 Bake the loaf for 10 minutes, then lower the oven temperature to 400°F, and cook for 20 minutes more, or until the loaf sounds hollow when it is tapped on the bottom. Transfer to a wire rack to cool.

NUTRITIONAL NOTES
PER PORTION:

CALORIES 367
FAT 5.36 g **SATURATED FAT** 0.60 g
CHOLESTEROL 0 **FIBER** 6.76 g

Saffron Focaccia

A dazzling yellow bread that is light in texture and distinctive in flavour.

Makes 1 loaf

INGREDIENTS
pinch of saffron threads
150 ml/¼ pint/⅔ cup boiling water
225 g/8 oz/2 cups plain flour
2.5 ml/½ tsp salt
5 ml/1 tsp easy-blend dry yeast
15 ml/1 tbsp olive oil

FOR THE TOPPING
2 garlic cloves, sliced
1 red onion, cut into thin wedges
rosemary sprigs
12 black olives, pitted and coarsely
   chopped
15 ml/1·tbsp olive oil

flour

garlic

rosemary

red onion

olives

saffron

yeast

1 Place the saffron in a heatproof jug and pour on the boiling water. Leave to stand and infuse until lukewarm.

2 Place the flour, salt, yeast and olive oil in a food processor. Turn on and gradually add the saffron and its liquid. Process until the dough forms into a ball.

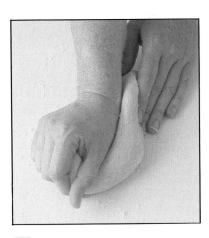

3 Turn onto a floured board and knead for 10–15 minutes. Place in a bowl, cover and leave to rise for 30–40 minutes until doubled in size.

4 Punch down the risen dough on a lightly floured surface and roll out into an oval shape, 1 cm/½ in thick. Place on a lightly greased baking tray and leave to rise for 20–30 minutes.

5 Preheat the oven to 200°C/400°F/Gas 6. Use your fingers to press small indentations all over the surface of the focaccia.

6 Cover with the topping ingredients, brush lightly with olive oil, and bake for 25 minutes or until the loaf sounds hollow when tapped on the bottom. Leave to cool on a wire rack.

Sun-dried Tomato Bread

This savoury bread tastes delicious on its own, but it also makes exceptional sandwiches.

Makes 1 loaf

INGREDIENTS

375 g/13 oz/3¼ cups strong white flour
5 ml/1 tsp salt
10 ml/2 tsp easy-blend dried yeast
50 g/2 oz (drained weight) sun-dried tomatoes in oil, chopped
175 ml/6 fl oz/¾ cup lukewarm water
75 ml/5 tbsp lukewarm olive oil, plus extra for brushing
plain flour for dusting

water

olive oil

strong white flour

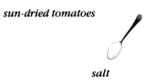

easy-blend yeast

sun-dried tomatoes

salt

1 Sift the flour and salt into a large mixing bowl.

2 Stir in the yeast and sun-dried tomatoes.

3 Make a well in the centre of the dry ingredients. Pour in the water and oil, and mix until the ingredients come together and form a soft dough.

4 Turn the dough on to a lightly floured surface and knead for about 10 minutes.

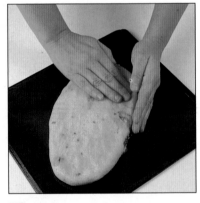

5 Shape into an oblong loaf, without making the top too smooth, and place on a greased baking sheet. Brush the top with oil, cover with clear film, then leave to rise in a warm place for about 1 hour.

6 Meanwhile, preheat the oven to 220°C/425°F/Gas 7. Remove the clear film, then sprinkle the top of the loaf lightly with flour. Bake for 30–40 minutes until the loaf sounds hollow when tapped on the bottom. Serve warm.

Rosemary and Sea Salt Focaccia

Focaccia is an Italian flat bread made with olive oil. Here it is given added flavour with rosemary and coarse sea salt.

Makes 1 loaf

INGREDIENTS
350 g/12 oz/3 cups plain flour
2.5 ml/½ tsp salt
10 ml/2 tsp easy-blend dried yeast
about 250 ml/8 fl oz/1 cup lukewarm
  water
45 ml/3 tbsp olive oil
1 small red onion
leaves from 1 large rosemary sprig
5 ml/1 tsp coarse sea salt

coarse sea salt

water

olive oil

plain flour

easy-blend yeast

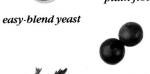

red onion

rosemary

1 Sift the flour and salt into a large mixing bowl. Stir in the yeast, then make a well in the centre of the dry ingredients. Pour in the water and 30 ml/2 tbsp of the oil. Mix well, adding a little more water if the mixture seems dry.

2 Turn the dough on to a lightly floured surface and knead for about 10 minutes until smooth and elastic.

3 Place the dough in a greased bowl, cover and leave in a warm place for about 1 hour until doubled in size. Knock back and knead the dough for 2–3 minutes.

4 Meanwhile, preheat the oven to 220°C/425°F/Gas 7. Roll out the dough to a large circle, about 1 cm/½ in thick, and transfer to a greased baking sheet. Brush with the remaining oil.

5 Halve the onion and slice into thin wedges. Sprinkle over the dough, with the rosemary and sea salt, pressing in lightly.

6 Using a finger make deep indentations in the dough. Cover the surface with greased clear film, then leave to rise in a warm place for 30 minutes. Remove the clear film and bake for 25–30 minutes until golden. Serve warm.

Olive and Oregano Bread

This is an excellent accompaniment to all salads and is particularly good served warm.

Serves 8–10

INGREDIENTS

300 ml/10 fl oz/1¼ cups warm water
5 ml/1 tsp dried yeast
pinch of sugar
15 ml/1 tbsp olive oil
1 onion, chopped
450 g/1 lb/4 cups strong white flour
5 ml/1 tsp salt
1.5 ml/¼ tsp freshly ground
  black pepper
50 g/2 oz/⅓ cup stoned black olives,
  roughly chopped
15 ml/1 tbsp black olive paste
15 ml/1 tbsp chopped fresh oregano
15 ml/1 tbsp chopped fresh parsley

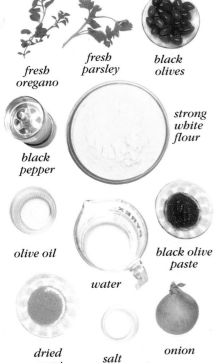

fresh oregano

fresh parsley

black olives

strong white flour

black pepper

olive oil

black olive paste

water

dried yeast

salt

onion

1 Put half the warm water in a jug. Sprinkle the yeast on top. Add the sugar, mix well and leave for 10 minutes.

2 Heat the olive oil in a frying pan and fry the onion until golden brown.

3 Sift the flour into a mixing bowl with the salt and pepper. Make a well in the centre. Add the yeast mixture, the fried onion (with the oil), the olives, olive paste, herbs and remaining water. Gradually incorporate the flour and mix to a soft dough, adding a little extra water if necessary.

4 Turn the dough on to a floured surface and knead for 5 minutes until smooth and elastic. Place in a mixing bowl, cover with a damp dish towel and leave in a warm place to rise for about 2 hours until doubled in bulk. Lightly grease a baking sheet.

5 Turn the dough on to a floured surface and knead again for a few minutes. Shape into a 20 cm/8 in round and place on the prepared baking sheet. Using a sharp knife, make criss-cross cuts over the top, cover and leave in a warm place for 30 minutes until well risen. Preheat the oven to 220°C/425°F/Gas 7.

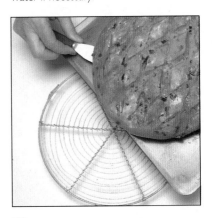

6 Dust the loaf with a little flour. Bake for 10 minutes then lower the oven temperature to 200°C/400°F/Gas 6. Bake for 20 minutes more, or until the loaf sounds hollow when it is tapped underneath. Transfer to a wire rack to cool slightly before serving.

Cheese and Onion Herb Sticks

An extremely tasty bread which is very good with soup or salads. Use an extra-strong cheese to give plenty of flavour without piling on the fat.

Makes 2 sticks, each serving 4–6

INGREDIENTS

300 ml/¹/₂ pint/1¹/₄ cups warm water
5 ml/1 tsp dried yeast
pinch of sugar
15 ml/1 tbsp sunflower oil
1 red onion, chopped
450 g/1 lb/4 cups strong white flour
5 ml/1 tsp salt
5 ml/1 tsp dry mustard powder
45 ml/3 tbsp chopped fresh herbs, such as thyme, parsley, marjoram or sage
75 g/3 oz/³/₄ cup grated reduced-fat Cheddar cheese

fresh herbs

sunflower oil

reduced-fat Cheddar cheese

salt

mustard powder

strong white flour

water

red onion

dried yeast

1 Put the water in a jug. Sprinkle the yeast on top. Add the sugar, mix well and leave for 10 minutes.

2 Heat the oil in a frying pan and fry the onion until well coloured.

3 Sift the flour, salt and mustard into a mixing bowl. Add the herbs. Set aside 30 ml/2 tbsp of the cheese. Stir the rest into the flour mixture and make a well in the centre. Add the yeast mixture with the fried onions and oil, then gradually incorporate the flour and mix to a soft dough, adding extra water if necessary.

4 Turn the dough on to a floured surface and knead for 5 minutes until smooth and elastic. Return to the clean bowl, cover with a damp dish towel and leave in a warm place to rise for about 2 hours until doubled in bulk. Lightly grease two baking sheets.

5 Turn the dough on to a floured surface, knead briefly, then divide the mixture in half and roll each piece into a 30 cm/12 in long stick. Place each stick on a baking sheet and make diagonal cuts along the top.

6 Sprinkle the sticks with the reserved cheese. Cover and leave for 30 minutes until well risen. Preheat the oven to 220°C/425°F/Gas 7. Bake the sticks for 25 minutes or until they sound hollow when they are tapped underneath. Cool on a wire rack.

VARIATION
To make Onion and Coriander Sticks, omit the cheese, herbs and mustard. Add 15 ml/1 tbsp ground coriander and 45 ml/3 tbsp chopped fresh coriander instead.

Sun-dried Tomato Plait

This is a marvellous Mediterranean-flavoured bread to serve at a summer buffet or barbecue.

Serves 8–10

INGREDIENTS
300 ml/¹/₂ pint/1¹/₄ cups warm water
5 ml/1 tsp dried yeast
pinch of sugar
225 g/8 oz/2 cups wholemeal flour
225 g/8 oz/2 cups strong white flour
5 ml/1 tsp salt
1.5 ml/¹/₄ tsp freshly ground
    black pepper
115 g/4 oz/²/₃ cup drained sun-dried
    tomatoes in oil, chopped, plus
    15 ml/1 tbsp oil from the jar
25 g/1 oz/¹/₄ cup freshly grated
    Parmesan cheese
30 ml/2 tbsp red pesto
5 ml/1 tsp coarse sea salt

Parmesan cheese · *red pesto* · *black pepper*

dried yeast · *wholemeal flour* · *sun-dried tomatoes* · *salt*

water · *strong white flour* · *coarse sea salt* · *tomato oil*

COOK'S TIP
If you are unable to locate red pesto, use 30 ml/2 tbsp chopped fresh basil mixed with 15 ml/1 tbsp sun-dried tomato paste.

1 Put half the warm water in a jug. Sprinkle the yeast on top. Add the sugar, mix well and leave for 10 minutes.

2 Put the wholemeal flour in a mixing bowl. Sift in the white flour, salt and pepper. Make a well in the centre and add the yeast mixture, oil, sun-dried tomatoes, Parmesan, pesto and the remaining water. Gradually incorporate the flour and mix to a soft dough, adding a little extra water if necessary.

3 Turn the dough on to a floured surface and knead for 5 minutes until smooth and elastic. Return to the clean bowl, cover with a damp dish towel and leave in a warm place to rise for about 2 hours until doubled in bulk. Lightly grease a baking sheet.

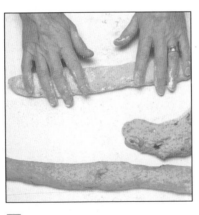

4 Turn the dough on to a lightly floured surface and knead for a few minutes. Divide the dough into three equal pieces and shape each into a 33 cm/13 in long sausage.

5 Dampen the ends of the three "sausages". Press them together at one end, plait them loosely, then press them together at the other end. Place on the baking sheet, cover and leave in a warm place for 30 minutes until well risen. Preheat the oven to 220°C/425°F/Gas 7.

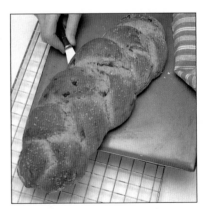

6 Sprinkle the plait with the coarse sea salt. Bake for 10 minutes, then lower the temperature to 200°C/400°F/Gas 6 and bake for a further 15–20 minutes, or until the loaf sounds hollow when tapped underneath. Cool on a wire rack.

Caraway Bread Sticks

Ideal to nibble with drinks, these can be made with all sorts of other seeds – try cumin seeds, poppy seeds or celery seeds.

Makes about 20

INGREDIENTS
150 ml/¼ pint/⅔ cup warm water
2.5 ml/½ tsp dried yeast
pinch of sugar
225 g/8 oz/2 cups plain flour
2.5 ml/½ tsp salt
10 ml/2 tsp caraway seeds

caraway seeds

dried yeast

plain flour

water

salt

1 Grease two baking sheets. Put the warm water in a jug. Sprinkle the yeast on top. Add the sugar, mix well and leave for 10 minutes.

2 Sift the flour and salt into a mixing bowl, stir in the caraway seeds and make a well in the centre. Add the yeast mixture and gradually incorporate the flour to make a soft dough, adding a little extra water if necessary.

3 Turn on to a lightly floured surface and knead for 5 minutes until smooth. Divide the mixture into 20 pieces and roll each one into a 30 cm/12 in stick. Arrange on the baking sheets, leaving room to allow for rising, then leave for 30 minutes until well risen. Meanwhile, preheat the oven to 220°C/425°F/Gas 7.

4 Bake the bread sticks for about 10–12 minutes until golden brown. Cool on the baking sheets.

VARIATION

To make Coriander and Sesame Sticks, replace the caraway seeds with 15 ml/1 tbsp crushed coriander seeds. Dampen the bread sticks lightly and sprinkle them with sesame seeds before baking.

Tomato Breadsticks

Once you've tried this simple recipe you'll never buy manufactured breadsticks again. Serve with aperitifs with a dip or with cheese to end a meal.

Makes 16

INGREDIENTS
225 g/8 oz/2 cups plain flour
2.5 ml/½ tsp salt
7.5 ml/½ tbsp easy-blend dry yeast
5 ml/1 tsp honey
5 ml/1 tsp olive oil
150 ml/¼ pint/⅔ cup warm water
6 halves sun-dried tomatoes in olive oil, drained and chopped
15 ml/1 tbsp skimmed milk
10 ml/2 tsp poppy seeds

plain flour

sun-dried tomatoes

honey

yeast

poppy seeds

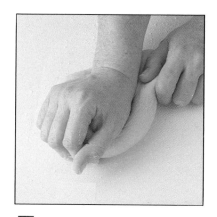

1 Place the flour, salt and yeast in a food processor. Add the honey and olive oil and, with the machine running, gradually pour in the water (you may not need it all as flours vary). Stop adding water as soon as the dough starts to cling together. Process for 1 minute more.

2 Turn out the dough onto a floured board and knead for 3–4 minutes until springy and smooth. Knead in the chopped sun-dried tomatoes. Form into a ball and place in a lightly oiled bowl. Leave to rise for 5 minutes.

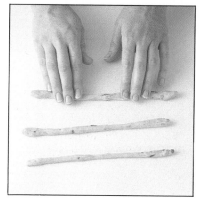

3 Preheat the oven to 150°C/300°F/Gas 2. Divide the dough into 16 pieces and roll each piece into a 28 cm × 1 cm/11 in × ½ in long stick. Place on a lightly oiled baking sheet and leave to rise in a warm place for 15 minutes.

4 Brush the sticks with milk and sprinkle with poppy seeds. Bake for 30 minutes. Leave to cool on a wire rack.

INDEX